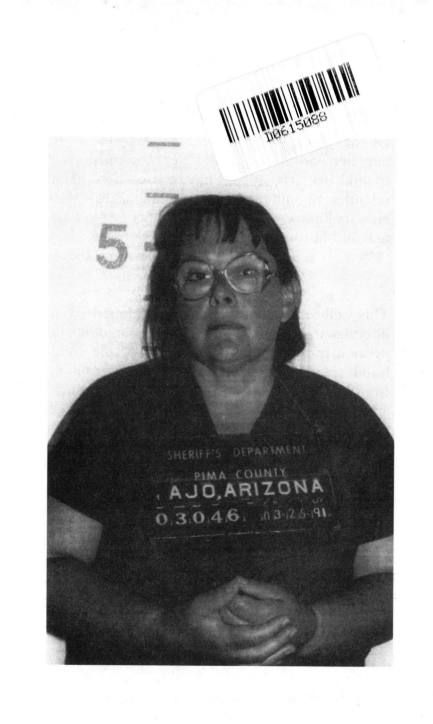

Hendry meticulously chronicles Marjorie's life, her behavioral problems, her compulsion to spend, her irresistible urge to set fires. That relentless pursuit of every last detail makes it clear Hendry knows what she's talking about from a factual and historical perspective.

— *Duluth News Tribune*

This well-researched narrative, developed from interviews with those who knew Congdon and previously published accounts, details the childhood, marriages and trials of this troubled woman, who has innumerable personality quirks and aberrant behaviors. *Glensheen's Daughter* will appeal to readers who want to know more about the twisted character of the woman still believed responsible for her mother's murder in one of Minnesota's best-known mansions.

— *St. Paul Pioneer Press*

Hendry gives us Caldwell in all her inexplicable malice and frenzy, a monster who might have been conjured from the depths of Shakespeare or Dostoevsky.

— *Minnesota Law and Politics*

Nominated for the Northeastern Minnesota Book Award.

Glensheen's Daughter

The Marjorie Congdon Story

Sharon Darby Hendry

Cable Publishing, Incorporated

Glensheen's Daughter
The Marjorie Congdon Story

Sharon Darby Hendry

Cable Publishing
14090 E. Keinenen Rd.
Brule, WI 54820

Printed in the United States of America

Library of Congress Cataloging-in-Publication Data
Hendry, Sharon Darby
     Glensheen's Daughter, The Marjorie Congdon Story
     by Sharon Darby Hendry—1st edition

Includes photographs and references.
ISBN 1-893088-34-0

                              98-93907
                                  CIP

Cover Design by Peter Hill, Axon Garside Hill
Printed by Bethany Press
Photographs courtesy of family members; Steve Kohls, Brainerd Daily Dispatch; Hastings Gazette; AP/Wide World Photos; Star Tribune/Minneapolis-St. Paul; and author's personal collection.

To Bruce, Amy and Jill
With all my love

AUTHOR'S NOTE

Glensheen's Daughter is a true story of Marjorie Congdon's life. The events, actions, and conversations portrayed here have been reconstructed from extensive research, using 4,000 pages of court documents, press accounts, interviews with police officers, attorneys, friends, foes and family members of Marjorie Congdon.

However, the reader should be aware that the author, for dramatic effect, created the few scenes that are set in *italics*.

**For more information and to
tour the Glensheen Mansion, visit:
www.glensheensdaughter.com**

CONTENTS

🦂 MORAL

This is a story of the frog and the scorpion:

The scorpion had to go home to visit his mother and was traveling cross-country to do that. When he reached the river, he was stymied on how to get across it. You see, scorpions can't swim.

Looking around, he spotted a frog and decided to ask him if he could ride on his back across the river. As the scorpion approached the frog, the frog backed up saying, "I know who you are and what you do. Stay away from me."

The scorpion replied, "Mr. Frog, I need a ride across the river. You see, I have to visit my ailing mother and as you know, I cannot swim."

The frog said, "No way. You sting and kill. Why would I want to give you a ride across the river?"

The scorpion answered, "Think about it for a minute, Mr. Frog. If I sting you, you will die, but I will drown. Why would I do such a thing?"

The frog thought about it for a minute and because he was such a nice frog, decided to give the scorpion a ride. About half way across the river, the frog felt a searing pain in his side and knew immediately what had happened. The frog asked the scorpion as they were going to their mutual death, "Why did you do that?"

The scorpion pondered the question for a moment and said, "I don't know. I guess that's just what I do."

Aesop's Fables
Circa 600 B.C.

🐝 *Prologue*

It was a warm fall afternoon, October 30, 1992. Two young police officers escorted a sixty-year-old woman to her home in Ajo, Arizona. She had been sentenced to fifteen years in prison on charges of arson, and she had asked the judge if she could make arrangements for her husband before she was sent away. He was old and sick. The judge had sympathized. What harm could there be in giving her one extra day? And so, he granted her a twenty-four-hour reprieve.

The officers were amazed at her present attitude, her light-heartedness. She joked and made small talk for the whole two-hour ride as if it were any normal day.

"My grandfather started this town," she boasted.

"Is that right?" They glanced at each other and smiled.

"It's true. Chester Congdon was filthy rich."

"Really? How did he get so rich?"

"He was a lawyer for one thing."

"Guess that explains it," said the driver. They all chuckled.

The driver could see her face in his rearview mirror. Although large sunglasses hid the expression in her eyes, her mouth smiled. Had she been younger or more attractive, he may have thought she was flirting or trying to impress him. But under the circumstances, he doubted it. At any rate, he was getting tired of her rather piercing voice and looked forward to dropping her off. So was his partner, who was rubbing his arthritic knee, the way he always did when he felt tense.

"He'd go up to the Mesabi Range, north of Duluth—that's in Minnesota—and buy up land for the Oliver Mining Company for almost nothing. The land was loaded with iron ore."

"So what's that have to do with Ajo?" asked the driver.

"Same thing. He bought up this godforsaken desert after

9

he discovered that it was loaded with copper and mined it. The man knew what he was doing, believe me!"

Ajo was nothing but an old, abandoned mining site, a dried-up sinkhole with cracker-box houses. As they approached the town, the officers mentally compared it to Tucson with its lush desert, rugged mountains, and gentle rolling hills—its population. It was like life and death.

Finally, they arrived at her house, which looked like a tiny wrapped gift, white with blue trim, and windows divided into squares. A green garden hose hung on a vinyl holder on the side of the house. The driver got out of the car and opened the back door for her. She shook his hand, thanked them both for the ride, and proceeded up a crooked walkway of cement blocks to her doorstep, where an elderly man greeted her with outstretched arms. The two embraced and went into the house while the officers turned off Palo Verde Drive and headed for Highway 86 to Tucson.

The next day, when the officers got the call, they couldn't believe it. Yesterday's passenger, Marjorie Congdon LeRoy Caldwell Hagen had been arrested again—this time for murder.

Elisabeth Congdon, Night Nurse Murdered

Elisabeth M. Congdon and her night nurse, Velma Pietila, were found dead in the Congdon mansion, 3300 London Road, today.

Duluth Police Detective Inspector Ernest Grams said Congdon, 83, apparently was smothered in her bed with a pillow. Pietila, 67, apparently died of head injuries she received when struck with a heavy candlestick.

Grams said that the situation officers discovered when they reached the mansion indicates the intruder or intruders were surprised on the staircase by Pietila, and she was struck. She apparently fell against a window seat on the landing but managed to climb up onto it where she died. He said blood on the pillow with which Congdon was smothered indicated she was killed after the nurse was slain.

Grams said the deaths occurred between 11 p.m. and 7 a.m., when bodies were discovered by the relief nurse, Mildred Garvue, reporting for the day shift.

He said the assailant or assailants apparently entered through a basement window. Investigators said drawers in Congdon's room had been ransacked, an empty jewelry box was found on the floor, and her ring and watch may have been removed from her body.

Police were holding no suspects late this morning. "If I had to estimate or guess," Grams said, "I would say one (suspect)...but we're not ruling out the possibility of more."

Son-in-Law Investigated in Duluth Slayings

Roger Caldwell, husband of one of Elisabeth Congdon's adopted daughters, is being investigated in connection with the slayings of the 83-year-old Duluth heiress and her night nurse, Velma Pietila.

A search warrant, requested by police in Golden, Colorado, was issued Sunday to search the residence of Caldwell and his wife, Marjorie.

Miss Congdon, the last child of mining and timber baron Chester Congdon, adopted Mrs. Caldwell and another daughter, Jennifer Johnson, as infants. Mrs. Marjorie Caldwell is 45.

Mrs. Caldwell has been in court on a number of occasions and has a reputation for living beyond her means, largely on the strength of her future inheritance from the Congdon estate, estimated to be about $2 million.

11

Part I

"You'll Like My Mother"

❧ *Chapter One*

Marjorie Congdon often claimed she was a descendent of Charlemagne, onetime emperor of the Western World. No one has ever discovered any truth to this. But she was raised in a family that had built its own kind of empire. She was the adopted daughter of Elisabeth Congdon, heiress daughter of the mega-millionaire Chester Congdon.

Chester Congdon was not born into wealth. His parents were Sylvester Congdon, a Methodist minister, and Laura Jane Adgate Congdon. The eldest of six children, Chester was born in Rochester, New York, on June 12, 1853, five years before Minnesota became the thirty-second state in the Union. In 1868, his family was struck with scarlet fever, and his younger sister and two brothers died. His father never fully recovered from the disease either. Worn out and emotionally distraught from the loss of his children, Sylvester died that same spring from a heart attack. He was only forty-two years old. At age fifteen, Chester became the head of the household.

To help his mother make the mortgage payments, Chester left his family in Ovid, New York, and moved to Corning to work at a local lumberyard. Although they wrote letters, Chester was homesick and lonely. A responsible boy, he grew into a serious man with a driving ambition and a fierce need to succeed. He never wanted to face the want, loneliness, and insecurity he knew as an adolescent.

By the fall of 1870, Chester had moved back to Ovid to be near his family, and he was able to enroll in the college preparatory curriculum at East Genesee

Conference Seminary. There he graduated as class valedictorian. In September 1871, he joined the law program at Syracuse University, a Methodist school. He preferred Yale, but he could afford Syracuse. Sons and daughters of clergymen only had to pay half the tuition—ten dollars per term. While attending college, he worked as an administrator at a girls' school to help pay his tuition. He still found time to write for the school newspaper and play on the baseball team.

In his mathematics class, Chester met Clara Hesperia Bannister, whose father was also a Methodist minister. Chester was impressed that "Clara always knew her lessons." She was a beautiful girl with long brown curled hair pulled back from her face and parted down the middle. She had large, dark eyes and a heart-shaped mouth. She studied art and architecture. They fell in love and planned to marry after they graduated from college. In June 1875, Chester and Clara both graduated Phi Beta Kappa from Syracuse University, part of the first graduating class. But Chester would not commit to marriage until he had his finances in order.

After graduation, he worked as an apprentice for a law firm for two years, and in 1877 he passed the bar examination for the state of New York. Clara continued her education in art and became an art instructor at a Methodist college preparatory school in Pennsylvania. Chester hoped to start an independent law practice, but until he could afford to do that, he taught school in New York state. Then he was offered the position of principal at a high school in Chippewa Falls, Wisconsin, and he accepted, even though he would have to move even farther away from Clara. His yearly salary would be $900.

Dissatisfied with the teaching profession, Chester resigned his post as principal before his first year was up and set out to explore more of the Upper Midwest. He wanted to test his chances as a lawyer. When he arrived in St. Paul, Minnesota, he had 31 dollars in his pocket. He loved the city and decided that this was where he wanted to settle down with Clara and raise a family.

In January 1880, he passed the Minnesota Bar Examination and joined a local law firm. Unfortunately, Chester found his work monotonous. He lived an austere life. He was overcome with responsibilities and self-doubt and was described as having negative aloofness. A former instructor from Syracuse wrote, "You indulge too much in cynicism," and advised Chester not to isolate himself so much.

All this time he had been sending money home to his mother to help her make her mortgage payments. In a letter to Clara he wrote, "I have $9.67 in cash, $5.00 receivable from my law firm, a month's prepaid rent at $8.00, a meal ticket worth $5.75, two pounds of crackers, two pounds of canned meat and one-half pound of coffee."

Things were moving too slowly for a man with Chester's ambition. By now, he and Clara had been engaged for five years, and she still lived on the East Coast. Chester was depressed, but Clara tried to boost his morale, congratulate him on his accomplishments, and look optimistically toward his career and their future together.

Chester's luck changed in 1881. In St. Paul he had struck up a friendship with William Billson, the United States District Attorney, and Billson offered Congdon a job as his assistant. This was the job security that he needed to get married.

On September 29, 1881, Chester and Clara were wed in Syracuse, New York. There was no money for a honeymoon. After the service, they boarded a train for

St. Paul to begin their life together. The couple lived in a very small home at 65 Wilkin Street near Irvine Park. One year later, in 1882, their first son, Walter, was born. After his birth, they needed more space and moved to occupy the bottom floor of a house at 325 South Franklin; another family lived upstairs.

Edward and Marjorie were born within the next five years. These first three children were named after Chester's deceased brothers and sister. The Congdons moved once more, to 546 Selby, on the west bluff, overlooking the city. Helen and John were born here, but like Chester's own siblings, John caught scarlet fever and died shortly before his second birthday.

In 1883 Chester resigned his position as assistant district attorney, realizing that there was no room for advancement, and he started his own practice, where he would remain for the next six years. His client list grew, and for the first time in his life, his finances looked promising. During this time, he traveled frequently to Duluth, where he visited his friend William Billson. Billson's federal office was in St. Paul, but he also had his own law firm in Duluth, Minnesota. It was at this time that Chester began investing in western mining stocks.

During these years, Duluth was growing rapidly. William Billson was enthusiastic about the city's future, and Congdon got excited when he heard Billson expound on the development plans for the city. Duluth was a major port on Lake Superior. Lumber businesses flourished at the mouth of the St. Louis River, railroads brought grain to Duluth's harbor elevators, and the real estate industry was growing rapidly. On top of that, a deposit of iron ore had been discovered sixty miles to the north in the Mesabi Range. Billson offered Congdon a partnership in his law firm, and Congdon had the good sense to accept. Clara and their children joined him in Duluth, where they found a house in the eastern section of the city at 1530 E. First Street. It was 1892.

Henry W. Oliver then entered the picture. Oliver had his own steel company in Pittsburgh. Hearing the announcement of iron ore on the Mesabi Range, he traveled to Duluth to investigate. Oliver, according to one historian, "saw in a flash that he had found what he was looking for, a vast body of high grade ore, cheaply mined." He needed legal counsel and was recommended to William Billson, but Billson was out of the office when Oliver arrived. With some reservation, Oliver agreed to meet with his partner, Chester A. Congdon.

The two men hit it off immediately, and Congdon was hired to be Henry Oliver's legal counsel. Now that Oliver knew his interests would be taken care of in Duluth, he went back to Pittsburgh and formed the Oliver Iron Mining Company. Soon, Andrew Carnegie, founder of United States Steel, the largest steel manufacturer in the nation, merged his interests with Oliver's. With new ore bodies being discovered almost daily, Oliver advised Congdon to lease additional iron ore land, in the company's name, whenever the opportunity arose. The addition of Carnegie's money to the venture made this expansion possible. In 1893, John D. Rockefeller entered the iron ore mining business. Competition was getting stiffer.

By 1899, Congdon had formed a partnership with another fellow Duluthian, Guilford Hartley, who also had an eye for obtaining leases on less-than-desirable iron ore properties on the Mesabi Range. Test drilling showed that this ore was mixed with silica (sand), a waste product. They took a risk and acquired leases on large tracts of land in the area, knowing that the ore was presently unusable. The silica would have to be removed. At great expense, Congdon and Hartley hired a mining engineer to construct a small washing mill, which removed the contaminating silica. They convinced Thomas Cole, the president of the Oliver Iron Mining Company, the mining subsidiary of United States Steel, that the ore could be washed and made marketable. Eventually, United States Steel bought the ore land. The Mesabi Range would be the source of the iron ore that built U.S. ships and tanks in both World Wars. Chester Congdon was on his way to becoming a very wealthy man.

On April 22, 1894, Chester and Clara had a daughter, Elisabeth Mannering, named after Clara's maternal grandfather. One year after her birth, the family bought a large brick house, the Redstone Building, at 1509 E. Superior Street, where they would live for the next thirteen years. Built by a Duluth architect, it was considered one of Duluth's most elegant and fashionable homes. Four years later, in 1898, Robert was born.

Though busy with six children, Clara was also very active in the Methodist church. She was a devout woman, a believer in long prayers before meals. She was a patient lady, intuitively understanding. Clara loved to sew and made certain that her daughters learned how to mend. She sewed with only the finest laces and materials.

Chester was warm and loving with his children, but he was also demanding of them. He required his daughters to study difficult subjects at school and expected his sons to perform difficult work. He regarded his wealth as a responsibility and the management of it a difficult task—he wanted his children to be up to it. Chester took a more stern approach with his children than Clara did. The children attended elementary schools in Duluth but were sent back East for preparatory and college work—the boys eventually graduating from Yale, where Chester had once wanted to attend. The girls studied at Dana Hall in Wellesley, Massachusetts, and two of them, Helen and Elisabeth, continued on to Vassar.

Chester had a penchant for big houses. In 1903, when Elisabeth was nine years old, he and Clara decided to build their dream home on the north shore of Lake Superior. Chester purchased twenty-two acres of land along Lake Superior and London Road. He hired a Minnesota architect, Clarence H. Johnston, Sr., to design their home, which was bordered by the lake on one side, a wooded area to the east, and a small cemetery to the west. Clara mused that they would have quiet neighbors.

Construction on the new home began in 1905. The Congdons modeled it after the English country estates that were popular in the early 1600's—England's Jacobean Period—with cement and steel beam supports. This technique was typically used for commercial structures rather than residential homes. But the Congdons wanted the house to be able to withstand fire as well as the fierce storms that could blow up on the lake. They oversaw every stage of the construction of their home, which was finally completed in 1909. At that time, their oldest child was twenty-six and Elisabeth was fifteen. Because she was away at school, she missed much of the construction of her parents' new home, but she must have been duly impressed with what she saw when she came home on her breaks. Her father not only spent lavishly on the home, but he was both practical and innovative. The house was piped for gas light fixtures, but provisions were made for adding electricity when it became available. The bedrooms had walk-in closets, and pocket doors were installed on the main level for privacy. Every room had windows to view the lake and the magnificent grounds. Her mother's artistic taste and talents showed throughout. A bird theme ran throughout the interior of the house, as well as pineapples, which represented hospitality. The home was totally harmonious in pattern and color. Even though most of the children were past adolescence, Glensheen was built with one room for each child. The cost was over $750,000 in 1909 dollars, the equivalent of $24,000,000 today.

With its thirty-nine rooms, it was a home beyond compare in Duluth. On the ground floor was the billiard room, with broad-grained white oak. The wallpaper had been lacquered to make it resemble japanned leather. Handmade Irish and Persian rugs lined the walls. Centered in the room was a St. Bernard billiard table.

On the first floor was the central entrance, dominated by a massive stairway of fumed oak with hand-carved newel posts and grills. Ascending the staircase, a panoramic view of the grounds and the lake was visible through stained glass windows, which featured a Tudor rose design and a stylized heraldic shield. This staircase led to the second floor, with the master bedroom suite, Marjorie, Helen and Elisabeth's bedrooms, two guest bedrooms, and three bedrooms for the female members of the staff.

The boys—Walter, Edward, and Robert—stayed on the third floor. Even if the Congdons had married guests, the husband would have to room on the third floor. There would be no males staying overnight on the second floor where Chester's daughters slept. Chester Congdon had a protective nature.

The living room had a beamed ceiling of gold japanned leather, wall coverings of damask made from goats hair, and a fireplace faced with red marble from Algeria. The library was of mahogany with a ceiling of wrought leather. Wall hangings were exquisitely embroidered in wools and silks, all custom designed for the room. The dining room had a plaster relief ceiling that was made in Italy and shipped to Duluth in three-foot sections. The walls were gold and green silk damask specially woven for the room in Portugal, and the fireplace was faced in yellow marble with a frame of silver.

The family's favorite, the breakfast room, was windowed on three sides with a view of the lake. The floor was a low luster green tile and the windows were crystal plate.

Travel lovers, the Congdons brought back wonderful artifacts from the Middle East and Italy to adorn their home. Italian alabaster shimmered in the light fixtures in almost every room, and Oriental rugs adorned the hardwood floors.

There was a carriage house and paddocks with high fences for the horses. Glensheen cows produced fresh milk for the family. Clara loved roses and orchids, so they installed a greenhouse where, in addition to flowers, they also grew their own bananas. The colorful gardens and lawns on the estate stretched across almost eight acres of land, gently sloping down to meet Lake Superior. Surrounded by tall evergreens, birches and oaks, the reflections of the mansion and its beautifully landscaped grounds shimmered on Lake Superior's surface, a mirror image. The Congdons affectionately named it "Glensheen." *Glen* represented the wooded lot and *sheen* was chosen for the Congdon family's origin in the village of Sheen in Surrey, England.

Elisabeth was away at school when her family resettled at Glensheen. Of course, she was home for the summers, but oftentimes would travel with her parents to New York to visit Clara's relatives. The Congdons also took family vacations to historical sites and national exhibitions—Seattle, Chicago, San Fransisco, and Portland. Traveling would become an important part of Elisabeth's life. She would go to Tucson in the winter, where the Congdons had their winter home, to the East Coast, and to Europe whenever she could.

Though Chester proclaimed his place in Duluth Society with Glensheen, he also believed in service to the community. A staunch Republican, he served two terms (1909-1913) as a Minnesota legislator in the House of Representatives. In 1915, he donated funds to the city of Duluth for the purchase of shore land along Lake Superior, which helped create a scenic drive along the North Shore, known today as Congdon Boulevard.

As available ore land in the Upper Midwest became more difficult to obtain, Chester Congdon and his associates began to expand their horizons, investing in copper mines in Bisbee, Arizona, and eventually, Ajo (pronounced ah-ho), Arizona, an old abandoned mining site about 120 miles west of Tucson. Situated in a dry basin, surrounded by hills, the mining camp had acquired its name from the wild garlic (in Spanish, *aho*) that grows like weeds after a rain.

A dear friend of Chester's, John C. Greenway, had managed mining operations and developed small communities where the Oliver Iron Mining Company's employees had lived. Congdon hired Greenway to oversee the Ajo mining operations. To accommodate the miners, Greenway built the town around a plaza, with houses far enough away from the mine so that there would be less noise, a modern school for the children, a hospital, and a retail store. The community had a water and sewage system, electric power, and paved streets.

At first, Congdon was skeptical that the mines

would be profitable, but he trusted Greenway's experience. In 1914 Greenway reported that Ajo would net them $60 million. As Europe prepared for war, the price of copper rose, and so did Chester Congdon's wealth. Congdon had already involved two of his sons in the mining business, and now he invested in copper for two of his daughters. Another wise choice.

In 1914, Chester built another home for his family in the Yakima Valley in Washington state. The house, built on a bluff, took two years to build and became known as Westhome. At the Westhome property, Chester was able to indulge his interest in farming. He studied irrigation and constructed what was called the Congdon Ditch.

Unfortunately, Chester only had a few years to enjoy his homes. On November 21, 1916, while on business in St. Paul, he died of complications from a blood clot on one lung and a dilation of the heart, which produced a pulmonary embolism. He was sixty-three years old. Before his death, Chester had created two trusts to remain in effect while any of his children lived. "It is my desire and direction that so long as any of my children shall live, Glensheen shall be thus kept open by the trustees for the equal use of my children and their families, if any there be, as may at any time wish to either live in it, or revisit it as they would be free to do were my wife and I still surviving [sic]." He wrote that he expected his sons would most likely marry and make homes for themselves. He ordered that unmarried children would have a stronger claim upon the use of the home. He added, "My daughters will have preference over my sons for Glensheen."

All of his children did eventually marry—except for Elisabeth, who would one day be murdered in her second floor bedroom.

✣ *Chapter Two*

Clara was sixty-two years old when her husband died. Elisabeth was a sophomore at Vassar but left school and moved home to be with her mother. They were extremely close. Clara had suffered a severe hearing loss in her early forties and carried a hearing aid and a large battery with a microphone around her neck. To communicate, Elisabeth would talk directly into Clara's microphone and write messages to her. Elisabeth tried forming letters with her hands, but Clara preferred lip reading, which seemed to work best.

Clara's hearing problem did not hold her back. She remained active in the Methodist church, and she continued to paint with watercolors, do needlework, and travel. She loved to read, and she studied history, botany, science, and painting.

Clara and Elisabeth cared for the staff almost as if they were family. They hired mostly immigrant girls from Europe who were about sixteen or seventeen years old. One of their servants, a young German girl, Else Wilke, journaled during her days at Glensheen. Else's daughter-in-law, Virginia Soetebier, transcribed her diary and printed it in a book titled *Footnote to History*.

"Our workday began at 7 a.m. with the cook preparing breakfast for the household staff, all of whom ate together. After our meal, while the dishes were washed by hand, the cook made the same meal for Mrs. Congdon and Miss Elisabeth, who were served by the butler in the lovely breakfast room. Special porcelain dishes and flatware were used for lunch and breakfast with fresh flowers, which were brought in each morning by the gardener—in the summer, from the gardens, and in the winter, from the greenhouse. Oranges, lemons, bananas and many exotic plants and flowers were grown in that building, which stood next to the much-used tennis court."

Else Wilke wrote, "In the daytime, Miss Elisabeth wore mostly white shirtwaist blouses made out of the finest cotton, lawn fabric with tiny handstitched tucks and a long skirt. In summer, she spent a lot of time at Northland Country Club and some time was spent at a summer house on the Brule."

Elisabeth loved to play tennis and, when in Brule, Wisconsin, pole the rapids with her friends in heavy wooden canoes. This was a popular sport at the time.

In her twenties, Elisabeth became engaged to Fred Wolvin, who also lived in Duluth. Considered a catch, he had a reputation for being a ladies man and a wonderful dancer—and he had his heart set on Elisabeth. He gave her a beautiful diamond engagement ring. Elisabeth must have been unsure of her feelings or his commitment because instead of wearing the ring on her finger, she pinned it inside her bra. The engagement was never announced. Eventually, Elisabeth broke up with Fred. She realized that she did not love him enough to marry him. When she gave him back the diamond engagement ring, he was so devastated he threw it into Lake Superior. Fred remained single for the rest of his life.

As for Elisabeth, she was part of the social set in Duluth. She was the president of King's Daughters when she was only twenty-six years old. She traveled to Brule and Tucson, and went abroad to spend time with relatives and her good friends the Marshall sisters, Julia and Caroline, who were her favorite traveling companions. Marriage did not make her priority list.

Caroline was three years older, and Julia two years younger than Elisabeth. Like the Congdons, the Marshalls also enjoyed great wealth and resided on London Road. They also wintered in Tucson. Their father, Albert M. Marshall, had moved his family to Duluth from Saginaw, Michigan, in 1892 and founded Marshall Wells, a wholesale hardware operation that became the giant of its day. The Marshalls' summer home, which the Congdons often visited, was on the Brule River in Wisconsin.

The Marshall sisters were inseparable, but at the same time, they were very different in nature. Caroline was small and always dressed like a lady—with nylons, fancy shoes, and jewelry. She was "pale and proper." Julia, who was at first more like a younger sister to Elisabeth, was more frenetic and bounced around from one thing to another. She was spunky and was described as "undeniably nuts. If she would do backflips across the yard, it wouldn't surprise anyone." Julia was a petite girl, only five feet, three inches with brown eyes and short dark hair. Always tan. She liked to dress in ordinary clothes, beat-up pants and plaid shirts, romping-in-the-woods clothes. She was a tomboy and she educed Elisabeth's outgoing side.

Eventually, Elisabeth began to long for children. What drove this desire is not known, but in any case, fulfilling her wish would not be an easy task without a husband—especially in the 1930s. At that time, it was almost unheard of for a single woman to adopt. In 1932, when she was thirty-eight years old, she came home from one of her vacations on the East Coast with a three-month-old baby girl. She told Clara and the rest of the family that she had adopted her. She was a tiny baby, with dark skin and straight, black hair.

Elisabeth named her Marjorie (after her older sister) Mannering (after her maternal grandfather) Congdon.

Rumors floated in back rooms in Brule. Miss Elisabeth's English butler and sometimes chauffeur, Jim Roper, told the cook, Sophie Boelter, that he had driven Elisabeth to New York. He said that Julia Marshall was there to greet them, and the next thing he knew they were driving back to Duluth with a baby girl. He believed that Marjorie was Julia's natural child and that she had given her to Elisabeth. No one else knew. Despite the rumors about Marjorie's adoption, nothing concrete was ever determined. In any case, Elisabeth had a child to love.

From the age of two, Marjorie was so nearsighted that she had to wear thick glasses. Elisabeth had to tie them on her so they wouldn't fall off when she played. Children don't like to feel different, and cumbersome glasses probably didn't help Marjorie's self-esteem. Her weak eyesight distanced her from other people. She was lonely.

Three years after Elisabeth brought Marjorie home, she took an extended trip out East where she adopted a second baby girl and named her Jennifer. She was a beautiful, blond, fair-skinned baby, and her arrival sparked more rumors. It was said that Elisabeth was Jennifer's biological mother. Jennifer was told that her natural parents were unmarried college students. As far as she was concerned, it didn't matter. Elisabeth was her mother and she was grateful for that.

Now, Marjorie had competition for her mother's love. It must have been emotionally confusing for her. It is not uncommon for an older child to feel jealousy when a new baby comes home, but from the beginning, Marjorie did not feel as though she fit into the Congdon family. Perhaps that was true. Jennifer would not suffer those insecurities. She was cheerful, easy-going, and flexible—characteristics that helped her adapt to a life that was not as easy for Marjorie.

As they grew, it became obvious that the sisters would never be close. Jennifer was an extrovert, loved to be outside and play with her friends. The staff at all of the Congdon households loved her. Three years her elder, Marjorie was an introvert and spent much of her time alone reading in her favorite chair. The staff rarely saw her. They assumed she was shy or that perhaps she was uncomfortable with adults. Marjorie seemed to be more at ease with horses and other pets than people. She loved to hide in the secret panels of Glensheen and play house by herself in the massive attic on rainy days.

Glensheen was a house of females. Although there were many relatives, the two Congdon girls lacked a father figure. Even so, Marjorie felt close to her mother's older brother Edward, or Uncle Ned, as he was called. She pretended that he was her father. He and his wife Dorothy were actually Jennifer's godparents, but both of the girls loved Uncle Ned. It was devastating for them both when he died of a heart attack in 1940, when he was only fifty-five years old. Marjorie was eight years old and Jennifer was five. About this time, Marjorie began to show noticeable problems. She would laugh in an odd way and pull out wisps of her own hair. She seemed to be alone and unaware that her schoolmates watched her.

Elisabeth's youngest brother, Robert, like many of Elisabeth's siblings, was very disturbed about Marjorie's behavior. He had disapproved of the adoption and now of the way Elisabeth handled her. He felt close to Jennifer but quite put off by Marjorie's growing behavioral problems. He felt that his sister was ill-equipped to deal with them. She overcompensated by giving Marjorie whatever toys, clothes or animals she asked for—a pattern that would become a way of life for Elisabeth as well as for Marjorie. Although close relatives could see what was happening, they felt powerless to do anything about it.

Growing up at the Glensheen Mansion was a privileged life for Elisabeth's daughters. They lived in a world of velvet drapes, gilded ceilings, Oriental carpets, and canopy beds. Tea was served promptly at 4:30 in the living room or at the tennis court on nice days. Clara would fix sliced cucumber and tomato sandwiches for Elisabeth and her girls. She also taught her granddaughters intricate needlework.

Elisabeth loved to read. She belonged to two book clubs. When her daughters were young, she spent hours reading to them. When Jennifer was a teenager, she would step in Elisabeth's room to say goodnight, and she would often find her mother sound asleep with her glasses on and a book face down on her chest.

Marjorie took French lessons from a governess. Jennifer learned to write in Chinese. In the fall, they attended a school called the Normal School in Duluth, which was connected to a teachers' college, and after the Christmas holidays, Elisabeth would take them to their winter home in Tucson, Arizona. Here, they attended another private elementary school, the Arizona Sunshine School. They had many friends and relatives in Tucson as well as Duluth, and the switching of schools was not a struggle for Jennifer. She was pretty and vivacious, the outgoing child who seemed to fit in anywhere. But it was more difficult for Marjorie with her sensitive and reserved nature. She did not make friends easily, and moving back and forth was stressful. This was a child who didn't feel as though she belonged in her own family, so being bounced around from house to house must have contributed to her growing vulnerabilities.

The girls also traveled with their mother to Europe, Mexico, to Westhome in Yakima, Washington, and of course, to Brule, where they spent many weeks during the summer. And there were rides on the *Hesperia*—Clara's middle name—the Congdon yacht. To some it would seem a charmed life. But Marjorie's problems were deeper than vacations, yachts, or summer homes could solve. She felt that her natural parents had abandoned her. She was embarrassed when she explained to her friends that her mother was a "Miss." But this was not something Elisabeth could totally protect Marjorie against, though she tried her best to shield her. While Elisabeth did her best to compensate, she may not have recognized that Marjorie needed boundaries. She needed to be rooted in one place. Like all children, she needed discipline.

Elisabeth was determined to make holidays memorable for her daughters. At Christmastime, Marjorie, Jennifer, and their cousins would gather ground pine and weave it into garlands, which would hang around the balconies, down the stair railings, and along the walls. There would be huge wreaths with satin ribbons on the doors. Then, on Christmas morning, they would wake early to go down to a huge breakfast in the main dining room with Clara and Elisabeth. Marjorie would be off-hand and reserved in her excitement, while Jennifer would be "chomping at the bit" to get downstairs to the amusement room where there was a roaring fire in the fireplace and a huge decorated tree adorned with ornaments and silver tinsel and loaded with presents. They had a tradition. After breakfast, the four "girls" marched into the amusement room in order of age—Clara, Elisabeth, Marjorie, and Jennifer—singing "Joy to the World" as they made their way toward the beautifully wrapped gifts.

Then they would sit down and take turns opening their presents, one at a time.

Later that day, the Congdon relatives would drive down London Road, some of them on horse-drawn carriages. They would be wrapped in buffalo robes, with hot bricks on the floor to keep their feet warm. Once they arrived at Glensheen, there would be a traditional turkey dinner, with dressing, gravy, mashed potatoes, yams, cranberries, and pumpkin pie. The older cousins were allowed to sit with the adults in the main dining room and the younger kids would eat in the breakfast room, which faced Lake Superior. They were happy not to be with the adults because the chairs in the main dining room were prickly, like horsehair, and made their legs itch. After the relatives left, Elisabeth would host a buffet for her friends who were alone on Christmas. Another lavish feast would be set up on the billiard table. While Jennifer would revel in all the relatives, Marjorie was never as comfortable. She didn't feel fully accepted because she knew she was adopted, and her cousins often reminded her of this. And, because she was dark, instead of fair like her sister and mother, she felt different.

Birthdays were special too. During the year, the maids would save all the string from packages and groceries so that Elisabeth could play "the string game" with her daughters. She would piece the ends of the string together and tie one end to the leg of a piece of furniture. The girls would find the end of the string, which was wrapped around sofa legs, tables, and chairs, and roll the string into a ball as they followed its path. When they got to the end of the trail, they would find their presents!

Throughout Marjorie's childhood, the Marshall sisters remained a part of Elisabeth's life. It is quite probable that Marjorie knew well the rumors about her birth and adoption. She complained that her cousins called her "bastard." Jennifer did not seem to have suffered from such name-calling.

Neither of the Marshall sisters ever married. Revered in Duluth, they were extraordinary women, artistic and generous. Julia was one of the founders of the American Indian Fellowship Association Center, a director of the St. Louis County Heritage and Arts Center, the founder of the Duluth Chapter of the League of Women Voters, and a member of the Model City Rehabilitation program. She also created the Duluth Art Institute, raised funds for the Canal Park Marine Museum, and she and her sister were instrumental in the establishment of the Marshall Performing Arts Center at the University of Minnesota in Duluth. In 1968, Julia was named Duluth's Woman of the Year. In 1972, Julia was added to the board of directors of the Duluth Area Chamber of Commerce, becoming the first woman director in the Chamber's history. Not surprising, she was named to the Duluth Hall of Fame that same year.

Caroline Marshall died at the age of 101 in 1992 and Julia died in 1994. She was 98 years old. If there is any truth to the rumor that Marjorie was Julia's biological child, it is buried now.

Despite being a single mother, Elisabeth, like Caroline and Julia Marshall, was a leader in Duluth Society, still active in many causes such as the Junior League. During World War II, the Northland Chapter of the American Red Cross became a large part of Elisabeth Congdon's family life. Since the majority of the country's doctors and nurses were sent abroad to attend to wounded soldiers, the Red Cross trained volunteers to replace them in hospitals at home. Women in Duluth became instant nurses, dedicated sewers, makers of care packages, and rollers of bandages. Everyone wanted to do their part. Elisabeth was no exception. She was the chairperson for the Red Cross Nurse's Aid Committee.

At home she was busy assisting her aging mother and two daughters, one of whom seemed to be presenting more and more problems all the time. Already, Marjorie liked to spend money. At the age of twelve she had started stealing money from her mother's purse and riding downtown on a bus to charge clothes at Walls Department Store. She would buy three or four cashmere sweaters at a time without Elisabeth's permission. These kinds of actions really stood out when everyone was cutting back for the war effort. Joyce Alsop* worked at the department store during this time. The president of the Erie Mining Company had adopted Joyce, and their families were social friends. Marjorie and Joyce attended the Normal School in Duluth, and because of their adoption, they felt a special bond. But, Joyce was sometimes astounded by her friend's behavior. Marjorie always seemed to be in a fervor, which made people feel uncomfortable. Their other school friends considered her aggressive and unpleasant. Joyce felt sorry for her.

Eventually, with the buying sprees continuing, Elisabeth called Walls Department Store and told them not to let Marjorie charge unless she had a note from her. This is when Marjorie learned to forge her mother's signature. And, this is when a small fire broke out in the store's basement. The cause was never determined.

---

* The names of some individuals have been changed. Such names are indicated by an asterisk (*) the first time each appears in the book.

As a young teenager, Marjorie and a friend, Ann Paine, rented horses from Skyline Stables, across from the Northland Country Club in Duluth. Marjorie's favorite horse was a Tennessee Walker named Greyhound. The girls used English saddles and rode up and down Snively Road, a winding rural road, about one mile long, that looked over Lake Superior. Greyhound was a large horse, about fifteen hands, or five feet, and had a running walk. He required an experienced rider. Marjorie loved him. Ann thought that Marjorie was an "excellent horse woman." When Skyline Stables closed down, Elisabeth bought Greyhound for Marjorie.

Another acquaintance recalled that Marjorie soon tired of Greyhound and refused to take responsibility for it. She told her mother she didn't want it anymore. Jennifer didn't want the horse, so Elisabeth told Marjorie that she was going to give it to someone who would love it and take care of it. Elisabeth did not realize that her solution was not acceptable to Marjorie. If Marjorie couldn't have Greyhound, neither could anyone else.

One day a caretaker at Glensheen walked into the carriage house to get a rake. He saw Marjorie using both hands to coax some oats into Greyhound's mouth. She was feeding him with such intensity that it made him stop and watch her. He said, "Hey, Marjorie, Greyhound doesn't look all that hungry right now." Marjorie had not seen him enter the carriage house. She turned around with a start, and the oats dropped out of her hands. She ran past him and out the door as if she thought he was going to chase her. Then he noticed what looked like small, white pills scattered on the floor with the oats she had dropped. He raked through the oats with his hands and saw that there must have been thirty or forty pills. He didn't know what they were, but it was obvious by the look on Marjorie's face and the way she ran out that she knew she was doing something wrong. He had to tell her mother.

He was worried about confronting Miss Congdon about the incident since he was only a caretaker, but she had always been so friendly, offering him lemonade on hot days and treating him "just like anyone else." Besides, he loved horses, and he was afraid that Marjorie might try it again. He thought she needed a good spanking. So, he knocked on Miss Congdon's door and explained what had happened. Elisabeth was very kind to him, as always, and thanked him for being forthright. To his dismay, that was the last he heard about it. Elisabeth was able to find a new owner for Greyhound, and in doing so, probably saved the horse's life. But now, it was obvious that Marjorie had a serious problem.

When Marjorie was in the eleventh grade, Elisabeth sent her to Wellesley, Massachusetts, to attend Dana Hall, the same school she had gone to as a girl. Perhaps Elisabeth hoped a change of location and the discipline of a boarding school might help her daughter. At first it seemed to be working. Marjorie proved an excellent student. She was intelligent and got good grades. One classmate said, "Marjorie read books way beyond her years. But she was no good at math. She was in my algebra class at Dana Hall, and I loved math, and she just couldn't understand it. Logic was beyond her. She would say, 'I just don't get it, I don't get it.' It was the only time I ever saw her defenseless." She didn't remember Marjorie as having any friends. "She reminded me of Judy Garland with that high forehead and fine hair, which I used to watch her pull out. Her body was squat, with a small waist and large hips and thighs. She was very talented, especially with needlework."

When Marjorie was eighteen, spending a winter break at their home in Tucson, the chauffeur saw her steal money out of her mother's purse. When he informed Elisabeth, she realized that Marjorie's actions had not changed in the new school. She had to do something more drastic. A friend of Elisabeth's who was a child psychiatrist advised her to send Marjorie to the Menninger Clinic in Topeka, Kansas, for psychological evaluation. She did. Marjorie was not there for long when Elisabeth consented to her getting outpatient therapy at Washington University in St. Louis Missouri. Elisabeth never discussed the outcome of Marjorie's treatment or her diagnosis with anyone. That was too personal. This must have been a very stressful time for her, not only because she had such a troubled daughter, but also because her mother died that same year. Clara's death was a terrible loss for Elisabeth. But she kept her problems to herself.

❧ *Chapter Three*

Richard Webster LeRoy was born in Somerville, Massachusetts, the youngest of eight children. Like the Congdons, his family was Methodist. When Dick was three years old, his family moved to Winchester where he graduated from high school in 1944. After a two-year hitch in the Navy, he enrolled at the University of Massachusetts where he graduated in 1949 with a bachelor's degree in political science and history. The economy was slow in Boston that year, so Dick accepted an invitation from his brother to come to St. Louis and seek work. He landed a job with the General Insurance Company of America and eventually became a casualty underwriter.

After a short time living at the downtown Y.M.C.A. in St. Louis, Dick moved to a rooming house on Washington Street. A few doors down was Mom and Pop Lippert's Boarding House, which served meals to boarders and neighbors. On a warm evening in September 1950, Dick sat across the table from Marjorie Congdon. They had a nice conversation over dinner, and he found her intellectually bright and stimulating. She told him that she had come to St. Louis to attend Washington University but decided that she didn't like it. She decided to take a nursing course instead, as well as a class or two at St. Louis University. He had no reason to doubt her. They began to date. They enjoyed eating at Parentés Cellar, a pizza place, and they became active at Centenary Methodist Church. Its YAKS (Young Adult Klub) hosted potluck dinners and volleyball games, and performed social service projects such as helping paint the church. Marjorie found Dick not only intellectually stimulating, but also attractive, standing nearly six feet tall with dark hair and huge, warm hazel eyes full of compassion. He had a calm voice, and he was a good listener. Marjorie needed a good listener.

Several months after they met, Dick proposed marriage and Marjorie accepted. He was twenty-four; she was nineteen. Elisabeth and Jennifer had been on vacation together in Europe, and on the way home they stopped in St. Louis to see Marjorie and meet Dick LeRoy. Elisabeth took to him immediately, but she told Marjorie that she would prefer that her daughter travel and have some life experiences before she settled down to marry. Marjorie wouldn't hear of it.

Eventually resigned to her daughter's wish to marry, Elisabeth emphasized to Marjorie that a husband and wife should have a relationship based on trust. She encouraged Marjorie to confess to Dick that she had been treated at the Menninger Clinic. Marjorie did mention the clinic to him, but she explained that Elisabeth was a doting mother, a worrier, and that she had been overly concerned about Marjorie's strong personality. Marjorie said she went along with the clinic appointments to pacify her mother, even though it was silly. Dick accepted her explanation.

On June 30, 1951, with about 150 people in attendance, they married in the living room of the Glensheen Mansion. Dick's hometown newspaper, the *Winchester Star*, covered the wedding:

> Before a fireplace, banked with caladium, ivy and maidenhair fern at the home of her mother, Elisabeth M. Congdon, 3300 London Road, Duluth, Minnesota, Miss Marjorie Mannering Congdon became the bride of Richard Webster LeRoy at 4:30 p.m. Saturday afternoon, June 30. Miss Congdon wore a gown of white Italian silk satin, a fitted bodice designed with a scalloped, portrait neckline edged in heirloom rosepoint lace and a bouffant, hoop skirt, extending into a cathedral train. Her veil was silk illusion, which belonged to her aunt, Mrs. Marjorie Congdon Dudley, and was cupped to a satin Dutch cap. An arrangement of lilies of the valley made up her bouquet.

The announcement went on to describe Jennifer Congdon's maid-of-honor's dress and the attire of the other four attendants—Helen Moore, Ann Paine, Caroline Lewis, and Betsy Congdon Mason. The bride's mother wore a floor-length gown of gray chiffon with bateau neckline.

After the reception at Glensheen, the bride and groom went to Swiftwater Farm in Brule, a house Elisabeth had purchased in 1947. It was near the Marshalls' summer home. They had a wonderful two-week honeymoon. Dick was looking forward to his new life. After the honeymoon, the couple moved into a new apartment complex in Brentwood, Missouri, a suburb of St. Louis. Dick returned to work. He was happy and everything seemed normal—for the first two months.

Suddenly, he started to get phone calls from unknown creditors asking why he hadn't paid his bills. He didn't know what they were talking about. He was making $260 a month, and he had given Marjorie the money to buy food and necessities. When he confronted Marjorie about the phone calls, she told him that her mother had run up these bills on their accounts with her permission.

Dick called Elisabeth, and she informed him that this was not true. She asked him, sadly, why he hadn't figured out "Marjorie's little problem" before he married her. She immediately sent him $3,500 to cover the obligations. This would be the first of many instances in which Elisabeth would bail him out.

Dick was overwhelmed with the situation. Clara Congdon had set up a trust for all of her grandchildren, and in order to help Dick, Elisabeth persuaded the trustees to pay Marjorie her interest from Clara's trust immediately rather than waiting until she was twenty-one. This provided an annual income of about $6,000, which over the years became about $8,000.

While the additional income helped, Marjorie continued to spend far beyond her means. When she was twenty-five, she became entitled to receive income from the M 1972 trust set up by Elisabeth in the 1930s after she had adopted Marjorie. At that time, inheritance by adopted children was a questionable legal matter. Elisabeth wanted to be sure that Marjorie was well provided for, and this trust provided another $25,000 annually. With that income, the $8,000 from Clara's trust, and Dick's salary, their combined income was well over $50,000 a year. Still, Marjorie's spending outpaced her income. They were now $25,000 in the hole. She took the trouble to hide bills, but when Dick confronted her she didn't deny what she had done. She left him to assume responsibility for her actions. Again and again, Elisabeth came to his rescue.

Stephen was born in 1952, eleven months after the wedding. The next year, Peter was born, and then Suzanne, Andrew, and Rebecca. Dick was teased a lot about having so many children. He was asked if he was a good Catholic or a passionate Protestant. He would laugh good-naturedly and say, "I guess I am a passionate Protestant."

After one year in St. Louis, Dick was promoted to the position of office manager at the General Insurance Company office in Minneapolis. His job required him to travel, which was unfortunate because he was away from Marjorie and the children, and he had less control over her spending sprees. After one year of traveling to small towns in northern and southern Minnesota, he decided that his absence was too much of a strain on the family. He resigned and started his own agency, The American Insurance Agency in Minneapolis. It was a difficult transition because money was tight, and that was a concept that Marjorie did not understand.

Mr. and Mrs. LeRoy and their four babies lived in suburban Minneapolis in St. Louis Park, in a 1750s replica with hand-pegged paneling and wrought-iron hinges on the doors—a typical two bedroom Early American house. One baby shared a room with Marjorie and Dick and the others slept in the second bedroom. Dick loved that house. But Marjorie wanted something bigger. She contacted the realtor that had sold them the house, and they began to search for something new. She found just what she wanted on Fremont Avenue South in Minneapolis. Dick told her that he had no interest in it because they could not afford to move.

Marjorie asked the real estate agent to write up an earnest money contract, but Dick refused to sign it. Undeterred, she took the contract back to the realtor, scratched his name off it, and gave the realtor a check for $1,000. She told the realtor that she was expecting many thousands of dollars from a trust fund in Duluth and that she would pay for the house herself. The check was no good.

Dick suspected that she might go behind his back, so he called the realtor to tell her that they would not be buying the house. Before he could tell her though, she congratulated him on his new home on Fremont Avenue. Elisabeth sent the LeRoys a check for $32,000. Dick promised her that he would pay her back someday. Her generosity amazed him.

The Glensheen Mansion soon became the venue for another beautiful wedding. In September 1955 Jennifer had met Charles (Chuck) William Johnson while he was a graduate student at MIT and she was attending Garland College in Boston. Though not close to her sister, Marjorie was Jennifer's matron of honor and Dick was one of the groomsmen. Jennifer felt obligated to have Marjorie in her wedding, and she did not want to hurt her mother.

After the wedding, Chuck joined the Army, and the newlyweds lived in Belvoir, Virginia, outside of Washington, D.C., for two years. Here, he started a computer lab that eventually evolved into a financially successful company, Visual Numerics, Inc., a scientific soft-ware business. They settled on Lake Michigan in Racine, Wisconsin, where Chuck grew up. Now there would be no reason for Jennifer and Marjorie to cross paths. Jennifer and Chuck enjoyed a happy marriage, had six beautiful children (five girls and one boy), and few money worries.

Marjorie was busy raising her own large family. In 1959, Heather LeRoy was born, and then Richard (Ricky), Jr., came along. By 1960, there were seven little LeRoys. When the children were young, Marjorie took care of them herself, but eventually she left them with sitters to go on her shopping sprees. Then she hired Hester Norwood to help care for the children and the house. Dick and the kids loved Hester and thought of her as a member of the family. She would arrive around 10:00 in the morning and stay until 7:00 p.m. She cooked lunch and dinner, and attended the kids' school events.

Marjorie developed a serious interest in antiques at this time—eighteenth century. She frequented antique stores and set out to decorate her house in that period. It was an expensive hobby. She complained to Dick that the living room was shabby and they needed new furniture. After Dick said they couldn't afford it she didn't mention it again for a while; Dick thought that she had finally seen the light. He was relieved, but not for long.

On a Sunday morning like any other Dick piled the kids in the car to go to church and waited for Marjorie. They waited so long before she finally came out that the family thought they'd be late. When they returned from church, they were shocked to see that the house and, most specifically, the furniture had been vandalized. Their dog and their neighbor's dog were in the house, and Marjorie blamed them for destroying the furniture. But it was clear that the chairs and sofas had been slashed with a knife. For the first time, Dick was alarmed. Marjorie called the same insurance company that Dick had worked for, submitted her claim, and re-decorated the living room.

The children's bedrooms were also redecorated with eighteenth-century furniture and antiques. The rooms had hardwood floors, and each bed had a quilt from that period. It was hard to believe that these were children's rooms—immaculate, without a toy in sight. They were like mini-museums. Marjorie did her re-search. She went to the trouble to find out what type of paint was used in that era and tried to duplicate it. Her compulsion to spend money escalated, and there was no end to fulfilling her needs. Dick knew that a lot of men would have walked out right then and there. But he had seven kids. And he did not want to leave them. Also, he had become very attached to his mother-in-law. She had been so good to all of them that he didn't want to disappoint her. One thing she had said to Dick stuck in his mind: "If it weren't for you and the chil-dren, I would just let Marjorie go." Even she had her limits.

❧ *Chapter Four*

Marjorie was a good mother, at least when it came to granting her kids' wishes, whether it be clothes, les-sons, pets, or material items. She wanted all the best for her children. She saw to it that they were always clean and well dressed, that they were disciplined, and that they had the best education that money could buy.

She wanted them to take up horseback riding and enter shows. She wanted them to be figure skaters. She wanted them to be competitors.

Mannette Allen remembers the day in 1962 that Marjorie arrived at the Ice Center in Minneapolis with her entourage, all seven children. She told Mannette that she wanted her to be their figure skating coach. Mannette was a tiny woman—about five feet, three inches, with short, dark hair, wide almond-shaped, light brown eyes, and a clear, waxy complexion, perpetually tanned, as if she lived in Florida, not Minnesota.

Most kids started out in group lessons, but Marjorie wanted nothing to do with that. She wanted Mannette to give her children private lessons as a family. Mannette tried to explain that this was not practical because each child was at a different level. It was obvious from the beginning that ten-year-old Stephen had the talent and the drive. Four of the kids eventually quit skating. Yet all of the LeRoy children made a favorable impression on Mannette. They were polite and well-behaved.

Every morning the skaters got up at 5:00 and practiced for one or two hours before Marjorie took them to school. She stayed at the Ice Center with them, watching and encouraging. Dick and the other children slept until 6:45 a.m. He saw that they had breakfast and got them off to school. (They all went to private schools, except for Peter who attended Minneapolis Vocational High School.) Ricky took a bus to Breck, and Dick drove Andy to Blake and Suzanne to Northrup School. Then, at 8:30, he went to work at his insurance company.

After school, Marjorie picked up the skaters and took them back to the Ice Center to practice. Or, if she had to take Suzanne to Jonathan Stables to ride, Dick would leave work at 4:00 p.m. to pick up the skaters. Oftentimes, Marjorie would not get home until 8:30 at night. Since Hester was there until 7:00, she helped pick up the slack. But it was getting to be too much for Dick to handle. His business suffered. Taking care of the children and trying to handle Marjorie's bills did not leave much time to sell insurance. He scrimped and saved to keep up with expenses, but there was no way to crawl out from under. Finally, he contacted the trustees of the estate, and they covered Marjorie's bills. Dick made house payments and paid utilities and groceries with the money he earned. He had to drop a $100,000 life insurance policy because there was no money to pay for it.

Eventually Peter, Andy, and Rick gave up skating. But before they quit, the *Minneapolis Star* did a story on them. The headline read, "Son's a Champion—Figure Skating Bug Hits Whole Family." There was a picture of Marjorie, Dick, and five of the children all posing in their skates. "The figure skating is as contagious as the twenty-four hour flu. When it hits one, the whole family gets it," Marjorie commented. Dick posed for the picture to be a good sport, but he had no interest in skating. Marjorie was not a skater either. Stephen would be the star.

In the beginning, when all seven kids were still taking lessons, Marjorie made sure that they were dressed in the most beautiful costumes of sequins, satin, and chiffon. It was difficult—almost impossible—to keep seven children (four of them boys) clean, no matter how careful they were. Yet it was important that they looked their best. Once in that first year, they all performed in the ice show. The seven LeRoy children marched into the arena, single file, each of them with their group number—representing age and skating ability—and all of them wearing a dry cleaner bag over their costume with slits cut out of the top for their heads to poke through. When it was their turn to perform, Marjorie yanked the bags off of them, and out they went to do their thing. Marjorie said to Mannette, "Well, it was the only thing I could think of, and it worked." Embarrassed as they were, if Marjorie told her children they were going to wear dry cleaning bags, they knew better than to question her. Her love for them was laced with discipline. She commanded their respect.

Mannette and Marjorie became close friends. Besides the fact that Mannette was an excellent skating teacher, she had three sons and one daughter who were close in age to Marjorie's children. Since they lived near each other, their kids played together, going back and forth to one anothers' houses constantly. Mannette felt like a second mother to Marjorie's children, and Marjorie felt the same. They helped each other out with car pooling and babysitting. They were there for each other in times of need. But, Marjorie and Mannette had problems too. There was no way to be Marjorie's friend and have everything run on an even keel. "Being Marjorie's friend was like riding a roller coaster."

There was a hierarchy in skating competitions. The regionals were the first round. If you came out in the top four, you would advance to the sectionals. There were hundreds of skaters who would never pass the regionals. If you came out on the top four of the sectionals, you would go on to the nationals. If you came out in the top four of the nationals, at the senior level, you made the world team. The competition was fierce.

"One year Stephen didn't win at regionals, but he qualified for the next level," explained Mannette. "I'm not a morning person. I sleep until 10:00 or 10:30 every morning. If you were my first competitor in the morning, it was your job to get me up or I might not be there. So if you wanted me there, you called, got me on my feet, and talked to me.

"Anyway, Stephen didn't do as well as Marjorie had wanted him to do at the regionals. She blamed me because I was his coach, so we went off to the next city to sectionals, and when I woke up the next morning, Stephen had already done his figures. She simply didn't call me. She told Stephen that I must have forgotten or overslept. He did it alone. He was hurt. Like I said, with Marjorie, you never knew if she was going to shower you with gifts, or pull the rug out from under you. But after you'd been very close for years, you learned to cope. 'Oh well, it's one of those days,' I'd say to myself."

Mannette's husband, Ken, was not comfortable with their relationship with the LeRoys. Dick and Ken got together with the families, but that was about the extent of their friendship. Marjorie was generous with her money, always giving gifts to Mannette and even paying for her airline tickets when they took Stephen to the various competitions around the country. The Allens would have the LeRoys over for backyard barbecues, and Marjorie would take the Allen family to the Athletic Club for Easter dinner. There was no way to pay them back. The families shared many experiences during those years when the LeRoys lived on Fremont Avenue.

The LeRoys had a Siamese cat named Sarah. Mannette's daughter, Stephanie coveted that cat, but the Allens had other pets—and did not need more. Marjorie decided to import an ocelot, a spotted, leopard-like cat, from down South to keep Sarah company. They named it Lancelot the Ocelot. Dick thought that "it was a ratty looking thing," white underneath and tan on top. When it was small it was striped, and when it got bigger the stripes changed into dots. Lancelot was about two feet long and would hang in the elm tree in their front yard on Fremont. The cat liked to ride on people's shoulders, so if some unsuspecting neighbor was out for a walk, the wild beast might leap out of the tree and onto their shoulder, looking for a lift. The neighbors were furious about the LeRoys' newest pet.

Lancelot mated with Sarah, the Siamese cat, and she had kittens, which they laughingly dubbed "simelots." The two cats should not have been allowed to mate. The ocelot was too big for Sarah, and naturally, the baby kittens would be too large for her to deliver. Sarah died in kitten-birth. The kittens were left without a mother to clean them or give them milk. Mannette took a couple of them and so did other friends who had female cats that would be able to mother these kittens. Despite their efforts, the kittens died. Some time later Mannette opened her door to see Marjorie standing on the porch with a beautiful Siamese cat in her arms.

"What's that for?" asked Mannette.

"For helping me."

"They didn't live, Marj, they died."

"I know, but you tried, and Stephanie has always wanted a Siamese cat, so I got her one."

***

In 1965, fourteen years after Dick and Marjorie's wedding, Elisabeth became partially paralyzed by a stroke. She would never regain the use of her right side. Elisabeth would need nursing care for the rest of her life. She could no longer read and had trouble speaking. Often, she would be unable to come up with a word, so the person with her would go through the alphabet slowly, and she would nod when the correct letter came up. Communicating with Elisabeth was reminiscent of her trying to communicate with her mother,

50

Clara, who had now been dead for fifteen years.

The next year, Suzanne LeRoy, twelve years old, was sitting on the porch when she looked over and saw that their garage was on fire. She ran in the house to tell her mother. Marjorie, who was sitting at the window that faced the garage, didn't even bother to look up from her paperback murder mystery. She said, "Don't worry about it." When Suzanne went back to the porch, she saw flames shooting out of the garage windows. Frightened, she ran back into the house to tell her mother. Marjorie repeated herself as if she were in a trance, "I said, don't worry about it, Suzanne."

Just then, Dick pulled into the driveway and saw that the windows in the garage were exploding. He quickly pulled the car out of the way and yelled at his neighbor to do the same because their garages were only a few feet apart from each other. He called the fire department, but they couldn't save the garage. It burned to the ground.

In 1967, Marjorie turned thirty-five and became entitled to all of the capital of one of the trusts, the Clara Congdon Trust. The money was composed of stocks and $288,000 cash. In 1968, Elisabeth would set up two other trusts and name Dick LeRoy as the person who could receive money on behalf of Marjorie and their children. She knew that if Marjorie was in charge her children would never see that money. What she didn't count on was that Marjorie could outsmart her husband.

One day in May 1967, Mannette got an emergency call from the skating rink. Stephanie had been practicing on the ice when she fell and hit her head. The caller said that Stephanie was lying on the couch and throwing up. She was ten years old. Mannette rushed to the rink to pick her up, and took her to the doctor. The doctor told her not to worry about it, it was a slight concussion, and to take her home and let her sleep. Mannette told the doctor that she'd read that you should never let someone with a head injury go to sleep. The doctor said, no, just take her home and put her to bed.

Mannette took her home and Stephanie began to have seizures. She lapsed into a coma. Mannette and Ken rushed their daughter to the hospital in the middle of the night and were told by the admitting doctor that Stephanie needed a brain surgeon. Mannette was horrified. Stephanie had a skull fracture and a brain concussion. She was hemorrhaging and the blood had to be drained from her head. During the operation, the doctors cut two circles in Stephanie's skull to drain the blood, and her parents were told that she had a 50 percent chance to live. At 3:00 in the morning, Mannette knew who she needed to call—Marjorie. Even though they had been out of touch, Marjorie came to the hospital immediately to comfort her old friend, and she visited Stephanie every day, bringing her gifts and keeping her company as she recovered.

But, just when she thought everything was back to normal, typically, Marjorie did an about face. Stephanie, within the year, had gotten back on the ice and had entered an ice-dancing test. Stephen and Stephanie had planned to be partners. It was important that the couples looked like a unit, and they were perfect together. But for some unexplained reason, Stephen wanted out. Mannette didn't remember why, but perhaps Stephen thought Stephanie wouldn't make him look good.

"At that point, I had to recruit whoever I could to be Stephanie's partner. She felt terrible."

"Stephen was a solid, good, strong partner. When

you took a dance test, you didn't always take them at the same time. You would find a partner who had already passed it, and then that partner skated you through it so that you could pass it. If I'd already taken the test, I'd find a young man who had not passed it and I'd skate him through as his partner.

"Marjorie pulled Stephen at the last minute, for some slight or other. Who knows? At this point, I was not about to cancel. Stephanie was a slight figure, and the only available partner was about six feet tall. I knew we'd get comments like 'Poor presentation' and 'Not enough alignment.'"

Mannette explained to the judges what had happened, and when Marjorie found out, she sued Mannette for defamation of character.

"She never liked to be beaten or bested. Ever."

Mannette called one of the dads in the club who was an attorney and asked him what to do. He told her to sue her back for breach of contract. She did. They settled out of court. Mannette won a minimal amount in the settlement, $500, paid for by Dick LeRoy.

"I didn't want a war. She started it. It was always a ride with Marjorie. You never knew which persona you were going to run into. She could be incredibly generous and she could be incredibly selfish. She had a volatile personality. She could be extremely dramatic, difficult, and then turn around and be the best friend you ever had. When you were close to Marjorie, you had to expect tidal waves, hurricanes, and sun showers."

❧ *Chapter Five*

To skate competitively required a huge amount of time, dedication, and money. If a skater missed his or her chance to get into a competition, they had to wait for six months to be judged again. The pressure was enormous. Oftentimes, children were in the sport because of their competitive parents, or "skating mothers," as they were called. Jealousy was a common emotion among skaters. Parents got to know one another because they spent so much time together, sitting in the stands, watching and waiting while their children practiced and competed against one another. This was how Marjorie met Helen Hagen. Marjorie and Helen spent hours together, knitting, chatting, and watching their kids practice. Mannette said that Marjorie could knit faster than any other human being. She never had to watch what she was doing, and "like a miracle, a sweater would grow."

Helen had three children, two boys and a girl. Her oldest son, Dick, was not a skater, but her other two, Tom and Nancy, were pair skaters. Helen attended all of their competitions. She did not believe in having her kids live in the "groupie homes" for skaters, which meant she did not want to leave her children unsupervised. She chaperoned them everywhere they went.

Mannette was Tom and Nancy's supplemental coach when they won their titles at the national competition. Some spectator parents called Helen a "tiger." Dick LeRoy believed that Helen and Marjorie were two of the most "vicious skating mothers that ever lived." The women were dubbed, "Two Strong-Minded Mamas." They were always looking for new places to send their kids to compete or looking for a new well-known coach, anywhere in the country. Luckily, Stephen skated as a single, and Nancy and Tom were a pair, so they did not have to compete against each other. Helen was married to Wally Hagen, a mellow, mild-mannered man. He was good-looking, and he was charming. Wally traveled for his work as an electrician, so he was not as involved in his children's skating life as Helen was.

Another skating mother, Arlene Luger*, said that Marjorie would take meticulous notes on all the skaters that competed with her children. She intimidated the other kids. She would sometimes yell, "You cheated, you cheated!" to the skaters on the rink if they got a better score than Stephen. She was infamous for her scenes. Points were posted along the way, and she would contest them before the first round. She would push her way through the crowds and intimidate not only the skaters but their parents as well. They called her a "carnival act."

Because there was only so much ice and so much ice-time, ice arenas were divided up into squares, or "patches." One arena might have twenty patches, each one about the size of a twenty-by–thirty-foot room. Each child would contract one patch to practice on.

The patches were used to practice "school figures" such as serpentines and figure eights. The length of a figure eight was supposed to be three times your height. So, if a skater was five feet tall, he or she needed to make fifteen-foot circles. Serpentines were three circles instead of two. These maneuvers would be practiced in a "patch session."

School figures were a strict discipline that is not used anymore. Working on a small square of ice was important to a figure skater for timing as well as precision. A serious, competitive skater would skate "patch" and "freestyle" every day.

Patches were hard to come by, and Marjorie wanted Stephen to be able to practice when the rink was less busy. At that time, he was in a public junior high school. Marjorie let him skip the afternoons so that he could have the rink to himself, to the dismay of school officials. They sent a truant officer to get him. At this, Marjorie pulled him out of the public school and enrolled him in Benilde, a Catholic school. But they were concerned about the absences too—until an anonymous donor gave a generous gift to the school, an in-circuit TV system. After that, no one questioned Stephen's truancy. He could skate whenever he wished.

Arlene described some of the underhanded methods used to knock out the competition. For example, skaters could get an exemption from a competition if they were ill, and Stephen often took advantage of this rule. He received many exemptions when it looked like he wasn't going to make the first round of a competition because the other skaters were better. Then he would proceed to the next level.

Equipment failures could knock a skater out of the competition too. Competitors' skates are like extensions of their feet, custom-made. They are carefully guarded. It was therefore devastating to the young girl who was about to compete against Suzanne to discover that her skates had disappeared. Like the good-fairy godmother, Marjorie came to the rescue. She lent the girl a nice pair of skates that she just happened to have with her. The girl couldn't skate in them, though, and she lost the competition. Suzanne won.

Skates could be ruined by running the blades over concrete. The blades would lose their critical edge—figure skating is all about edges, making the right cuts on the ice. Without the edge, "You were dust."

That's what happened to a boy who had been third

place in Stephen's division. The serpentines counted as two-thirds of the score. Free skating, the program with a music accompaniment, counted for one-third. Stephen was in fourth place after the school figures when there was a sudden crash. The boy in third place had slid into the boards. He suffered a concussion and had to withdraw. Marjorie was down in that corner of the rink, beet red, crying her eyes out, seemingly upset over the boy's accident. Someone had "borrowed" this boy's skates and ruined his edges. Stephen won the competition and went on to the nationals.

Stephen's clothes were always the brightest and the most expensive. This was another way to intimidate the other skaters, "another way to make the other children feel inferior." Marjorie hired a professional seamstress to sew her children's costumes. The seamstress sewed everything except the hems, which Marjorie worked on as she sat in the stands. The idea was to let everyone think that she had made the entire outfit. If she saw a bolt of fabric she liked, she would buy up the entire bolt so that nobody else could use it for their children's costumes.

In those days, the skaters brought record albums to the competitions to play music for their routines. They carried them in a hard box, usually two, in case something happened to one of them. Of course, their routine was choreographed with their music, and they couldn't compete without their records. If anything happened to the records, such as being scratched or broken, or stolen, the skater would be out of the competition. Whenever something of this nature happened, everyone suspected Marjorie.

Although Helen was Marjorie's friend, she did not seem to need the attention that Marjorie commanded. She was often alone, but happy and secure. Her life revolved around her children. As an electrician, Wally sometimes hired out to Venezuela for jobs. Once he was stationed in Greenland for three years. Helen was lonely and thought nothing of calling the LeRoys' house in the middle of the night. Marjorie would always get out of bed and talk to her for hours.

It wasn't easy for Helen and Wally Hagen to keep Tom and Nancy in the skating competitions. The costumes and the traveling were expensive, and it was a struggle for them to work it into their budget. However, they believed that their children had a gift and it was their duty as parents to keep them in the competitions. Marjorie, on the other hand, seemed to have limitless funds. The Congdon legacy was common knowledge in Minnesota, and Helen and Wally naturally assumed that Marjorie lived off a trust fund or some kind of allowance from her wealthy mother. What the Hagens didn't know was that Marjorie was drowning her husband in debt.

✤ *Chapter Six*

Dick never complained about Marjorie's spending. Even with all her income from the trusts, Marjorie cut into his meager earnings, and he got to the point where he couldn't take it anymore. He was overrun with interest payments, and he had to mortgage their house to cover Marjorie's bills. His wife was out of control, and he was carrying the emotional burden alone.

He talked her into getting counseling. She saw a doctor from the University of Minnesota who suggested that Dick get help too. He went to a different doctor and was told that he didn't seem to have any feelings. This surprised him, although Marjorie had once told him that he "had a great big shell" around him, and he wouldn't let anybody in. He thought about that and realized that if he let *her in*, she would destroy him. He never found out what Marjorie's doctor had said about her.

Dick believed that many of Marjorie's problems stemmed from the fact that she was adopted. Soon after they were married, Elisabeth had told Dick's mother, Beth LeRoy, that she had burned all of the adoption information about Marjorie before she married Dick. He didn't understand why anyone would do such a thing, but was under the impression that her attorney or the trustees of her estate had advised her to do so. Elisabeth told him that Marjorie's natural mother was a teacher who got pregnant out of wedlock. Elisabeth said that she had received that information from the Children's Home Society in Greensboro, North Carolina, in 1932. Of course, that information was ashes now.

Out of desperation, Dick decided to do his own research. He petitioned a judge in Duluth to issue a court order to the vital records office at the North Carolina Department of Human Resources to obtain a copy of her birth certificate. The judge complied with Dick's request and the birth certificate was released. The baby's name on the certificate was Jacqueline Barnes. It showed her mother as being Florence Barnes. A father was not named. When he got this information, Dick called the Children's Home Society. They wrote him a three-page letter full of general information: The natural family was of Anglo-Saxon stock, from a rural community. The last thing they had heard about the natural mother was that she had been a clerk in a store and was fired for stealing from the owner. Obviously, this information would be of no help to his wife.

Dick's irritation with the "skating bug" had been growing yearly. He believed that Marjorie pursued figure skating so that she could be the "mother of a champion," and he worried that since Peter, Andy, and Rick had quit skating, Marjorie was neglecting them. He wanted to do something special for them. He thought that Marjorie was strict with the children but "she did not show them much emotion." He had three sensitive boys who were all but abandoned by their mother because they did not shine on the skating rink like their brother Stephen.

Stephen wanted to quit figure skating, but Marjorie would not hear of it. He continued to work hard and the awards rolled in. In the late sixties, he won the American Gold, the Canadian Gold, and the International Gold. He repeated his achievements in the dance category and won three more medals. He became the Upper Great Lakes Juvenile Men's Champion and finally qualified for the nationals at the Senior Men's Midwestern competition, where he twisted his ankle and came in eleventh out of twelve. That was the end of his skating career. He had to quit. Marjorie was extremely distraught; it was as if she had lost her *own* identity.

In 1970, Dick took Peter, Andy, and Rick to Alaska for a two-week vacation. They flew from Minneapolis to Seattle and on to Fairbanks. They visited the University of Alaska, its museum, took a boat trip down the China River, and visited an Eskimo village. They rode the Alaskan Railroad and ate in a dining car, stopping at McKinley Park to climb a small mountain and then reboarding the train for Anchorage. Here, they got on a bus for a three-day trip to Valdez, the Yukon Territory, and finally to the Port of Haines, where they boarded a ferry and traveled down the Inland Passage to Victoria, British Colombia. "Kids should have good memories," he said after they returned home to Minneapolis. The boys got to experience a lot of "firsts" with their dad.

By the end of 1970, Dick felt as though he had *eight* children and "one of them was a real problem." He tried to manage the trusts as Elisabeth had requested, but between that and his job and trying to be a father to seven children, he couldn't handle it anymore. Marjorie's spending had surpassed being out of control. She bought horses that they could not afford to feed or board, and a car for each child when they turned sixteen. It was as if she were obsessed. He decided that his wife was a habitual liar and had "gone off the deep end." The physical and emotional stress had taken its toll on him. He decided that he would "step out of the picture." In 1971, after twenty years of marriage, Dick LeRoy sued Marjorie for divorce on the basis of cruel and inhuman treatment.

During his depositions to attorneys, Dick described his life with Marjorie. He told of her financial scheming and her dishonesty.

"We had attended the Hobart United Methodist Church for several years. Another member of the church, Mrs. Schnoor, asked Marjorie to bake some cookies for a church event. Later I heard from the minister that my wife told Mrs. Schnoor that I had left her, and that she didn't have any money, that there was no food on the table, and certainly no materials to make cookies. This was just a couple of weeks ago!

"In January 1969, I came home to find a beautiful Oriental rug being put down in my living room. I asked the man who was laying the rug how much it cost. He said, '$4,000.' I told him that he had better roll up his rug and take it back because we didn't have the money to pay for it. He told me that he couldn't do that because it was actually two rugs, which had been cut and sewn together and my wife had special-ordered it.

"In the spring of 1969, she went to a figure skating competition at the Broadmoor Hotel in Colorado Springs, Colorado. She took my son Peter, and my daughter Suzanne. They were there for about two weeks. During that time, she ran up a hotel bill of $2,000. On top of that, she went to Mahan's, a jewelry store nearby, and purchased $8,000 worth of jewelry. Someone from the jewelry store called to make sure that he was designing the jewelry in the way that Marjorie had specified. She wasn't home and that is how I found out about these expenses. There was another bill for $10,000 from a jewelry store here in town.

"When Elisabeth put me in charge of Marjorie's trust money, I opened a checking account for her called the Marjorie C. LeRoy Trust Account. I discovered that Marjorie had to immediately sell $50,000 worth of the stock to pay her outstanding debts. I deposited the proceeds from the stocks into the account and paid her bills. With this new account, I was the only one who could sign the checks. The dividends from Clara's trust came quarterly. Marjorie would endorse the checks and I would deposit the money. Before I set it up, Marjorie had tried to have her own checking account but it was constantly overdrawn. We had a joint account, which was also constantly overdrawn. Even though she couldn't withdraw money from the account without my signature, her spending sprees continued. Eventually I had to sell off more stock to cover her bills. And then more stock. Those proceeds went into the checking account. At one point, she spent $17,000 to buy six horses. In two and a half years, $288,000 was gone.

"We kept records from 1958 until now, and I have

determined—conservatively—that Marjorie has spent approximately $1 million over the last twelve years. Her mother has bailed her out of approximately $365,000 of debt.

"Marjorie alienated all of our friends. Several months ago we attended a Sunday school class at Hobart Methodist Church. There are a number of minority groups there; there was a mulatto woman married to a man who was part Indian and part African American. Somehow we got to talking about dissenters and protesters and Marjorie got very emotional about it. She blasted away at them, making derogatory remarks about minority groups. The woman was so upset, she got up and left the room.

"My wife does not seem to have the ability to get along with people and frequently makes them uncomfortable by displaying her wealth or extolling the fact that she came from a fine background. One of our acquaintances told me that he had never invited us to his home because he never knew what Marjorie was going to say or do. I knew what he meant. Marjorie can become extremely emotional when she talks about controversial subjects, and she can become quite obnoxious.

"She has caused all the children except Stephen to turn against me. Rebecca called me one night and asked me why I was running around with other women. She asked me why I was telling the bank in Duluth not to send money to her mother. She wondered why I was telling lies about Marjorie. None of this was true. Peter wanted to know the name of the woman I was running around with. There was no woman. I was never unfaithful to Marjorie. I don't believe she was unfaithful either.

"Marjorie created tension in our household. Every time she came into the house she brought up controversial topics. There was never any quietness or smoothness in the house when she was around. She was gone so much of the time with the skating activities and I liked it when she was gone. There was not such an ordeal. As long as you would go along with what she wanted to do, she was happy and everything was all right. But if you disagreed, then there was immediate stress in the household and things would get very uncomfortable," explained Dick.

"Marjorie did everything full force. She couldn't do anything in moderation. And that showed in the children's activities, figure skating, and horseback riding. The children were constantly on a treadmill. There was no point in discussing my concerns with her because she would do exactly what she wanted to do anyway. I tried to get her to cut down on all of the skating lessons, or on the number of horses, but she ignored me."

After his parents separated, Stephen decided to come home from Stanford University in California and take his winter quarter at the University of Minnesota so that he could help with the family. He tried to be impartial. Elisabeth had invited Dick to Glensheen for Thanksgiving dinner, but she did not invite Marjorie. Dick went to Duluth on the Wednesday before Thanksgiving. When he got there, he got a call from Stephen saying that his mother had thrown him out of the house. Stephen took the train to Duluth the next morning and spent Thanksgiving with Elisabeth and his dad. Marjorie had been furious with Stephen for wanting to spend time with Dick. She screamed at him and kicked him. He pushed her and she landed on the floor. Hester later told Dick that Stephen hadn't done anything wrong and that Marjorie provoked him. After Thanksgiving, he moved out of the house and stayed with a friend. He and his friend dubbed his mother, "Major."

At first Dick disagreed that the children should attend private schools. He had gone to public schools. However, he soon realized that private schools did have some advantages, and the children were doing so well. Stephen got almost straight A's at Benilde High School, and he was not only the first Methodist but also the first sophomore to get a varsity letter in figure skating. His father was very proud of him.

Marjorie did not want a divorce. She thought that she had a "great marriage" until Dick walked out the door. She was angry, bitter, and depressed. Dick tried to get custody of his children, but the fact was, Marjorie could support them and he could not. The judge granted Marjorie custody. Dick turned over six bank accounts for his children—Stephen had already been given his—and seven insurance policies that Elisabeth had given the children. Marjorie also got seven horses and all of the antiques. As in the old cliché, Dick got the old Buick. She even took a collage of the children that Dick had hanging in his office. And, Marjorie also took the file that contained the information about her adoption.

Some of the children took their parents' divorce harder than the others. Peter was already married and lived with his wife in their own home, and Suzanne had graduated from high school and lived with Marjorie. Rebecca left home in the summer of 1973 and moved in with Dick. After two months, she moved back in with Marjorie so that she could continue her ice-skating lessons. Marjorie bought her a new car, which was later repossessed. The two youngest children, Heather and Rick, also lived with Marjorie.

Andy dropped out of high school, and Marjorie initiated an action to have him declared incorrigible and put in a state institution. Dick learned of this action and contacted the Hennepin County authorities, who released him to Dick's care. Andy then got a job, but as soon as Marjorie discovered that he had been released, she had him picked up for being absent from school and he was detained in a juvenile detention center over the weekend. Again Dick contacted the Hennepin County authorities and retrieved his son. The following Monday, Marjorie did not show up for the court hearing, the charges were dismissed, and Andy was allowed to live with his father. Under Dick's care he studied and qualified for his high school GED so that he could attend a junior college that fall.

In May 1974, three months before his eighteenth birthday, Andy applied for a loan of $5,000 from the insurance policy that Elisabeth had set up for her grandchildren. Elisabeth had specified that this money was to be used for her grandchildren's education, and Andy planned to use the money to help with college expenses. He was denied the loan. Three months earlier, his mother had forged his signature and withdrawn all of the money—there was nothing left. Later, it was discovered that she had cleaned out all of her children's funds. No one knows what happened to the money, but it was estimated to be $250,000.

Dick was allowed to see his children on scheduled visitations, but never in Marjorie's home. He knew his children believed that he had deserted them, which was the last thing he had wanted to do. Little by little, though, they began to see that Marjorie had lied to them, and they slowly reconciled with their father.

While the LeRoy family was in the midst of separating, Nancy and her brother Tom were training at Lake Placid and won the American and Canadian Pair Medals. Soon after, they too quit skating because Tom, who was seven years older than Nancy, wanted to get married. Without skating competitions to draw them together, Helen and Marjorie had no reason to see each other. Unfortunately, for Helen, those quiet years were only temporary.

❧ *Chapter Seven*

In 1974, Marjorie bought a house on Norell Avenue in Marine-on-St. Croix, Minnesota, and named it the "Homestead." Marjorie had always needed to name things. She had the house remodeled and built a separate guesthouse on the property for Suzanne, who was now twenty-one years old.

Marjorie hired Mike Billingsley to do the remodeling. She had met him through her realtor the previous year. It was not long before Mike confided to Marjorie that he was unhappy in his marriage, and by the Fourth of July, 1974, he and Marjorie had begun an affair. Mike told Marjorie that he was going to leave his wife; they planned to get married as soon as his divorce was final. They told their friends. They told Elisabeth. They told Mike's wife, Lorraine, who did not want a divorce. In September, Mike moved into Marjorie's house on Norell. During their time together, Marjorie gave Mike jewelry to "borrow on." She bought presents for him and his children. She loaned him money. They went so far as to order a wedding ring at Hudson's jewelry store in Minneapolis. But when March 1975 rolled around, Marjorie asked him to leave, having decided that they were no longer compatible.

That same year, she bought another home, in Englewood, Colorado. Three of her children—Heather, Rebecca, and Rick—moved with her. Her reason for moving to Colorado, she said, was that Rick, who was thirteen, had asthma and needed to be checked into an asthma clinic there.

Coincidentally, Tom Congdon, Elisabeth's nephew and one of the administrators of her estate, also lived in Colorado. Two other Congdon relatives, by marriage, William Van Evera and Salisbury Adams, shared in that responsibility, although they lived in Minnesota. These men were accustomed to Marjorie's asking for money just as they were accustomed to turning her down. Elisabeth could not say no to Marjorie, even though she knew it was the right thing to do, and these trustees were hired to protect Elisabeth's interests.

Perhaps Marjorie hoped to gain Tom's sympathy when she moved to Colorado with Rick. If he saw what a good and caring mother she was, he might release the money from her trust. She was tired of begging. As far as anyone knew, Marjorie spent all of her time in Colorado and left Suzanne to take care of the house in Marine-on-St. Croix. But a strange thing happened on May 12, 1975.

Joyce Alsop, Marjorie's childhood friend who had worked at Wahl's Department Store in Duluth, was at the Minneapolis–St. Paul International Airport with her eight-year-old daughter waiting for a flight to arrive from Salt Lake City, Utah. She was surprised to see Marjorie LeRoy in the terminal. Joyce said that she was excited because she had not seen her in years. Marjorie was very tan and wearing a chrome-yellow dress. When she approached, their eyes met and Joyce called, "Marjorie!" But Marj flew past her without stopping. As Marjorie vanished amidst the airport crowd, Joyce's daughter said, "Mom, that lady didn't want to see you." Joyce was hurt, because she'd had fond memories of Marjorie in Duluth.

That same morning, Mike Billingsley pulled into the driveway of the Homestead. He was shocked to see a woman who looked like Marjorie carrying things out of the house—pieces of furniture, antiques, and trophies that Suzanne had won in her horse competitions—and moving them into the guesthouse. She was obviously in a hurry. What was she doing back in Minnesota? He thought that she had moved to Colorado with Heather, Becky, and Rick. He did not want to see her, so he slowly backed out of the driveway and drove away. She was so absorbed with what she was doing that she didn't see him.

Minutes later, a neighbor was driving by and saw a huge cloud of smoke. He associated the huge billowing black cloud of smoke with burning gas or oil and thought that a neighboring farmer was in trouble. He sped to the source of the smoke and saw that it was coming from Marjorie LeRoy's house. He tore into the driveway, honking his horn to warn anyone that might be in the house. When no one came out, he sped home and called the fire department. By now the trees and shrubs had caught fire and the only thing left of the house was the shape, a vague imprint of what used to be. What the neighbor didn't know was that Marjorie owed Billingsley $100,000 for the remodeling, and he had put liens on the property. Marjorie's house was the one asset that Billingsley could claim in order to recover his money. Also, Billingsley's wife, Lorraine, was suing Marjorie for alienation of affection. By the time the fire department arrived, the Homestead had burnt to the ground.

There was a lengthy investigation by the Fire Marshall, and the facts about the fire were brought before the Washington County Attorney's office: The Homestead had been insured for $430,000. Marjorie LeRoy had been on the passenger manifest of Western Airlines on the evening of May 11, 1975, en route from Denver to the Twin Cities with a roundtrip ticket. She had rented a car from Hertz at the Minneapolis–St. Paul International Airport at 12:16 a.m. on May 12 and returned the car at 6:20 a.m., having driven seventy-four miles in the interim, the distance between Norell Avenue and the airport.

Ray DiPrima from the Minnesota Bureau of Criminal Apprehension was called on the case. Since Marjorie had been seen at the house that morning, she was questioned and later accused of having started the fire. However, because of a quirk in the law at that time, which said that if a person didn't have an insurance policy they could not be charged with damaging their own property, the charges were dropped. Marjorie's insurance policy had lapsed. DiPrima tucked her case away in his files, but he had a feeling that he might run into her again someday.

On September 29, 1976, more than one year after the Homestead fire, a fire was reported at the First National Bank Building in Englewood, Colorado, Marjorie's new hometown. One janitor on duty extinguished the fire while another one went to the elevator to call for help. By the time the firefighters arrived, the fire was out, but they noticed a burned spot on the rug about four inches in diameter. A loose edge of wallpaper that had been partially unglued was burned away, and there were soot marks where the fire had run up the wall. When the night supervisor at the bank building heard the emergency bell on the elevator—his call signal—he ran to the elevators on the ground floor. As the doors opened, a woman stepped out, smiled at him, and told him there was a fire on the fifth floor. The supervisor described the woman as a Caucasian, five feet, three inches tall, with short brown hair, and wearing large sunglasses. She had on a boxy, brownish-colored dress that was above her knees, and he noted that her legs were short and squat. She carried a brown paper bag.

Marjorie had been identified in the vicinity of the bank that day and was questioned by the investigators. Her excuse for being there was that she had accounts at First National Bank. Small pellets, used to ignite logs for fireplaces, were discovered in various areas of the carpet and underneath a couch in the bank. But since no witnesses had actually seen her start the fires, Marjorie was not charged.

❧ *Chapter Eight*

Heather and Rebecca had been unhappy living in Colorado and moved back to Minnesota to live with Stephen. Rebecca was fifteen and determined to resume her skating lessons, even though she had no transportation and was too young to drive. On top of that, her dad had no money to pay for lessons. She called her former teacher, Mannette, and explained her dilemma. Mannette would not let her down. As busy as she was with her own career and her own children, she not only gave Rebecca skating lessons, but also picked her up and brought her home. Rebecca scrubbed floors and cleaned houses to pay for her skating. When Stephen learned how important skating was to his sister, he began sending Mannette regular checks for $100 to pay for Rebecca's skating lessons. He told Mannette to tell Rebecca that she was contributing the lessons. Rebecca paid for ice time and the club membership with the money she earned cleaning houses.

When Rebecca was about to graduate from high school, Marjorie would not come back from Colorado for her graduation ceremony. Rebecca asked Mannette, "Will you come and be my mom for my graduation?" Mannette did.

Alienated from much of her family, Marjorie felt lonely. She wanted to marry again, to have a companion and someone to help raise Rick. She attended a Parents-Without-Partners meeting in Golden, Colorado, and met Roger Sipe Caldwell.

He must have been lonely, too, because he was divorced and didn't have custody of his own children. Perhaps he was looking for another lonely person, someone who had children that he could adopt as his own family. If that was the case, he found what he was looking for. Marjorie told him that she was an heiress with seven children. Two months after they met, they were married in a quiet ceremony on March 20, 1976.

Roger Caldwell was born on September 20, 1933. He grew up in Latrobe, Pennsylvania, about forty-five miles east of Pittsburgh. Latrobe is a quiet, pastoral town, surrounded by the forested hills of the Laurel Highlands, a part of the Allegheny Mountains. It is the home of Arnold Palmer, the noted golfer who owns the local country club, and Fred Rogers of the *Mr. Rogers* television program. Latrobe is also the home of Rolling Rock Beer and Valvoline Oil. Soon, it would be known in the Midwest for being the home of Roger Caldwell.

Caldwell played football on his high school league in 1953. He was not a big man, only 180 pounds and five feet, ten inches. There was nothing remarkable about his looks. His face was flat, as though it had been stamped on. His light blue eyes were set too close together. His hair had a widow's peak. It wasn't blond, it wasn't brown, but it was trimmed regularly. He was meticulous about his hair. His mouth was forgettable. A girl he had liked in high school had dubbed him "no-lips" after he kissed her.

When he was twenty years old, he eloped with a local girl and then studied for the ministry at a Lutheran college. He left college after a year and held various jobs, mostly as a salesman, in Indiana, California, and finally, Colorado, where his first marriage broke up. His wife got custody of their two children. Drinking had become a problem with Roger Caldwell after he left Latrobe, and he blamed alcohol for the failure of his first marriage.

Marjorie and Roger moved to a small ranch in the mountains in Bailey, Colorado. Rick, who was sixteen years old now, lived with them. Not long after that, the bank foreclosed on the ranch, and they were forced to move down to Golden, where the three of them set up housekeeping at the Holland House Motel. Marjorie had gone from a thirty-nine-room mansion to a two-room motel with one bathroom.

Roger worked as a salesman for the first two months of their marriage. His drinking increased. The more he drank, the angrier Marjorie became. He would disappear for days at a time, and she felt the need to explain away his absence, even to total strangers. He embarrassed her and he knew it. Roger discovered that his wife was a "terrible liar." The truth was no impediment for her. When he went "off on a toot," Marjorie made up stories to cover for him, even when nobody questioned his whereabouts. He didn't care what she said. He had his meal ticket. So on his sober days, he followed Marjorie around, visiting real estate offices and looking at properties, ranches, horses—things he'd had no interest in before he met her.

In fact, Roger hated horses. He had been stepped

on, bitten, butted, and kicked by the beasts and said, "I never got along well with the damned horses. Marjorie was a horsy person." She had tried to teach him how to handle a horse so that he wouldn't get stepped on, to get the horse to bend its leg up so he could clean out its hoof with "some kind of picky instrument" so that the horse wouldn't get dry rot. He never did catch on, and furthermore, he didn't give a rip if the horse had dry rot or not. Never the less, Roger began to resemble what he thought a Colorado rancher should look like. He dressed in ranch-style clothes, cowboy boots and shirts with appliqués and fringe. He was rarely seen without his gaudy turquoise jewelry—necklaces and even bracelets. This was not the shy, unassuming football star from Latrobe.

Marjorie had told Rick about Roger's drinking problem before the marriage. It turned out that Roger had more than a drinking problem, he was a violent drunk. Many nights, Marjorie and Rick would flee to another motel to get away from him. On January 23, 1977, Rick was in a car following Roger and Marjorie home from a real estate office when he noticed them fighting in the front seat of their car. He stepped on the gas and pulled his car in front of theirs, forcing Roger to slam on the brakes. Rick had to fight off Roger so that Marjorie could get out of the car. Roger pulled a twelve-inch chain out of the back seat and thwacked it across Rick's chest. Rick slugged him, pushed him away, and Roger stumbled back into the car and sped off. A highway patrolman happened to drive by, and Rick and Marjorie told him what had happened. The police picked Roger up and arrested him. Marjorie filed assault charges, but later dropped them on the promise that Roger would get chemical dependency treatment. It didn't work. Rick witnessed many more incidences of Roger's drunkenness and was afraid of him.

Marjorie's bad-check writing and expensive tastes had not changed since her first marriage. She and Roger argued about it constantly. One day, Marjorie came up with a scheme to get more money. She decided to ask the trustees of her estate for $750,000 so that she could become a horse rancher. She knew that she had no credibility with the attorneys who were in charge of the money, so she decided that Roger should go to Duluth to meet with them. He was supposed to convince them that he, Roger, would be in charge of handling the money, not Marjorie. Roger was supposed to appear to be a responsible businessman. As they planned the visit, Rick asked Roger if he could accompany him to Duluth because he wanted to see his brothers and sisters, and he missed his grandmother. Roger said no.

***

Nan Wisherd had been the cook at Swiftwater Farm, Elisabeth Congdon's summer home on the Brule River, for three years. Her husband, Scott, was in charge of upkeep and maintenance of the buildings and grounds. She was in charge of menu planning, cooking, and cleaning the "Big House." Nan was also a member of the spring cleaning crew at the Van Evera property, the Lodge, two houses down from Elisabeth Congdon's. Mary Van Evera was Elisabeth's niece and her husband, Bill, was one of the trustees for Elisabeth's estate.

On May 19, 1977, Nan was going to help her friend, Ina, open up the Marshalls' house so that Caroline and Julia could use it in the summer months ahead. On the way to the Marshalls, they stopped at the Van Evera Lodge to put out some plants. There had been a storm the night before, with rain and high winds. When they went into the house, they noticed a broken lamp on the floor. The Dutch doors that separated the screen porch from the kitchen were opened. They attributed that to the storm. Then, as Ina tried to close the Dutch doors, she noticed that the door was broken. Ina looked over the kitchen, living room, and dining room. It was obvious that the Lodge had been broken into. She thought about going into the bedrooms, but the door separating the bedrooms from the living room was cracked open, and she became frightened. The two women left the Lodge immediately.

The next day, when Ina and her husband, John, went back to the Van Evera Lodge, John mentioned that he and Scott had closed the dining room door when they had been there the morning of the break-in. Now, it was opened. That meant that whoever had broken into the Lodge was still there when Nan and Ina had arrived. When they left the Lodge, the intruder had fled.

Even though Marjorie lived in Colorado, Nan suspected that she was the intruder. Marjorie did not like Bill Van Evera. He was one of the trustees of her mother's estate—responsible for keeping the money out of Marjorie's hands. The summer homes all lined the Brule River, parallel to Congdon Road and off of Highway B. Marjorie could have parked on Highway B unnoticed because canoeists and fisherman frequently left their cars on either side of the bridge for hours at a time.

Nan and Scott were the only permanent residents of the area, and Marjorie would have known that weekdays in May, the Van Everas were not likely to be at their Lodge. Marjorie could have seen Nan through the bedroom door and would have recognized her as Elisabeth's cook at Swiftwater Farm. Marjorie had spent all of her summers at the Brule River and was familiar with the trails. The dining room door that was opened pointed directly back to the Winneboujou Bridge, which would have been a hasty escape route. She probably fled as soon as Ina and Nan drove away.

Nan's belief that Marjorie was the intruder was more than an educated guess. Several weeks after that incident, she and her friend were walking along the riverbank and came upon a partially burnt pillow, a pillow that had come from the Van Everas' house. The bank was quite steep going down from the Lodge. The landscape was natural, brushy and overgrown. If a fire had started on that bank, it would have quickly spread uphill and burned the house. It could have been blamed on a careless canoeist or fisherman flipping a cigarette into the brush. However, the heavy rains the night before had left the grass and brush saturated. It was too wet to burn.

After finding the pillow, the Van Everas had the dining room door dusted for prints, but it was too long after the event. Silver jewelry was missing, which was never recovered. In the end, they dropped the investigation. Perhaps they feared that Nan was right.

On May 25, 1977, less than a week after the break-in at the Van Everas', Roger flew to Duluth to meet with Bill Van Evera and another attorney to convince them that he and Marjorie were going into a "horse breeding and racing ranch operation" in Colorado. They needed $750,000 to get started. The trustees did not give Roger the money. As long as he was there, though, Roger decided to visit his mother-in-law, Elisabeth Congdon, for the first time. Marjorie had sent a gift along, a carved horse. He took a cab to Glensheen and was granted fifteen minutes with Elisabeth by Vera Dunbar, her social secretary. Elisabeth did not ask for any more time. Afterwards, she asked Vera to drive

Roger back to the Radisson Hotel where he was staying.

🐝 *Chapter Nine*

At least once in her life—briefly—Elisabeth Congdon stepped out of character. A woman who guarded her privacy, she allowed Universal Studios to move into Glensheen in the winter of 1972 to film a movie, *You'll Like My Mother*, starring Patty Duke and Richard Thomas. The story involved a young, pregnant Vietnam War widow who went to meet her dead husband's mother in the family mansion. There was a murder. Elisabeth was at her winter home in Tucson during the filming of the suspense thriller, but came back for the premier in Duluth, which she attended with her daughter Jennifer. All Elisabeth could mutter at the showing was "Oh, my word."

***

At age eighty-three, Elisabeth was still a tall, fair woman, large-boned. She was imposing, yet not intimidating. Because of her size and the fact that she was partially paralyzed, it was a task to get her ready for the day.

Mildred Garvue was fifty-eight years old and had been Elisabeth Congdon's day nurse for one month. Nurse Garvue's duties included a daily bath for Elisabeth; applying hot packs to her right paralyzed side, arm, and leg; and exercises including parallel bars. She changed the sheets on her bed daily and dressed her every day in a dress and neutral nylons. Elisabeth was meticulous about her dress, although she wasn't showy. One time, Elisabeth's slip was hanging below her dress. She was in her wheelchair and pointed to her slip. With a distressed look on her face she mouthed, "awful, awful." She wore very little jewelry, except for some pieces that had sentimental value.

Although she had only known Elisabeth for a short time, Mildred sensed that she was lonely. Sometimes she would look at portraits of her family, point to the people and say, "I'm the last." The two women played gin rummy together every day. Elisabeth enjoyed cards and she could beat all the nurses. Unable to hold the cards, she used a special board with a groove in the middle. She also managed to shuffle and deal, though laboriously.

Occasionally Elisabeth had an opportunity to indulge in her other passions. She still loved books, and now, after her stroke, when Jennifer came to visit they would sit together while Jennifer read to her mother from her favorite books. She also loved music, especially classical. When the hairdresser came to the house, she'd bring a tape recorder and play Chopin. Elisabeth would mouth, "Wonderful, wonderful."

Every Friday, Nurse Garvue packed Elisabeth's bags so she could spend her weekends at Swiftwater Farm. Although Swiftwater was just thirty-five miles east of Duluth in Brule, it was like being in a different country. After crossing Minnesota's border to Wisconsin on Highway Two, the land became hillier, the trees taller, the aroma of the northwoods stronger. The red-shaked summer home with white trim served as a retreat from city life. Surrounded by white and red pines, balsam, and birch trees on the banks of the Brule, the house had wide porches on all sides that looked onto the well-kept English gardens to the south and faced the rushing river to the north.

On June 24, 1977, Mildred prepared Elisabeth for her trip as usual. She packed the same thing every week into a large wicker suitcase: several dresses in a plastic garment bag, underwear, her exercise shoes, and walking shoes. In a smaller matching wicker case she packed small pillows and Elisabeth's medication. Mildred rode along with the chauffeur as always to escort Elisabeth to Brule and then returned back to Duluth with the chauffeur. She looked forward to seeing Elisabeth again when her shift began on Monday morning.

The weather was beautiful in Brule that weekend, not foggy as it was in Duluth. Nan Wisherd had made Elisabeth a special breakfast of substitute scrambled eggs, careful to make sure they looked like regular eggs—Elisabeth did not want anyone to go to extra trouble for her. After breakfast, Hanna, the night nurse, wheeled her out to the porch to watch the Brule river rush by. Elisabeth loved the roar of Halls Rapids. Sometimes it was so loud it was hard to hear anything else. From there, Elisabeth could see the wooden bridge that crossed the river. Nan caught a glimpse of her from the dining room window. With one foot, she managed to drag her wheelchair to the other side of the porch. She must have wanted to see her flowers. Red geraniums tumbled over moss-lined hanging baskets on both sides of the main entry doors. The red and yellow tulips and purple irises planted all around the house were in full bloom. She loved her garden. Nan watched as Elisabeth wore a "See, I can do it" grin on her face.

She loved to be wheeled out to the small bridge where she could watch canoeists float by. Perhaps it reminded her of the days when she was young, poling up the river. She had been so strong, so active, so independent. She enjoyed the sounds and the smells of the river and the blossoming trees, and she would mouth, "Nature, nature."

She valued her independence and insisted that the screen be removed from the fireplace so that she could wheel herself to the hearth and throw logs in with her good left arm. The staff worried that a spark might fly out and start the house on fire.

Every night, Elisabeth would pull her wheelchair up to the television to watch the 10:00 news on an old TV with rabbit ears wrapped in tinfoil, the picture barely visible through the wavy lines. The vacuum cleaner was old, too, and so was the lawnmower. Elisabeth did not want new things. She wanted things to stay the way they had always been. No new-fangled gadgets and no paved roads, thank you. When it was time to get ready for bed, Hanna would wheel her up to the bathroom sink so that Elisabeth could brush her own teeth and wash her own face. She never asked for help.

Spending weekends at Swiftwater Farm must have given Elisabeth a taste of freedom. Like many retreats, it was relaxing and free of schedules. Her diet was not as closely monitored as it was in Duluth. Elisabeth loved Dairy Queens and she was not prohibited from having an occasional cone on her Brule weekends. Nan and another cook at Swiftwater, Sophie Boelter, loved cooking for her. She was appreciative of their efforts. She always made sure that everyone who visited and worked at the house was well-fed, including the staff and their children.

Stephen, Marjorie's twenty-seven-year-old son, had business in Duluth that week, and Elisabeth was thrilled when he told her that he'd like to spend the weekend with her at Swiftwater Farm. He had graduated from Stanford University and was a zone manager for 7-eleven stores. He tried to visit her in Brule once or twice each summer. The staff at Swiftwater Farm loved Stephen. He was polite and unassuming. And they loved to see how happy Elisabeth was when any of her thirteen grandchildren visited her. Marjorie and Jennifer never visited Swiftwater Farm at the same time. Even if they had been close, thirteen children, all at once, would have been a burden for Miss Elisabeth—even with a staff to help.

That Sunday morning, Elisabeth's old friend Julia Marshall brought over some watercolors, ready to teach Elisabeth how to paint. Hanna had thought it would be good therapy for Elisabeth. The staff often mused that Elisabeth probably had some untapped talent. After all, her mother had been an accomplished artist.

Elisabeth had wanted to stay at Swiftwater Farm until Monday morning, but she decided that she might as well go back to Duluth that evening since Stephen was going back to Minneapolis. She knew that she would be back in Brule the following week. Stephen stood in the driveway watching as his grandmother's wheelchair and suitcase were loaded into the trunk. He kissed her goodbye on the cheek. She said her farewells to the staff and left Swiftwater Farm with the chauffeur and a nurse at about 3:00 p.m., heading back to Duluth. When they arrived at Glensheen, Elisabeth rested in her bedroom while a nurse unpacked her clothes and put her small wicker basket away in the closet. Elisabeth went to sleep at about 11:00 p.m.

Mildred always made arrangements for a nurse to attend to Elisabeth on Sunday nights, but she had had trouble finding anyone for June 26th. One of the regular relieving nurses was on vacation with her husband, and the other one was having company and asked Mildred if she could find someone else. Finally, she asked

Velma Pietila, Elisabeth's previous nurse who had retired, if she could help out. Velma had trained Mildred. Velma was reluctant to fill in at first because she
hated working nights and she knew her husband
wouldn't like it. He wanted her to "stay retired." She
told Mildred, "I'll do it this once. I miss Miss Elisabeth."

On Monday, June 27, 1977, Mildred came to work
as usual at 7:00 a.m. She parked in front of the main
doors of Glensheen as always. She walked in and left
her sweater and her purse on the settee in the corri-
dor, as usual, and proceeded to the kitchen to get Elisabeth's insulin from the refrigerator. Elisabeth had been
diagnosed with diabetes when she was in her late seventies. Mildred headed for the staircase.

"I climbed up and I saw nurse Velma's bare legs
dangling on the seat there on the bench in front of the
landing of the staircase. Her shoes were off. I thought,
'My gracious, Velma is resting,' and then I proceeded
to look at her, and just automatically, I took her pulse.
Somehow, something protected me from really seeing
details, but I knew that it was terrible. Velma was covered with blood. Holding her wrist—it was like holding cement. My immediate thought was of Miss Elisabeth, so I hurried up to the second floor. I almost
stepped on Velma's glasses.

"The nurses' room is to the left of the landing. I saw
Miss Elisabeth in her bedroom, and all I could see was
bare legs. She always kept her covers tucked under her
chin, and so then when I saw her legs, I knew something was drastically wrong. I spied the satin pillow
over her face, and I just picked up the corner very
gently and peeked underneath and saw her purple
face—saw that she was dead."

Mildred ran down the stairs to find Hazel Conger,
the maid.

"I told her that Miss Elisabeth was dead, and she said, 'Heart attack probably' and I said, 'No, she's been murdered, and Velma is dead, too.'" She spoke softly because she was afraid to upset Prudence, the cook who was in the kitchen preparing breakfast for Miss Elisabeth. Afraid that the murderer was still in the house, Hazel accompanied Mildred to the phone in the main lobby to call the police. Wringing her handkerchief in her hands, Mildred waited for the police to arrive, watching Hazel pace back and forth chanting, "Oh, my God, Oh my God."

As Mildred sat there, the impact of Velma's battered body and the details began to sink in—blood everywhere, dripping down the carved railing, soaking into the oriental carpet, splattered on the stained glass window.

Ernie Grams was Inspector of Detectives at the Duluth Police Department. Fifty-two years old, he was balding and had watery, brown cocker spaniel eyes. A cigar was his prop. He arrived at the murder scene at 7:30 a.m., following several other police officers, uniformed and in plain clothes. When he first arrived, his main concern was to assign the various officers to protect the crime scene. He assigned them to interview Mildred Garvue, Hazel Conger, the chauffeur, the gardener, and the cook.

The cook had been sleeping in the servants' quarters that night, which were separated from Elisabeth's bedroom by a wall and heavy door. She explained to Detective Grams that at 2:45 a.m. she heard her poodle Muffin barking. She picked him up and took him with her to the bathroom. She carried him back to her room, and he whined until 5:00 a.m.

The staircase was sealed off until the medical examiner arrived. Next, the ambulance appeared. Two tracking dogs began searching the grounds, and directions were given to identification technicians.

One of the detectives called Velma's husband, Loren Pietila, and without explaining what had happened, told Pietila to come right over to Glensheen. "I broke the news to him," said Grams. "It was terrible. At first, I didn't think he heard what I said. He just looked at me as if I was talking about something I'd seen on TV. And then, his eyes squinted as if the words had slapped him, and both hands flew up to his temples. He kept saying, 'No, no,' over and over again. I put my arm around him and led him over to a bench on the porch. He said, 'I didn't want her to go. She promised it would just be this one time.' He was sobbing. I asked him how his wife had gotten to work and he said she drove. That's when we realized that her car was missing."

❧ *Chapter Ten*

Jennifer was at home in Racine, Wisconsin, when she heard that her mother had been murdered. Painters were painting the walls in her bedroom. She was in the kitchen and her husband, Chuck, was down at the beach when the phone rang. It was Bill Van Evera. "Your mother has been murdered," he said. Just like that. Jennifer's first words were, "Marjorie did it." She couldn't speak anymore and hung up the phone and ran outside to call Chuck. They dressed and headed for Duluth that day.

When Dick LeRoy heard that Elisabeth Congdon had been murdered, he immediately suspected that Marjorie was involved. When asked why he thought so, he said, "Because I was married to her for twenty years."

Jennifer planned her mother's funeral, which was held at the Glensheen Mansion on June 30. It was rainy and cool for June. Congdon relatives flew in from all over the country for the service. One of Elisabeth's friends played the piano. Bill Van Evera helped with all of the arrangements. Jennifer and her family were distraught and stayed upstairs until the private service began. Marjorie greeted guests at the door. She acted "bouncy and was chatty" as if she were hosting a party. She wore white slacks and a blue flowered blouse. Elisabeth would have been horrified. Her daughter should have worn appropriate clothing. Roger had shown up in his "rancher's get-up," and Marjorie took him to Allenfall's Clothiers to purchase a suit. They charged it to Elisabeth Congdon's account.

The service was simple and meaningful, as Elisabeth would have wanted it to be. The minister talked about her generosity, her convictions, and her love of picnics and of exploring. He called her one of life's "peculiar treasures." Unfortunately, her funeral turned into a media event. Reporters were everywhere, jamming microphones into people's faces and asking cruel questions about the circumstances of her death. They broadcast the funeral live. A close relative spied one of the photographers aiming his lens at the casket. She opened her umbrella in front of his camera to block his view.

Amid all the furor over Elisabeth Congdon, the mansion, and the wealth, Velma Pietila seemed all but forgotten, at least by the media. But Velma would be dearly missed, too. She had lived in Duluth with her family for forty-three years. She left behind two sons, a daughter, a brother, four sisters, and six grandchildren. She was a member of Pilgrim Congregational Church, the Lakeside Chapter of the Order of Eastern Star, and the Ridgeview Country Club. "Velma was a fighter," Mildred Garvue said. "I'm sure she fought for her life and to protect Miss Elisabeth. That was her nature."

Velma Pietila's family was devastated over their loss. Loren, who was seventy-two, and his three grown children believed that these deaths were preventable, and they filed a wrongful death suit against the trustees of Elisabeth Congdon's estate. The family contended that the mansion was inadequately protected. Loren claimed that the murders resulted from the failure of the defendants to install a security system at the mansion and to hire bodyguards. In their suit, they asked for damages amounting to $475,490.

The Congdon's defense attorney expected the Pietilas to be awarded damages for the loss of comfort, companionship, "and to some extent, her homemaking services to her husband." He thought that they should get between $40,000 and $90,000. He was shocked when a jury awarded the Pietilas $225,000 in 1982.

But, in 1985, the Supreme Court would overturn the verdict in a seven-two vote. They said that there was no evidence that a security system or bodyguards would have prevented the murders. In its nearly seventy year history, the mansion had never been invaded by burglars or vandals. It was not in a high crime area, and the last crime to have occurred in that area was six or seven years prior to the murders.

On July 8, 1977, less than two weeks after the murders, the Norshor Theater in Duluth decided to rerun the movie, *You'll Like My Mother*. Some Duluth residents were outraged and said that the theater could win the Oscar for the Bad Taste Award. They believed that the theater's management "should take gruesome relish in knowing that its profits are, quite literally, blood money."

Newspapers throughout the area acknowledged that Duluth had lost a great lady. The *Duluth Herald* recognized some of the contributions of her life in a detailed obituary.

"But her greatest gifts may have gone to persons who even yet are unaware of her kindness," said a former provost at the University of Minnesota, Duluth, after her funeral. "She anonymously helped many students over the past twenty years. . . . The Mannering Scholarship Fund at UMD was completely financed by Miss Congdon." One week before her death, Elisabeth received a package in the mail. It was a homemade afghan. With it was a note that read, "Miss Congdon, you helped me thirty years ago when my family was in need of cash." It was not signed.

Part II

"The name of the game was to build a case around him."

🐝 *Chapter Eleven*

The first time Ernie Grams, who was dubbed "the Duluth sleuth," met Marjorie Caldwell was on June 29, two days after the murders. She and Roger appeared in his office unannounced. Not surprising—it is natural for family members of a murdered relative to want to follow the progress of an investigation. However, by that time, Grams had received calls from various members of the Congdon family who had known about Marjorie's compulsive need to spend. She had never been liked or accepted by the Congdon relatives, and they told Grams that she and Roger had a motive for the murders. They informed him that the Caldwells were in serious financial trouble and that Marjorie stood to inherit millions of dollars upon her mother's death.

Marjorie was wearing a short-sleeved black dress, cut above her knees, and a silver and turquoise necklace on a long chain, which he described as "clunky." She was very talkative, as if she'd had about five cups of coffee. Roger wore a plaid shirt, jeans, and cowboy boots. He seemed extremely interested in wanting to help solve his mother-in-law's murder. Grams noticed that Roger had a swollen right hand and a slight cut to his upper lip.

Marjorie asked Grams if the FBI had been called in to investigate the case. She wondered if any jewelry was missing from the mansion. She wanted to know about the security arrangements in her mother's house. Why weren't there more security provisions? Then she ranted and raved that the other members of the family would not let her participate in the funeral arrangements. She was not even allowed to go into the house to select a burial dress for her mother, she told him. Grams thought that "she was very distraught, the way you'd expect a grieving daughter to be. For some reason, she also wanted me to know that she had called her mother that Friday night before the murders, but was told her mother was in Brule, Wisconsin."

During their investigation, police learned that Marjorie had visited at least three realtors, people who could swear that she had never left Colorado on the weekend of the murders. She seemed to be covered. But her husband could not account for his whereabouts. The evidence against him was piling up. The police investigated the various places in which Roger and Marjorie had stayed during the crucial days before and after the murders.

In the Radisson Hotel in Duluth, where the Caldwells stayed during the funeral, the police found a receipt from the Hosts International shop stamped "Minneapolis-St. Paul International Airport" for 56 dollars, dated June 27, 1977, the date of the murders. The sales clerks at this gift shop identified Roger from a photograph. She remembered that he had purchased a garment bag and stuffed it into a wicker basket similar to the basket that was missing from Elisabeth Congdon's bedroom.

A Duluth taxi cab driver identified Caldwell by a photograph and remembered taking him to London Road the night of the murder.

They found the car keys to Velma Pietila's 1976 Ford Granada in a trash can at the airport and also a receipt that had been stamped at 6:35 a.m. at the short-term parking lot where the Pietila vehicle was found. Someone obviously had no intention of leaving the lot.

Most incriminating was an envelope in Roger Caldwell's handwriting addressed to himself on a Duluth Radisson Hotel envelope that was sent to the Holland House Motel in Golden where he lived with Marjorie. In the envelope was a 300 A.D. Byzantine coin, which was missing from Elisabeth Congdon's bedroom. A thumbprint on the envelope was determined to belong to Roger Caldwell.

On July 5, 1977, eight days after the murders, knowing that the Caldwells were staying at the Holiday Inn Airport South in Bloomington, Minnesota, the police entered their room, armed with a search warrant. They found, in plain view, a wicker case that matched the description of the one missing from the Glensheen Mansion. They also found a Tiffany pin with moveable flowers that had belonged to Elisabeth, and a cameo ring that fit the description of the one that had been taken off of Elisabeth Congdon's hand when she was murdered.

Hanging in the closet of that same hotel room, the police found the leather carryon garment bag, the one purchased at the Host International shop at the Minneapolis–St. Paul Airport. A person would have to believe that Roger Caldwell was asking to be caught, to be accused of murdering his mother-in-law. And that is exactly what happened.

But another drama occurred first. One month before the murders, Marjorie had gone to a physician in Denver, Doctor Zuckerman, and gotten a prescription drug called Antabuse, which produces sensitivity to alcohol. The combination of Antabuse and alcohol may produce chest pain, palpitation, cardiovascular collapse, acute congestive heart failure, unconsciousness, convulsions, or even death. She told Roger that if he wouldn't do something about his drinking, she would. According to Roger, the first thing every morning, "she would shove a couple of these things down my throat and say, 'There, damn you, you go and drink and you will be so sick you'll wish you hadn't.'"

Roger had been sober since the funeral and was craving a drink. Once he started, he couldn't stop. They went to a restaurant for dinner, and he had not taken the pills beforehand. The next morning, as they were eating breakfast in the hotel's coffee shop, she "pumped a couple of pills" in him and he became violently ill and collapsed. He was checked into Methodist Hospital and treated for a possible heart attack.

On Thursday, July 7, it was conclusively determined that Caldwell had not had a heart attack. At that point, he was discharged from the hospital, arrested for the murders of Elisabeth Congdon and Velma Pietila, and transported to the Hennepin County Jail in Minneapolis. His bond was set at $200,000.

Roger's older brother, Howard Caldwell, Jr., who lived in Latrobe, Pennsylvania, was shocked. "I can't see my brother being a party to such a thing." He and his brother were raised in a hard-working Lutheran family, and Roger had been a good brother and a good son. (A third brother, David, was an officer on the Latrobe Police Department.) Howard said that their parents were elderly, and he was afraid that their mother might not survive the shock of Roger's arrest. "He's a regular fellow," Howard said, "a real nice guy. He always had a lot of friends, both boys and girls, around the house. He was a leader and one who would not be influenced by others to do something wrong." He said that Roger was extremely dutiful to his parents, calling them frequently and sending them cards and small gifts. Howard did concede, though, that Roger had a drinking problem and had been convicted on October 10, 1976, on a drunken driving charge in Colorado.

Three days after his arrest, on July 9, wearing gray

prison overalls and soft green slippers, Roger Caldwell appeared in St. Louis County Court. Marjorie did not appear at her husband's arraignment, and Caldwell, slightly disheveled, did not speak before his short hearing before the judge. His request to have his bail lowered was denied. Deputy sheriffs led him through a tunnel connecting the jail and the county courthouse and across the hall to a holding cell.

On August 5, 1977, a grand jury indicted Roger Caldwell on two counts of first-degree murder.

***

When Ann Paine, Marjorie's childhood friend, heard about the murders, she did not imagine that her old horse-riding companion could have had anything to do with it. She had admired Marjorie. "She was bookish, had a huge imagination, was vibrant and full of curiosity." She described Marjorie as a "woman-child" of extraordinary intelligence with many diverse talents. She had no idea there was any strife in Marjorie's life. As the story began to unravel, she was shocked. Perhaps she didn't know Marjorie as well as she thought she had. "There are many people in this world who appear to be perfectly normal and fine people. They hide bitterness and their private agonies from the people that love them the most."

When Mannette Allen heard about the Congdon murders, she could not believe it. Marjorie had been there for her when she needed help, and now it was her turn to reciprocate. She called Stephen at his apartment in Fridley, and Marjorie answered the phone. She was living with him and his new wife. Mannette went to see Marjorie and could not believe it was the same woman. "Marjorie used to be like June Cleaver, shirtwaist dresses with full skirts, Capezio flats, and an hourglass figure. She had heavy hips and thighs and legs, and always wore tight belts to show off her tiny waist. She wore her hair in a bun."

The Marjorie she found at Stephen's wore short, cropped hair, jeans, and boots. She had become a "Western Person, dressed Colorado." She was talkative, as she had always been, rattling on about her schedule at the time of the murders, as if to convince Mannette that she was not responsible for her mother's death. She seemed very upset about her mother's murder and about her husband's arrest. In tears, she told Mannette how guilty she felt that she hadn't called her mother that Sunday. "Marjorie kept going back to that, saying, 'We were going to call her and it got too late,' and then, 'If I had only called her.'"

Mannette wanted to say, "Who are you?" But she decided that Marjorie had been through so much, with her husband in jail, accused of murdering her mother, that of course she would have changed. Mannette took her for what she was and decided to stand behind her.

On the first week of August, Marjorie called Mannette, sobbing. She was hysterical. She said she'd been assaulted, cut with a razor, and that she needed Mannette. Mannette rushed to her old friend and found her in the living room covered with small, superficial cuts on her arms, face, and neck. There were bloody handprints all over the walls. Mannette noticed that there was blood in the front hall and the bathroom, but not in the hall that connected the two rooms. There was no trail. Mannette was upset, and she did not want to be there. Marjorie had Mannette drive her to her attorney, Ronald Meshbesher's office, and that was the last she heard of Marjorie's assault until she read the story in the newspaper.

Marjorie described the attack to the Fridley police and Anoka County authorities.

Chester Adgate Congdon
Circa 1910

Elisabeth Congdon, age twenty

1976. Elisabeth Mannering Congdon at
Glensheen. She is wearing a diamond and
sapphire ring that Roger Caldwell stole the
night he murdered her, one year later.

Glensheen Mansion, 3300 London Road, Duluth, MN

June 30, 1950. Marjorie and Dick LeRoy's wedding at the Glensheen Mansion. Elisabeth stands by Dick. Jennifer is next to Marjorie.

1964. The LeRoys pose for a *Minneapolis Star* photographer.
Headline: Son's a Champion—Figure Skating Bug Hits Whole Family.

LeRoy family picnic 1960s

The LeRoys' garage on Fremont Avenue, which Marjorie burned to the ground.

The Cranberry House in Mound, Minnesota, which Marjorie set on fire.

Swiftwater Farm in Brule, Wisconsin, where Elisabeth spent her last
weekend before she was murdered.

The Swedish graveyard where Roger Caldwell waited for dark the night of the murders. Glensheen is in the background.

Courtesy of Steve Kohls, Brainerd Daily Dispatch

Sentenced to two consecutive life terms, Roger Caldwell, flanked by Crow Wing County Sheriff's deputies, walked to the car that transported him to Stillwater State Prison.

Courtesy of Star Tribune/Minneapolis St. Paul

Doug Thomson defended Roger Caldwell for the murders of Elisabeth Congdon and Velma Pietila.

Convicted murderer, Roger Caldwell walks out of the Crow Wing County courthouse with his attorney Doug Thomson (Right) after the jury pronounced its verdict of guilty.

Ronald Meshbesher defended Marjorie
for conspiring with her husband,
Roger Caldwell, to murder her mother.

Duluth Herald April 2, 1979. Marjorie Caldwell and Ronald Meshbesher
entering the Dakota County Courthouse in Hastings, MN, for the beginning
of her trial.

John DeSanto successfully prosecuted Roger Caldwell for murdering Elisabeth Congdon and Velma Pietila.
He wouldn't be as fortunate with Marjorie.

Marjorie Caldwell was found *not guilty* after a sixteen week trial, the longest criminal trial in Minnesota history.

Ray DiPrima, BCA agent who arrested Marjorie for the Cranberry House fire.

Dan Mabley prosecuted Marjorie for the Cranberry House fire. He's now the highly respected Chief Hennepin County District Court Judge.

July 21, 1979. Marjorie Caldwell is escorted by her son, Rick, leaving the Dakota County Courthouse shortly after the jury in her murder conspiracy trial ends its first full day of deliberations.

1970. Helen Hagen getting her nurse's degree.

1965. Tom and Nancy Hagen at skating competition. They won the gold medal for pairs.

Highway 86. The copper mines before entering Ajo, Arizona

Entering Ajo, Arizona from Highway 86

Ajo: The Plaza

A side view of Marjorie and Wally's house on Palo Verde Drive.

Ajo Federated Interdenominational Church, one of several churches where Marjorie worshipped.

The kerosene soaked rags that Marjorie placed in Mark Indivik's bedroom window.

The green garden vinyl hose holder nailed to the side of the garage. Marjorie carried the hose into the house and attached one end to her Progressive gas stove and the other end to Wally's nose as he lay sleeping in their bed.

October 30, 1992. This picture of Marjorie and Wally's bedroom was taken after Wally's body was removed.

July 1987. From left: Ken Kaufmann, Nancy Hagen Kaufmann, Dick Hagen, Judy Hagen, Marjorie Hagen, Wally Hagen, Tom Hagen, and Julie Hagen at family reunion.

A MEMORIAL SERVICE
FOR

WALLACE HOWARD HAGEN

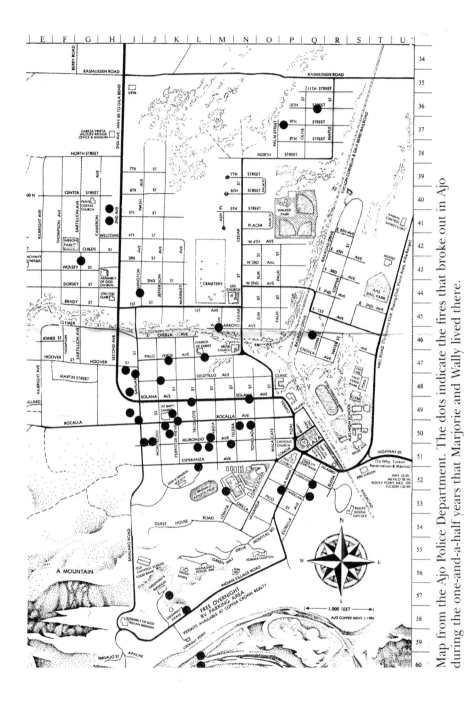

Map from the Ajo Police Department. The dots indicate the fires that broke out in Ajo during the one-and-a-half years that Marjorie and Wally lived there.

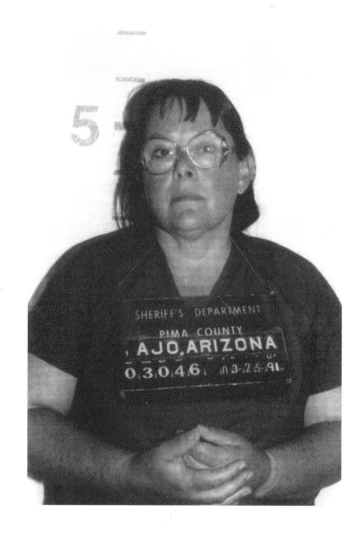

1998. Dick LeRoy at his home.

Then she went to Duluth and repeated the story to a *Duluth Herald* reporter, walking into his office unannounced with the left side of her face, her neck, and her left shoulder heavily bandaged. She claimed that "a man wearing a badge and gun" entered Stephen's apartment and slashed her with a razor-like instrument. The man said he would come back again and scar her for life if she did anything to help her husband. She allowed the newspaper's photographer to take her picture on the condition that he would focus on the bandaged side of her face.

It turned out that Marjorie had called another friend before she called Mannette. This woman said she could not come over but advised Marjorie to call 911. Instead, Marjorie called Mannette. Based on that information, the lack of a blood trail, and the fact that the wounds were superficial and looked to be self-inflicted, the police did not pursue an investigation.

❧ *Chapter Twelve*

After Roger's arrest, Marjorie went to Duluth and proclaimed that her husband was innocent. "Framed," she said. She complained that he had been harassed and mistreated by the police. Her husband was in Colorado at the time of the slayings, she stated, and though she could not account for his whereabouts the night of June 26, he woke her at 6:00 a.m. on June 27 in their motel room in Golden, Colorado. That was 7:00 a.m. Duluth time. She claimed he could not have driven from Duluth to Minneapolis and then flown to Colorado between the time of the murders and when he woke her.

The press hounded Marjorie for interviews, and she didn't let them down. Marjorie loved to talk, always had. Histrionics and hyperbole were her trademark. In one interview, she informed the reporters that she was "particularly unhappy about the way police have been taking specimens of hair from my husband under the authority of search warrants." She said, "the hairs are not to be cut but are to be pulled out by the roots—from his armpits!"

Marjorie complained she was penniless. She could not find a job because of the publicity about her and she had turned to the Salvation Army for food. "I am not employable," she cried. She asked the attorneys handling the Congdon probate case, in a deposition, for monthly funding from the estate. She said that Stephen was helping her financially, which was the only way she could stay off public assistance.

"If there was any doubt about my husband's innocence, I would turn on him," she said. "We're talking about my mother. We're talking about the woman who took me from an orphanage.

"Three years ago," she continued, "my mother did not have any gold coins; yet a gold coin was reported missing from the mansion after the murders and a coin matching its description was reported mailed to us at our motel in Golden, Colorado." She said that her husband had been in Duluth in May to discuss a possible loan with officials of the Chester Congdon estate. She said he had been asked to leave a number of self-addressed envelopes with them, and he used envelopes from the Radisson Duluth Hotel.

Marjorie said Roger had been a good husband. She said that he had spent his own money to buy her son, Rick, a horse and a car when funds were not available from the Congdon trust. She did not elaborate on where Roger got that money, though, since he had not worked since two months after their marriage. She also told the press that Rick's sports activities were limited to horseback riding, motorcycling, and downhill skiing because of his health. She complained that the jailers, whom she believed were acting on orders of the Duluth Police Department, refused to allow Roger to receive a pair of Hanes briefs on which she had written, "I love you." She said, "There are too many things that don't fit—it's too pat." She claimed that witnesses could account for most of her husband's time on the day of the murders. "We will prove that Roger was framed, who framed him, and why he was framed," she said.

The police did not agree. They suspected that Marjorie had conspired with Roger to murder her mother. Upon her mother's death, she stood to inherit a lot of money, about $4 million, plus $50,000 a year for a maximum of twenty-one years. There were additional assets of $45 million. On June 16, eleven days before Elisabeth's death, Marjorie had hired attorneys to file a demand for notice of any orders or filings pertaining to the estate. The will would have to be probated.

The Glensheen Mansion was given to the University of Minnesota by Chester and Clara's heirs in 1968 with the provision that Elisabeth would have "life's rights." Elisabeth's will covered the monies she possessed and was dated December 29, 1976. She specified that her estate be handled through the Elisabeth Congdon Living Trust agreement. Twenty percent of the estate would go to charity, and the rest would be shared by her two adopted daughters. Her trust was valued at $4,078,101. In addition, she was the heir to $45,106,453 in trusts set up by Chester before he died in 1916. She bequeathed "all of my jewelry, personal effects and all other articles of tangible personal property to my daughters, Marjorie Congdon Caldwell and

Jennifer Congdon Johnson, equally to be divided among them, as they shall mutually agree." She left Jim Roper, the retired chauffeur, and Robert Wyness, the gardener at the estate, each $25,000. In her will, Elisabeth stated that Jennifer was to get her inheritance immediately but Marjorie's was to go into a trust.

Marjorie was furious. She accused that her mother's will discriminated against her. She filed petitions objecting to the probate of the will, saying that her mother was under "undue influence" at the time the will was executed and that it was a mistake. Marjorie said in petitions filed in court that William Van Evera had sought to "disgrace and discredit" her.

In July, following the murders, trustees Thomas Congdon, William Van Evera, and Salisbury Adams asked the probate court to determine whether Marjorie and Jennifer were eligible to inherit from the estate in light of the fact that they were adopted. Chester's will did not stipulate "adopted children." It took the judge one month to decide that adopted children were eligible to inherit. These actions by her relatives did not upset Jennifer. She agreed with them that Marjorie should be stopped—at any cost.

To counter the trustees' petitions, Marjorie filed a seventy-nine-page deposition of her own with the probate court in St. Louis County, claiming that William Van Evera hadn't followed the terms of her trust and caused her "financial embarrassment" and "medical hardship." She said, "He dislikes me to the point of hatred" and has vowed he will "do everything in his power to see that I am cut out of any bequests left to me either by my mother or by my grandfather, Chester Congdon." She added that there were derogatory comments made about her by Van Evera. She said that her information came from Thomas Congdon, Robert Congdon, and Julia and Caroline Marshall.

In her deposition, she included an argument she had had with Van Evera in the library of the Congdon mansion before she moved to Colorado three years ago. Van Evera said he didn't want her talking to her mother without the supervision of her nurses. She said that at the Glensheen Mansion, Van Evera had "personally, to my face, called me a bastard." The argument was prompted by a pair of bank notes cosigned by Elisabeth, one for about $300,000 and the other about $125,000. Marjorie had obtained her mother's signature without going through Elisabeth's financial advisors. When Jennifer heard about that, she knew that her mother needed a financial conservatorship to help her conduct her affairs. She was confident that the trustees were doing a good job.

Five of Marjorie's children turned against her in September 1977 in private depositions to attorneys before Roger's murder trial. Jennifer and her husband, Charles, helped them finance their suit. Citing the Minnesota statue that states, "No person who feloniously takes or causes or procures another to so take the life of another shall inherit from such person or receive any interest in the estate of the decedent or take by devise or bequest from him any portion of the estate," Peter, Suzanne, Rebecca, Andrew, and Heather asked that Marjorie not be allowed to share in the Congdon fortune until a police investigation was completed. They said they did not believe their mother should inherit their grandmother's money if she was responsible for her death.

Rick and Stephen remained loyal to their mother. In his deposition, Stephen lauded his mother's generosity toward his grandmother. "She made a needlepoint rug that had fifty squares for the fifty states with the state bird and the name of the state and the date the state was admitted to the Union. It was about five feet by ten feet," he said. "She'd won a prize at the state fair before giving the rug to her mother.

"She didn't like to buy her things because she wanted Grandmother's gifts to be personalized, and Grandmother got such great pleasure out of getting things that people had made for her."

Stephen detailed his mother's support during his years of figure skating. "It was an expensive sport and probably cost around $10,000 or $15,000 a year. But, Mom was always generous. She used to pick up the tab when we were out to dinner with other people, giving people things, expensive things, and not expecting anything in return." He said that his mother's relationship with his grandmother was excellent.

Rick reiterated Stephen's comments about Marjorie's relationship with Elisabeth. At eighteen years old, he had lived with Marjorie longer than any of the other children. She bought him horses, she gave him money when he wanted it, and he had almost total freedom to do whatever he wanted.

Years later, in 1983, the probate court would settle the dispute between Marjorie and her children over Elisabeth's estate. Marjorie would get about $1.5 million from the estate. Her children would share about $6 million. Marjorie would also be entitled to income for the rest of her life from a fund created with one-third of her children's share. The settlement would also pay $1.3 million in attorney's fees and at least $158,924 in claims against the estate by Marjorie's creditors. Under the terms of another trust, the Chester Congdon Trust, which was valued at $19 million (in 1983 dollars), the principal would be distributed to his heirs twenty-one years after Elisabeth's death, or June 27, 1998. Although Rick and Stephen did not participate in the lawsuit, they would still share equally the money that was distributed.

***

Helen and Wally Hagen first heard about Elisabeth Congdon's murder on the six o'clock news. Up until that time, it was the shock of their lives. Details of Roger Caldwell's life and the accumulating evidence against him made good copy, and the Hagens joined the rest of Minnesota in soaking up every juicy detail. Helen and Wally couldn't get over the fact that their friend Marjorie had married a loser like Roger Caldwell. Dick LeRoy had been such a nice man—a hard worker, a good father, and a doting husband.

Nancy Hagen heard the news on her car radio. She hadn't thought of Marjorie in years. The radio announcer said they were questioning Marjorie's second husband about the murders. Nancy had not been aware that Marjorie had remarried. It was the first time she had heard the name Roger Caldwell. It would not be the last.

Helen decided to call her old friend and let her know that she was there for her. She had never believed the rumors she heard about Marjorie. When Marjorie was accused of setting the fire at Marine-on-St. Croix, Helen and Wally thought of her as the victim—a woman who was unfairly persecuted because of her wealth. In spite of everything that had happened, there were still some people who believed in her. Marjorie was grateful.

✎ *Chapter Thirteen*

On May 8, 1978, it was 55 degrees and raining in Brainerd, Minnesota, when Roger Caldwell went on trial for the murders of Elisabeth Congdon and Velma Pietila.

Brainerd is about 110 miles southwest of Duluth. Caldwell's trial was moved there because of all the pretrial publicity. Thousands of Minnesotans flock to this resort community every summer to enjoy the 464 freshwater lakes in a 30-mile radius, with fabulous walleye and bass fishing, and twenty-one golf courses. Now, Brainerd would also be recognized for the Congdon murder trial.

This was the most sensational crime in Minnesota since the T. Eugene Thompson case from the 1960s. Thompson was a well-known lawyer who had contracted for his wife to be brutally murdered in their home. Not since then had the local press been blessed with an ongoing soap opera to tantalize their readers. The courtroom was full of spectators and reporters. It seemed that everyone was there except for Roger's wife. After courting the press so adamantly about her husband's innocence, Marjorie was conspicuously absent.

The prosecutor was thirty-two-year-old John De-Santo. He was of medium build, about five foot nine, with dark wavy hair and a full mustache that covered his top lip. His smile was wide and natural. He wore large square-framed glasses, which did not hide his youthful appearance.

He had decided he wanted to be a lawyer while in Duluth Cathedral High School, where he was a student council member and president of his junior and senior classes. He had majored in psychology and business administration at the University of Minnesota-Duluth and worked two summers for the Duluth Mesabi & Iron Range Railroad. Out of UMD in 1968, DeSanto served a two-year hitch in the Army as a clerk-typist with the 3rd Armored Division in West Germany. Then he went to the University of Minnesota Law School, graduating in 1973. He was admitted to the Minnesota bar that fall and got a job with the St. Louis County Attorney's Office. At the age of twenty-nine, he ran the office's criminal division. DeSanto had a passion for his work.

His greatest courtroom thrill came in the 1975 murder trial of Ed Reilly who was accused of raping and strangling a woman in Duluth. DeSanto got a subpoena to get an impression of his teeth to match them with teeth marks on the dead woman's body. It was one of the first times this type of evidence had been used in Minnesota. John DeSanto wanted to be known for representing a case that he believed in.

Marjorie contacted a well-known defense attorney, Ronald Meshbesher. She knew well that she would need a criminal attorney. Meshbesher had worked on cases having to do with inheritances, and he thought that hers would be an interesting case. She called in another well-known criminal defense attorney, Doug Thomson, to represent Roger. Thomson had an immediate dislike for Marjorie. Their personalities clashed, he said. He described her body as "corpulent," her voice as "shrill and penetrating," and her attitude as "pushy and dominating."

Thomson was forty-five years old at the time of the trial. He had prematurely gray hair that receded on the right side. He combed the sides straight down, over the top half of his ears. He'd obviously had thick hair at some point in his life. His glasses were wire-rimmed, large, and cut straight across his eyebrows. Thomson was recognized as one of the top defense attorneys from Minneapolis and he had seventeen years experience at the time of the trial. Divorced, he drove a Mercedes and wore expensive clothing—stylish, heavily-starched collars on white shirts with wide, conservative silk ties.

In the courtroom he could be ruthless. He once caused a witness on the stand to become so shook up that he began to stutter. When the questioning was over, someone asked Thomson why he had been so cruel to the witness. He answered, "You know where you'll find *fair* in the dictionary? It's between *fart* and *fuck*. You know where you'll find *sympathy* in the dictionary? Right between *shit* and *syphilis*."

After four weeks of jury selection and pretrial motions, the trial began. Thomson did not make an opening statement. He said that he didn't know what the defense was going to be at the time, nor did he know what the prosecution had as evidence against his client. He didn't want to lock himself into a corner and make a lot of promises he couldn't keep. The burden of proof to solve the murder was not on him. Thomson's only goal was to create a reasonable doubt.

In his opening remarks, DeSanto claimed, "Roger Caldwell killed his mother-in-law last June because he was faced with an almost unimaginable build-up of financial pressures and needed his wife's share of the Congdon inheritance to alleviate that pressure. These murders were motivated crimes." The jury of five men, seven women, and two women alternates watched DeSanto grip the lectern tightly as he went on to deliver a two-hour opening statement.

As expected, DeSanto first went over the medical testimony that would be presented, detailing the autopsies performed on the "beaten bloody body" of Mrs. Pietila and the "smothered" Miss Congdon. The jury shifted uneasily in their chairs as he described in detail how Velma Pietila had been beaten to death with a brass candlestick, suffering a severely fractured skull and twenty-three facial lacerations. He said that he would call about 100 witnesses. He outlined some of the physical evidence he would use in an attempt to show Caldwell's involvement in the crimes and numerous accounts of Caldwell's indebtedness.

"In September 1976, Caldwell signed a contract to buy a $290,000 ranch near Denver, Colorado. When he couldn't pay the $45,000 down payment, a $335,000 civil judgment was entered against him.

"He tried again. In March 1977, he made an offer for a $195,000 ranch in Golden, Colorado. Caldwell told the real estate agent on the sale that he was going to Minnesota in May to get the money for the purchase. Caldwell did indeed go to Duluth in May to ask the trustees of the Congdon estate for a $750,000 loan," DeSanto told the jury. "The request was denied, and the ranch deal was forfeited."

DeSanto explained how, on June 18, Caldwell had visited Thomas Congdon at his office in Denver, asking for money. Caldwell had told Congdon that he and his wife were thousands of dollars in debt. (Tom Congdon ended up paying their bills at the Holland House.) Their three jeeps had been repossessed. Caldwell's only income was his $97-a-week unemployment check.

"This was a very extravagant, spendthrift, dream-world type lifestyle for this unemployed fortune seeker. Finally, on June 24, just three days before the killings, Marjorie Caldwell prepared and signed a will giving Roger control of more than $2.5 million of her expected inheritance. That would be a carrot not too hard to swallow."

DeSanto admitted that his case was not perfect. "It is all circumstantial evidence, and none of the fingerprints found in the thirty-nine room Congdon mansion matched Caldwells." But then DeSanto laid out the evidence he did have.

"Although Congdon, Caldwell, and Pietila all have type-O blood, some of the blood found at the scene does match Caldwell's when broken down into enzyme groups. And three hairs found in the mansion match favorably with Caldwell's.

"Caldwell's right thumbprint was also found on an envelope, hand addressed by Caldwell to himself at his Colorado hotel and postmarked June 27 in Duluth. In the envelope was an odd-shaped gold coin," he said. "A similar gold coin was missing from the Congdon mansion after the slayings. And Caldwell is a coin collector."

The next day, after DeSanto's opening arguments, the trial began in earnest. DeSanto called Police Sgt. Gary Waller as his first witness. Introduced as evidence were: bloody sunglasses and teeth fragments matched to Mrs. Pietila; an earring found on the stairs near the body, along with a hairpin and a heel pad from a shoe; and gruesome color photographs. One of the photographs was from the basement area and showed a broken window near a recreation area, through which the intruder was believed to have gained access to the mansion. But out of thirty-seven exhibits, the most dramatic was the murder weapon, the brass candlestick holder, which was fractured at its base.

Ernie Grams testified that he interviewed Roger and Marjorie on June 29 at the Duluth police station. At that time, he noted the swelling of Roger's hand and the cut on his lip.

Next, Mildred Garvue testified. Dabbing an occasional tear, but speaking in a voice that never faltered, she told DeSanto how she had discovered the bodies.

Then there was testimony about the basement window. The hole in the window measured about six feet above the floor of an enclosed concourse. Glass found inside the mansion, more than sixteen feet from the window, indicated that a projectile could have made the hole. A police officer who had investigated the scene said that the basement window had two types of locks, a conventional thumb latch in the middle of the sliding panels and a metal sash lock designed to prevent the window from being raised beyond a certain height. He testified that neither he nor another officer could reach through the broken pane to the sash lock on the opposite side.

This testimony made it necessary to discuss the length of Roger Caldwell's arms. DeSanto tried to show that Caldwell's arm *could* reach through a small hole to unlock a basement window in the Congdon mansion. A police officer said that his arm fit through the window and could reach the sash lock, stating that his own arm was 31 inches long. Caldwell's arm measured 31⅝ inches.

Thomson countered by using a cardboard model of the broken window in order to show that Caldwell's arm could not fit.

There was confused testimony about footprints. The police officers had apparently contaminated the murder scene by walking around the grounds underneath the broken window with the dogs. If Caldwell had left prints, they were not identifiable.

A waitress at the Holland House Motel in Golden where the Caldwells lived testified that Marjorie usually came to breakfast earlier than Roger did, and that they usually ate separately. But on Sunday, June 26, the day before the murders, the couple came in together, dressed up more than usual, with look-alike red-checkered shirts, and Mrs. Caldwell wore earrings, which was unusual. They customarily dressed with a "western look, denim jeans and jackets, something you'd see out on the ranch." Marjorie had made a comment that they were in a hurry. She added that she saw Marjorie in the coffee shop twice on Monday, June 27. But she hadn't seen Roger at all.

And next, the mystery of the gold coin, which had been taken from Miss Congdon's room. Miss Congdon's private secretary testified that she noticed the coin was missing several days after the murders. And then the desk clerk at the Holland House Motel in Golden, Colorado, testified that she had found an envelope in the Caldwell's mail slot, postmarked June 27 from Duluth. It was addressed to Caldwell in handwriting that she recognized to be his. She said she notified police about the envelope and was asked to hold onto it until a handwriting analyst was called in.

Under cross-examination by Thomson, Elisabeth's staff coordinator and social secretary, Vera Dunbar, confirmed that on May 25, 1977, Caldwell met Elisabeth Congdon for the first time. He had come to the mansion alone. He brought Miss Congdon a small, reclining, antique ivory horse and told her about his life with Marjorie in Colorado. She said that Miss Congdon was not impressed with him. When Caldwell left, Miss Congdon was upset and signed with her hands, "Bad." This was probably not what Thomson had hoped to hear from her. Caldwell had not given Mrs. Dunbar a self-addressed, stamped envelope when he had been in Duluth in May, she added.

A banker from Golden said that in late 1976, Roger Caldwell had taken out a loan of more than $21,000 for three vehicles. He soon defaulted on the loan, and the bank repossessed the vehicles, which were pickups or similar, suitable for ranching. Roger had met payments of some $700 monthly in December 1976 and January 1977, before he defaulted on the three-year contract. On March 9, 1977, Caldwell came to the bank with a briefcase full of cash and made two months' payments. Those were the last payments the bank would receive.

The banker testified that Caldwell appeared normal on the Monday of the murders. Caldwell had visited the Golden State Bank at 9:30 a.m. that day to explain that his stepson, Rick LeRoy, had taken one of the vehicles repossessed by the bank. The Caldwells had had an arrangement to use one of the three repossessed vehicles if they checked with the banker in the morning and returned the car to the bank's parking lot every night. The banker had seen Rick drive the vehicle from the bank parking lot earlier that Monday at 7:30 a.m.

Under cross-examination, the banker explained that Caldwell generally came to the bank between 9:00 and 9:30 a.m. to check about the use of a vehicle for the day. The banker found out later that Monday that Miss Congdon had died and $300 had been wired from a bank in Minnesota for the Caldwells to buy plane tickets to go back for the funeral. The next morning, Caldwell returned to the bank about 9:00 and was "very nervous" the banker said. "His hair was uncombed and he seemed to be somewhat apprehensive." Caldwell told him that he had cut his lip shaving and that a horse had stepped on his hand.

During the ninth week of testimony, a real estate agent from Denver told of a 1976 contract the Caldwells entered into for 272 acres of mountain land and a modest house near Bailey, Colorado. She said the Caldwells put $10,000 down on the $300,000 property and moved into the house in November 1976. They were to pay $45,000 more in January 1977, but the payment was never made.

Another real estate agent said that Marjorie had looked at expensive properties on June 25, June 26, and June 27. Marjorie had signed three purchase agreements, and the realtor was told that the properties would be paid for by a trust fund. All the deals fell through.

Testimony about the Caldwells' financial difficulties went on and on, piled up, like their bills and defaulted loans, stacking evidence against Roger Caldwell. At the rate they were spending money, according to the testimony, Elisabeth Congdon could not have died soon enough for Marjorie to collect her inheritance.

Rick LeRoy, Marjorie's youngest son, was called to the stand. He resembled both his mother and his father, stocky, with dark, thick hair. He testified that on the night of the murders he had been out with his girlfriend. When he got back to the Holland House, at about 1:00 a.m. on June 27, he peeked in their room. "It looked to me like there were two people sleeping in the bedroom," he told Doug Thomson. Then, DeSanto pressed Rick about the figures in the bed.

"Did you see Roger Caldwell in that bed?" DeSanto asked.

"I seen some hair, yes, it looked like him," he responded.

DeSanto asked, "What did you see when you looked at the bed?"

"Two bodies—well, two lumps under the covers." He admitted that he did not actually see Caldwell's face. Rick explained that he had lived with his mother all his life and met Caldwell two months before the couple's 1976 marriage. He said he was "pretty friendly" with Caldwell and usually called him "Roger or Rog."

At 12:30 a.m. Saturday, June 25, Rick found 50 dollars and a note on his bed at the Holland House Motel in Golden. The note said, "Mom and I will be with real estate people all day Saturday and Sunday. . . . Here's fifty bucks for gasoline, dates, whatever through Monday. . . . Love, Mom and Dad." DeSanto asked him if Roger usually signed his notes, "Dad." Rick admitted that no, it would be signed, Rog or Roger.

After almost six weeks, Doug Thomson began his defense. He promised the jury that one defense witness, an examiner of questioned documents, would conclude, "The envelope has sufficient inconsistencies with the known handwriting of Mr. Caldwell. It will be her conclusion the envelope was written by someone who was familiar with Mr. Caldwell's handwriting." He promised that the witness would reach a similar conclusion concerning a printed address label found on a suede garment bag that Caldwell allegedly purchased at the airport.

Thomson also promised that another major witness would be an anatomy professor and crime lab analyst from Milwaukee who examined the hairs introduced as evidence by the state. As opposed to the prosecution, this analyst used an electronic scanning microscope, which could detect the actual chemical content of hair. The conclusion of that witness, Thomson said, would be that hairs found on the sheet in which Mrs. Pietila's body was wrapped and on a rug near her body did not compare with Caldwell's hair. Also contrary to state testimony, Thomson said, the witness would conclude that the dark hair found in Mrs. Pietila's hands did not come from her own head, or Caldwell's, but from another source. Thomson kept his promises to the court.

Finally, after eight weeks and 106 witnesses, the testimony ended, DeSanto rose to sum up his case. He stood at a podium in front of and facing the jury box, and repeated again and again what he called "inescapable conclusions" resulting from the prosecution's case. In the heat of his summation, several times, he struck the jury box banister with his clenched fist to drive home a point. He emphasized a handwritten will from Marjorie to Roger giving him $2.5 million. The promised money, he said, was a "desperate attempt to persuade the defendant to go to Duluth and commit murder."

He also blasted the defense witness called in connection with three hair strands found at the murder scene. The defense's microanalyst witness, DeSanto claimed, gave arbitrary answers that changed all the time. The expert, DeSanto told the jury, said he was a microanalyst because he had looked through a microscope. "By that definition, I guess I'm a microanalyst because I once looked through a microscope in eleventh grade in high school."

He also questioned Rick LeRoy's integrity. DeSanto said that Rick gave "frequent glances and smiles to the defendant and had some convenient memory lapses."

DeSanto described the case against Caldwell as "overwhelming," and asked the jury to "evaluate the evidence and it will lead you to one conclusion: Guilty as charged."

It was Thomson's turn. He was known to have pioneered the great closing argument. Even prosecutors copied his style. He reminded the jury that the experts that he and the defense team had used had concluded that it was not Caldwell's writing on the envelope, but a forgery, and that the hairs from the death scene were not Caldwell's. He implied to the jury that Caldwell was the victim of a frame-up by the real killer who was seeking to prevent Roger and his wife from realizing the benefit of the Congdon inheritance. He reminded the jurors that DeSanto had not produced evidence to show that Caldwell traveled by air between Colorado and Minnesota and had introduced only the disputed hair strands as evidence that Caldwell was ever at the mansion.

He proclaimed that his client was the hapless victim of a frame compounded by negligent police work. He emphasized that the frame was possibly planned by Caldwell's wife, Marjorie, and aided by his stepson, Rick. It was the only thing that made sense. He argued that the police were "tipped" as to Caldwell's alleged role in the murders—a tip that came fifteen minutes before nurse Velma Pietila's body was removed from the Congdon mansion.

"On what basis did the Duluth Police Department decide that Roger Caldwell was a prime suspect?" Thomson asked the jury. "Somebody who was either directly or indirectly responsible for the murders contacted the Duluth police and said 'There's your man.' Someone fed the police something and they fell for it hook, line, and sinker."

Thomson blasted the Duluth police department, saying that once a suspect was found they conducted a slipshod, incomplete investigation aimed only at convicting Caldwell. "They had blinders on. They had a suspect and the name of the game was to build a case around him—and they had a lot of help," Thomson said.

"The prosecution claims that the two murders were an attempt by Caldwell to speed up his wife's expected inheritance of $8.2 million, part of a Congdon fortune estimated at a total of $45 million." Thomson, in a style that had become his trademark, illustrated his argument against accepting such a motive with a story: He told the jury of a boy who after stealing and eating a blueberry pie from a farmer's kitchen looked out the window and saw the farmer approaching. The boy grabbed the family dog and rubbed its muzzle in the pie plate. The farmer, seeing the obvious evidence, kicked the dog to death.

Next, he dealt with the crime-scene evidence: "A broken window, which the prosecution claims was the killer's point of entry into the Congdon mansion—Caldwell's arm had been shown to be too large to go through the shattered glass and unlatch the window," he said. "Fingerprints, all of which eliminated Caldwell as a suspect—the police never tried to match the prints with anyone else once it was found they weren't Caldwell's. Hair strands—instead of analyzing strands found clutched in nurse Pietila's hands—that may well have been the calling card of her murderer—police analyzed instead some strands found on a rug and in the sheet used to transport the nurse's body. An analysis of drops of blood found at the scene showed only that it was Caldwell's type—and the blood type of some thirty million other people in the United States. There was not one shred of evidence uncovered at that crime scene that would point at Roger Caldwell," Thomson said.

He looked next at several items found in the Bloomington hotel room occupied by Caldwell after the murders, items such as jewelry, the rare coin, and a wicker case, all of which came from Miss Congdon's bedroom.

"Picking up these items from the murder scene and leaving them in a hotel room didn't make sense," he said, "unless the mission of the murderers was to point the finger at Caldwell."

He argued that the address on the envelope itself, written to "Mr. Roger Caldwell," also indicated a frame because people do not use the term "Mr." when referring to themselves.

Thomson put forth his own sequence of events for

the night of the murder. "The murderer, or murderers, entered through the front door, because they were recognized. The broken window was a red herring to throw authorities off the track. After committing the two murders, the killers left in nurse Pietila's car. They took several items from Miss Congdon's bedroom in order to plant them in Caldwell's hotel room. The murderers purchased a garment bag at the airport, leaving a nametag with Caldwell on it inside the bag. They knew the store employees would remember only the bag and not the purchaser's face."

He ended his argument by once again blasting the police, accusing them of stopping short before the real killers were revealed. "The minute they had arrested Caldwell, they had gone too far not to go on. Anything in this case that didn't point to Roger Caldwell as a suspect was ignored," he said. Later, though, he would admit that he believed that Roger was framed because he didn't think that Caldwell had the wherewithal to do the job alone.

By the time he was finished with his closing statements, Thomson's voice was rasping from the strain of nearly five hours with only one short break. He repeatedly drove home the point that only the presumption of innocence stood between a man charged with a crime and the power of the state. He ended his summation by reminding the jury that the prosecution's case was based only on circumstantial evidence.

Finally, after twelve long weeks, the case went to the jury. They had to consider not only a first-degree murder charge in connection with Elisabeth Congdon's death, but also a first–and second–degree charge in connection with Velma Pietila's death. Caldwell could be found guilty or not guilty. But, there could be one other outcome: a deadlocked or hung jury. All twelve jurors had to agree to convict or acquit Roger Caldwell, the man who had sat next to Doug Thomson, mute for the entire twelve weeks, as if he were merely a spectator and had no important reason to be there. Did Roger have some premonition of what his fate was going to be? It was impossible to read the man.

It was partly cloudy on Saturday, July 8, 1978. The temperature was in the 70s, the streets busy with summer tourists in shorts and sandals, and cars towing boats on trailers. The town buzzed with the headlines from the *Brainerd Daily Dispatch*: "Caldwell Found Guilty on Two Counts of First-Degree Murder". The verdict was reached on the seventh ballot after twenty-four hours of deliberation. Roger would be sentenced the following Monday.

After the clerk read the word *Guilty*, Caldwell broke his silence. He deadpanned the jury and said, "You're wrong." This was a profound statement. The court reporters, the bailiffs, and other court officials believed that Roger was telling the truth. His eyes scanned the gallery as if looking for someone. Outside of curious spectators and reporters, he was alone. Marjorie was not there. She had not been there for one day of his trial.

On the following Monday, Roger Caldwell was sentenced to two consecutive life terms in prison. Asked if he had anything to say before sentencing, Caldwell said, "Only that I'm not guilty of these charges." He was taken to Stillwater State Prison to begin serving his sentence.

DeSanto was pleased with the result of what he called "Step One." He told reporters that "it was a fair and just verdict, certainly an intelligent one." Now he intended to go after Marjorie. On July 11, 1978, Marjorie Caldwell was charged with conspiring with her husband to kill her mother. She was released on

$100,000 bond. Since bail bondsmen charge only 10 percent of that amount, Marjorie only had to come up with $10,000 to remain free until her trial. If she skipped bail, she would owe the bondsman the remaining $90,000 when she was apprehended.

In spite of DeSanto's youth and his inexperience compared to his formidable opponent, Ronald Meshbesher, DeSanto believed that he had a no-lose case. Roger Caldwell had been convicted of killing Elisabeth Congdon and her nurse. But, it seemed obvious to DeSanto that Caldwell could not have pulled off this crime by himself. He had to have had help.

One scenario was that Marjorie put Roger on the plane to Minneapolis from Denver. She probably kissed him goodbye, as if he were going off to work, and then set out to meet with at least three realtors who could verify that she never left Colorado during the time of the murders.

DeSanto figured Marjorie knew that Roger would not be able to handle the stress without booze. He would leave a trail a mile long to incriminate himself. She sent him to the Glensheen Mansion a month before the murders to ask her mother for money. Alone. He didn't even know Elisabeth Congdon, and Marjorie didn't go with him? Of course not, because that was part of the plan. Make it look like this was Roger's idea to butter up the old lady and talk her out of some money. She probably had an outline, all written down, step-by-step. It could have been titled, *The Framing of Roger Caldwell*. As for the murder, she must have told him to make it look like a burglary, simply put a pillow over her mother's face, ransack the bedroom, and get the hell out of there. "Oh, and as long as you're there, I've always wanted that cameo ring she wears, so after you've killed her, just take it off her hand and bring it home."

DeSanto thought Marjorie probably hadn't counted on Velma hearing him in the house. If by some miracle that had entered her mind, it wouldn't have mattered anyway. Roger was there to murder her mother, and how it got done was beside the point. It was clear, Marjorie was sick of his drinking, sick of always having to make excuses for his behavior, his absences. She wanted to get rid of him. She needed money, why not kill two birds with one stone? Roger would go to jail for a long time, and Marjorie would get her inheritance. It was only common sense. DeSanto knew it. All he had to do was prove it in court.

Thank God for that one shred of physical evidence that definitely connected Roger to the crime—his fingerprint on the envelope he had mailed to himself. Or had he? It was hard to believe that Caldwell would have had the presence of mind to steal only one coin, load it into an envelope bearing a Radisson Hotel logo, and then mail it to his home address, calling himself "Mr." But the motivation was so clear, and the fingerprint that put Roger away was really just the icing on the cake. Now, all DeSanto had to do was to prove that Roger Caldwell could not have acted alone.

Marjorie should go to prison for life for having her mother killed.

❧ *Chapter Fourteen*

When Marjorie hired forty-four-year-old Ron Meshbesher to defend her, he was one of the Midwest's top defense lawyers. This was probably one of the best choices she ever made. Meshbesher was slick, he was shrewd, he was competent. He used homespun language, such as "you folks," and had a look-you-in-the-eyes kind of smile custom-tailored for conservative Midwest juries. Meshbesher stood about five feet, ten inches with a shock of thick gray hair, matching beard, only more salt-and-pepper, eye-glasses with black plastic frames, and a commanding, resonant, James Earl Jones–like voice. His silences were just as commanding. He had a way of letting just enough time lapse before his client or his adversary would fill in the empty spaces with words, oftentimes revealing things they never intended. It was far more effective than asking a lot of questions point-blank. An impeccable dresser, he could wear three-piece Southwick suits without being pompous.

He was well-regarded for his meticulous preparation, incisive cross-examination, and an engaging manner that built rapport with juries. He sported metaphors to plead his case, and he let his feelings show when warranted. "There have been several times when I've caught myself shedding tears in a final argument," he said.

But another colleague warned people not to get too carried away with style. "His style is his preparation. He's indefatigable—an indefatigable digger. He's skeptical of everything in the government's case."

He pointed to a murder case Meshbesher had about seven years earlier. "It looked as though his client was cooked, based on the results of a new scientific test called 'Neutron Activation,' which measured the amount of gunpowder on a person's skin.

"Meshbesher didn't trust the test," he recalled. "So he started making calls, first locally, then all over the country. Somehow he got in touch with a University of California-Irvine doctor who not only knew about the neutron activation test, but also had developed it.

"Meshbesher told the professor of his client's test

results," he recalled. "The professor listened and said, 'It can't be. What did the gun shoot? A cannon? A 105 howitzer? Something's wrong with the reading.'"

"From there," he said, "it was easy for Meshbesher to blow away the results of the test in court. His client was acquitted."

To a law enforcement official who worked with him, he was the top graduate of the "Dial a Witness School," coming up with witnesses no one had heard of before to say the right thing at the right time. "A never-ending supply of new witnesses. They're dug out of the bushes," the investigator said angrily.

One of Meshbesher's friends, a former Hennepin County attorney who went up against him a number of times, called him the toughest defense attorney he had ever faced. Meshbesher would "bluff you right out of your socks" if you weren't paying attention, he said. "You just gotta be watching yourself all the time with Meshbesher. He's very tricky and very good. He's a great, great user of the needle. You have to keep your back to the wall at all times or else he'll nail it in quite securely."

Outside the courtroom, Meshbesher was described as a "very droll, witty, serious, thoughtful guy. Very bright, very well-read." Few defense lawyers were the Renaissance man Meshbesher was. He had a delightful sense of humor and he was stable. Unlike many of his colleagues, he seldom drank. It was said, though, that he had a certain compulsion about whatever he did, whether it was work or play.

Meshbesher attended North High School in Minneapolis, the University of Minnesota, and the University's law school. After graduating, he worked as a prosecutor in the Hennepin County Attorney's office. He and his first wife had three daughters before they divorced. He married the second time at the Fairmont

Hotel in San Francisco, the same building in which he was attending the National Association of Criminal Defense Lawyers convention. He was efficient.

Ronald Meshbesher had begun his ascent to the upper echelons of the Minnesota criminal bar in the enemy camp, as an assistant prosecutor for Hennepin County. Fresh out of the University of Minnesota Law School in the late 1950s, Meshbesher tried forty-five felony cases in three years—invaluable experience for a young attorney learning his way around a courtroom. He went on to co-found Meshbesher & Spence, where he became the lawyer of choice for clients with deep pockets and desperate circumstances. Marjorie Caldwell certainly matched his client profile.

The first question before Meshbesher was whether Marjorie Caldwell would go to trial at all.

A few days after Roger Caldwell was convicted, prosecutor DeSanto called Meshbesher to say he was filing a complaint against Marjorie Caldwell. At the same time, DeSanto offered a deal: If Marjorie would plead guilty to conspiracy, the state wouldn't seek a murder indictment against her.

Conspiracy carried a maximum term of twenty years in prison, but Meshbesher said that under the parole system, Marjorie probably would not have "done worse than three or four years, so it was a hell of a thing to turn down, even if you're innocent. She always maintained her innocence, but even innocent people have a right to avoid a gamble." However, when Meshbesher conveyed the offer to Marjorie, she "flatly rejected it." That's when Meshbesher's defense began in earnest.

The fact that Marjorie's trial was held in Hastings, Minnesota, was a plus. As with Roger, there had been so much pretrial publicity that her trial had to be moved. Hastings is about thirty miles south of Minneapolis and 180 miles south of Duluth. One of the oldest cities in the state, Hastings is a small river town built up against the Mississippi. Her trial was held in the new government center, a modern building with lots of large windows, chrome railings, terracotta tiles, and skylights. Dakota County (Hastings) had one of the youngest populations in the state of Minnesota. This was ultimately reflected in the selection of her jury, whose members averaged about thirty-five years of age. Older jurors were thought to be more likely to vote for a conviction than younger jurors, who may be more skeptical of prosecution claims. Roger's jury had been older than Marjorie's.

The contemporary courtroom had been built with blond wood with a large "well area" for the attorneys and an even larger area for the spectators. The judge sat in the middle of the room at a blond bench, which was long enough to seat three judges. Marjorie sat at a long table next to Meshbesher. Her legs were too short to reach the floor and she sat there, every day, swinging her feet back and forth the way a child would. She always had a paperback book with her, as if she were disinterested in the proceedings.

Reporters from all the major TV stations in Minnesota flocked to the courtroom every day even though the actual trial was not televised. Town residents as well as people from Duluth stood in line for hours every day to get a seat. The trial would last for sixteen weeks, yet would not lose a juror. One juror's father died and they buried him on a weekend so that the juror would not have to be replaced.

Another of the pluses for Meshbesher was that he had the transcript of Roger Caldwell's trial in front of him. This gave him the incalculable advantage of hindsight. An even bigger edge for him was that he had access to more than sixty police reports and other documents that, for some reason, had never been turned over to Roger's defense attorney during his trial.

Despite all this, Meshbesher had some big minuses to overcome in defending Marjorie. One was the effect of the enormous publicity surrounding the case. A survey conducted for Meshbesher in the Duluth area showed more animosity toward Marjorie than toward her husband, and a widespread belief that she was the schemer behind the murders. Another problem facing Meshbesher was the fact that Marjorie was charged with conspiracy as well as murder.

"Conspiracy as we know it in this country has been labeled the 'prosecutor's darling' because when they can't prove anything else, they resort to conspiracy charges, which are easily proved and very difficult to defend against," Meshbesher said.

Marjorie's statements also complicated Meshbesher's defense—some of them were admittedly lies that Marjorie made to police shortly after the murders. Roger Caldwell, he noted, made no such statements. For those reasons, Meshbesher said he thought "the case against Marjorie was a tougher case than Roger's."

Meshbesher faced a mountain of paperwork. He and the other members of the defense team had to absorb hundreds of police reports, review scores of pictures and exhibits, read the 5,400-page transcript of Roger Caldwell's trial, and somehow keep all the salient details in mind. They developed a reference system—modeled on one used by Doug Thomson—to organize this information. One part of the system was a thick book containing the names of more than 300 potential witnesses. Below each person's name was a code telling where that person's name appeared in a police report, a grand jury transcript, or any other document pertaining to the case.

Meshbesher's preparation also included an analysis report he commissioned on the jury that had convicted Roger Caldwell in 1978. A group called the National Jury Project Midwest interviewed four of the Roger Caldwell jurors. From those interviews, Meshbesher learned what pieces of evidence had been most convincing to that jury.

The fingerprint on the envelope that Roger had allegedly mailed to himself in Colorado had been perhaps the most damaging evidence against Roger. Meshbesher knew, instinctively, that if he could create some doubt in the jurors' minds about Roger's guilt, his client would have a good chance. This thought was strengthened when he learned that a majority of the jurors at Roger's trial had at first favored acquittal, only to change their minds under pressure from the jury's strong-willed foreman.

All of this interviewing and research cost money, so much in fact that by the opening day of Marjorie's trial, Meshbesher had already spent $60,000 defending his client. That was a lot of money in 1978. It would take years before the attorneys would get paid. Some of the legal fees for the murder trial would be paid from Marjorie's inheritance. Marjorie had guaranteed Doug Thomson $100,000 for representing Roger in the murder trial. But that didn't cover his fees or expenses after the trial, which easily amounted to $250,000. Meshbesher's fee was $100,000, with expenses of $84,000.

Meshbesher went to court to seek $137,813 in legal fees and expenses from one of the trust accounts that had been set up for Marjorie. He said that if the motion was not granted, the state would end up paying. He noted that the trust that Elisabeth had set up in 1968, the Marjorie C. LeRoy Family Trust, the one that Dick LeRoy was to manage for his wife, had about

$750,000 in principal and had an annual income of about $45,000. Part of Meshbesher's legal fees would have to come from the principal. Marjorie's children objected to his proposal, stating that the trust agreement did not allow the principal to be used for their mother's benefit. The judge ruled that Marjorie could receive payments from the income of the trust but not from the principal. Eventually, it would be this income that would cover her legal fees.

"The first tactical decision to make," Meshbesher said, "was whether we should more or less stipulate that Roger had committed the murder, and just place our defense in the fact that Marjorie had no part of it, or whether we should fight Roger's case, in effect, all over again." He decided on the second course because, it seemed to him, it was the only one that fit the facts of the case as revealed by his investigation.

"You can't conjure up a theory," Meshbesher said. "The facts dictate it."

And as Meshbesher envisioned the Caldwell case, it came down to one simple question. Had Roger actually committed the murder and mailed that coin to himself, for whatever reason, or had someone wanted to frame Roger? The "frame" would later be dubbed "The Colorado Connection." Meshbesher would imply that Marjorie's cousin Thomas Congdon, his attorney, and others had good motives to kill Elisabeth Congdon: "Control, power, and money."

"There was no other way to handle the case because of the incriminating evidence that was found in Roger and Marjorie's possession. It was really bad stuff and you couldn't just hide yourself and say, 'Well, it's there, so what?' You had to give the jury, although you are not required to, a rational alternative."

Meshbesher's strategy also entailed painting a far different picture of the relationship between Roger and Marjorie Caldwell than had been presented by Thomson in Brainerd. Thomson had depicted Roger as a "patsy" who was dominated and finally framed by his wife. But to Meshbesher's way of thinking, there was a giant flaw in that theory. "That theory to me was fallacious because it would mean that Marjorie would have framed herself at the same time. Because if she were going to frame Roger, why in the world would she have that incriminating evidence (jewels stolen from Miss Congdon) in her jewelry case, not too well-hidden, in the night-stand at the Holiday Inn?" To counter this theory, Meshbesher's strategy was to show that Roger was not a weakling dependent on his wife, but a strong and sometimes abusive figure in his own right, although still not a killer.

Before the trial began, he talked with Caldwell at Stillwater Prison and told him how he intended to proceed. "I told him up front that we were going to represent Marjorie to the hilt even if it meant in some respects painting him as not such a nice guy. I told him that we knew about his drinking problems and we knew he had attacked his wife and that some of these assaults had resulted in her hospitalization. He understood that and he said, 'Well, you do what you think is right.' He maintained he was not involved in the murder and felt he was framed."

There was one other strategic decision that Meshbesher had to make and that was whether to put Marjorie on the witness stand.

"I think we had decided from the beginning that she had to take the witness stand to explain certain things away, such as her statements to police with respect to finding Miss Congdon's jewelry in her jewelry case."

But Meshbesher also knew that putting Marjorie on the stand posed great risks. "Marjorie is a very unusual person," he said. "She is very outspoken and not afraid to speak her mind, and she's the type of person you might lose control over in the courtroom."

It took three weeks to pick a jury. The trial would last for sixteen weeks; 141 witnesses would testify.

❧ *Chapter Fifteen*

After lengthy opening statements by both attorneys, the testimony for Marjorie's trial finally began on May 1, 1979, nine months after Roger had been sentenced to two life terms in prison.

John DeSanto called Mildred Garvue, Ernie Grams, and all the people that were at the Congdon estate the day the bodies were discovered. They went over, step-by-step, everything that happened that day.

One witness, Dr. Elizabeth Bagley, who had been Elisabeth Congdon's personal physician, told the jury about an incident that occurred at the Glensheen Mansion in 1974.

"Can you relate to the jury what happened?"

"Well, Marjorie came over to Glensheen, she said she wanted to see her mother. The nurse on duty that day, I don't remember which one, let her in. Marjorie had some homemade bread and some marmalade that she said she'd made herself."

"What happened?"

"Well, Elisabeth was diabetic—Marjorie knew that, of course—and the nurse told her that Elisabeth couldn't eat the marmalade."

"And what did Marjorie do?"

"She wouldn't listen. She insisted on giving that bread and marmalade to her mother. Well, the nurse called me and I knew how Marjorie could be, of course, so I told the nurse to let her give just a small amount to Elisabeth, and it would probably be all right. So Marjorie went in the kitchen, alone, made the sandwich and then she went upstairs and fed it to her mother."

"What happened?"

"Well, the next morning, the nurse couldn't wake Elisabeth. She became frightened and called me. I went over there immediately and I took a blood sample from Elisabeth's arm. By then she was beginning to wake up but her heartbeat and blood pressure were very low. Elisabeth was unresponsive and she didn't really come around until later that day."

"Dr. Bagley, what did you deduce from that incident?"

"Well, I knew something was very strange at the time. But when we had the blood sample tested, it revealed traces of meprobamate, a form of tranquilizer. I believed that Marjorie had tried to poison her mother."

DeSanto called Vera Dunbar to the stand. She was sixty-four years old and married with two sons. Elisabeth's brother Edward had hired her in 1968 to manage Elisabeth's business and social affairs. Since her stroke, it had been difficult for Elisabeth to coordinate affairs at the Glensheen by herself. Mrs. Dunbar explained that she did not live at Glensheen but worked from 9:00 in the morning until late afternoon. The only staff that actually lived in the house was the maid and the cook. The maintenance man and his family and the gardener and his wife lived in other buildings on the grounds.

Mrs. Dunbar also assisted Elisabeth in her winter home in Tucson along with two registered nurses. In 1977, Elisabeth had spent February until April in Arizona. In the summer, Vera would accompany Elisabeth to Brule. They normally left Duluth on Friday after lunch and returned late afternoon on Sunday. Dr. Bagley was the deciding factor on how long they would stay, depending on how Elisabeth was feeling. Mrs. Dunbar accompanied Elisabeth to Swiftwater Farm on Friday, June 24, 1977, along with Mildred Garvue.

Vera recalled Roger Caldwell's one visit to Elisabeth. He showed up around 2:00 p.m. for an appointment that he had scheduled the day before. They met for about thirty minutes in the library. Mrs. Dunbar assured DeSanto that Roger did not go anywhere else in the house that day.

During Meshbesher's cross-examination, Mrs. Dunbar told him that the last time that Marjorie had been to Duluth to see her mother was in August 1975. She described Marjorie's relationship with her mother as a "reserved closeness." Before Elisabeth's death, Mrs. Dunbar had helped her go through her jewelry, which Elisabeth planned to leave to her daughters after she died. One ring that had been willed to Marjorie was a platinum diamond and sapphire strawberry dome ring containing fifteen well-worn sapphires and six diamonds of .08 carats each. This was the ring stolen from Elisabeth's dressing table the night she was murdered.

Meshbesher called Hyman Zuckerman to the stand. He was a physician who specialized in internal medicine and had been practicing in Denver since 1975. He first met Marjorie Caldwell when she was hospitalized at Beth Israel Hospital in Denver on June 17 for five days. She told him she had fallen off a horse and then been kicked. She complained of pain in the left side of her body. The next time he saw her was in April 1977 when she told him that she had been crushed against a wall by a horse and complained of severe pain in her right chest.

"Was there any other conversation with her as to how those injuries occurred?"

"When she returned on May 3, she admitted to me that the injuries had been the result of her having been beaten by her husband."

Meshbesher asked Dr. Zuckerman if he was aware of Roger's drinking problem. Zuckerman told him that he was and that in January 1977 Roger was admitted to a hospital in Denver for treatment. The following May, Dr. Zuckerman gave a prescription of Antabuse to Marjorie for Roger Caldwell. He did not know if it had stopped Caldwell from drinking.

Roger DeSanto called Ruth McDermott to the stand. She had met Marjorie in May 1975 when Marjorie lived in Bailey, Colorado. Ruth's son had become friends with Marjorie's son Rick. On their second meeting, Marjorie had told Ruth that a spinster had adopted her. She received a monthly stipend, which came from several trusts, she confided.

"What did she relate to you about the status of her inheritance, based upon her adoption?"

"She related to me that the other Congdon relatives and heirs objected or had taken to court the fact that she was an adopted child on the basis that an adopted child should not inherit under the same terms as a natural born child. She said that she had gone to the Supreme Court and that they decided that she would inherit the same as any other heirs."

She recalled one night when she had Marjorie and Roger for dinner at her home before they were married. Marj had confided to Ruth that Roger had a drinking problem, and she had requested that Ruth serve wine so that she could see how Roger would react. Roger had gone through a drying-out process and was trying to get his life together, but she was afraid of his drinking. She told **Ruth that she was lonely and tired of hassling with the trust accounts and battling with the** "powers that be" **and the rest of the family.** She thought Roger was good with Rick, and although she did not love him, he would be a good companion. He would also serve as a buffer, she said.

"What does that mean? A buffer?"

"There had been a continual battle over the amounts of money and the way it was being received. Marjorie felt that the money was being mismanaged, and she thought the family, including her own children, were trying to disenfranchise her. She thought that the people handling the trusts might relate better to Roger than they did to her."

Ruth had been at Roger and Marjorie's wedding. They were married at the Littleton Methodist Church in Littleton, Colorado, on March 20, 1976. She and another neighbor were witnesses. After the wedding day, Ruth said, she saw Roger intoxicated on many occasions.

DeSanto changed the subject. "Did Marjorie ever talk to you about her accessibility to seeing her mother?"

"Yes, many times. She said that the family did not want her to visit her mother. She said that her mother had had surgery for cancer and strokes, and that she was very ill. She told me that she felt her mother was being kept alive in order to support Doctor Bagley and some of the Congdon administrators of her mother's funds."

The last time that Ruth saw Marjorie, in September 1976, Marjorie told her that it was a shame her mother was still living because she—Marjorie—could use the money.

When Meshbesher cross-examined Ruth, he got her to talk about Marjorie's generosity, the fact that she was still depressed from her divorce from Dick LeRoy, and how worried she must have been being married to an alcoholic.

DeSanto called Barney Johnson to the stand. He practiced law in Duluth and his firm specialized in corporations, trusts, and estates. Johnson had been an attorney for the trustees of the Chester Congdon Trusts since 1969. Elisabeth had been his client since 1974.

On May 25, 1977, he met Roger Caldwell with two of Marjorie's attorneys in his office. Bill Van Evera was also there. They met for two hours. This was the meeting requesting the $750,000. Caldwell made an articulate proposal with financial projections and even blueprints for the buildings they intended to put up. However, there was no collateral—only a mortgage on some real estate was offered as security. The real estate had much less value than the amount of the loan they were proposing. They decided to reject Caldwell's request. Elisabeth was never told about the proposal.

Johnson was an expert in probate and estate law and he knew if adopted children were excluded by a court ruling, neither Marjorie nor her children would get any funds from the Congdon trust. Their share would go to the other direct descendants of Chester Congdon.

In regards to the lawsuit filed by the trustees to keep Marjorie from collecting her inheritance, Meshbesher got Johnson to admit that Marjorie and Jennifer had *each* filed a brief in opposition to any attempt to exclude adopted children. If Marjorie and Jennifer could not collect, approximately $16 million would go to the remaining beneficiaries. Thomas Congdon would be one of the direct recipients. William Van Evera's wife would be another, as would Salisbury Adam's wife, because they were blood members of the Congdon family.

DeSanto called William (Bill) Van Evera. He was a sixty-two-year-old lawyer married to Mary Congdon, Elisabeth's brother's daughter. Mary was also Thomas Congdon's sister, and Marjorie's first cousin. Bill practiced law in Duluth. He explained that he was a trustee along with Thomas Congdon and Salisbury Adams (who had also married into the family and practiced law in Minneapolis).

Bill and Mary had been at Marjorie's wedding. Other than that, they saw each other rarely, at family functions. Mary's parents also had a summer home on the Brule, he said. The break-in and the burned pillow were not mentioned. Bill had seen Marjorie and her family in Brule occasionally when she had been married to Dick LeRoy.

In 1968, Bill had informed Marjorie and Jennifer that their mother planned to set up two identical trusts for them and their families. He met with her again in 1972 when Marjorie decided that Marquette Bank in Minneapolis should administer the trust.

Bill first met Roger Caldwell on May 25, 1976, when he came to his office in Duluth and asked for the $750,000 loan to "start a ranch of some sort." He said that the request was denied for a few reasons: It was a request for cash assets, which were not readily available; he was aware of Marjorie's substantial debts; and he did not believe that the money was going to go for the purposes that Roger proposed. Bill stated that he was at home the morning that Vera Dunbar called his wife to tell her that something terrible had happened at Glensheen. He immediately called Mary's brother in Denver, Tom Congdon.

On May 22, 1979, DeSanto called Thomas Congdon to the stand. His father, Edward, was Elisabeth's brother. Congdon was fifty-two years old and married with two children. He was Marjorie Caldwell's first cousin. He had been born and raised in Duluth but lived in Englewood, Colorado, a suburb of Denver. Tom Congdon had his own company, Congdon & Carey, which engaged in the business of looking for new ore bodies to mine.

At DeSanto's request, Congdon diagrammed a family tree to show the generations effected by the trusts. Remarkably, he named all of Clara and Chester's children in order of age and all of their children, including Elisabeth. He remembered that there were 120 surviving relatives.

He explained numerous trusts that were set up by Chester Congdon and Clara Congdon to care for their family after their deaths. The income from Clara's trust was to be distributed to her grandchildren when they turned thirty-five. In 1967, when Marjorie was thirty-five years old, the Clara B. Congdon Trust paid her stocks and bonds worth $300,000. These stocks could be sold through a broker for cash at any time.

In 1968, Elisabeth, under the direction of her trustees, set up more trusts for her daughters. This was when Marjorie was married to Dick, and Elisabeth requested that he handle her trust money. This was not only to protect Marjorie from running out of money, but also to protect their children's interests.

One of the trusts, called the MCL (Marjorie Congdon LeRoy) Trust was for $490,000. The MCL Family Trust was for $990,000. Marjorie was to get the income from these trusts, which would be disbursed by Tom Congdon, William Van Evera, and Salisbury Adams. But Marjorie resented that these men had control over her money and changed the trusteeship to Marquette National Bank in Minneapolis. Since their divorce, Dick LeRoy was no longer in charge of the money. By 1974, Marjorie had received the income and the principal of the MCL Trust—the $490,000 was gone.

There was still another trust at Marjorie's disposal. In the 1930s, after Marjorie had been adopted, Elisabeth had set up a trust called the M 1972 Trust. From the age of twenty-one onward, Marjorie had received income from that trust. Then, when she turned forty in 1972 she had the option to take the principal. She did. She cashed in her stocks for $1,050,000. During that year, Marjorie received over $2.8 million of *principal* from the trusts. That did not include her yearly *income* from the other trusts.

Thus, by 1974, Marjorie had received about $3 million out of the $4 million that had been placed in trust for her and her family. What remained was $900,000 principal left in the MCL Family Trust being run by the Marquette National Bank to provide her income.

Tom Congdon explained to DeSanto that he was six years older than Marjorie and they therefore had nothing in common. They saw each other at weddings, family reunions, and funerals. She had never been happy about his being trustee of her mother's estate and was irate and threatening whenever he turned down her requests for money.

Bill Van Evera had informed him of the murders. His next call was from Marjorie. She pointedly told him everything she was doing the day of the murders, from washing clothes at the laundromat to running around town with her realtor looking for a place to live. She said that she had planned to call her mother just the night before, but remembered that it was an hour later in Duluth, and anyway, "Mother was still at Brule. Now, I'll never be able to call her again."

Tom Congdon was concerned that Marjorie had had something to do with her mother's death. He hired a private investigator, William Furman, to watch over his house until the murders were solved.

Meshbesher called William Furman to the stand to testify for the defense. Furman had brought his own attorney from Denver who was very concerned about Furman's upcoming testimony, stating that it might result in some discovery of alleged wrongdoing, not in Minnesota, he said, but in Colorado. His attorney warned that Furman would be taking the Fifth Amendment (I refuse to answer on the grounds that it may incriminate me.) whenever appropriate. He said that Furman's testimony was irrelevant. Meshbesher was irate, calling Furman a hostile witness. They argued it out in the judge's chambers.

DeSanto objected to Furman being called. "The defense can only be calling Furman for two reasons: To confuse the issues in this trial, whether Marjorie Caldwell is guilty of conspiracy, in aiding and abetting in the murder, or number two, to mislead the jury to make Mr. Furman look like the scapegoat in this trial."

Finally, they entered the courtroom and Meshbesher began his direct examination of William Furman. He gave his address in Denver and stated that he had been a private investigator for eight years. Before that he had worked with a retired Denver policeman named Captain Walter Lawless.

"You were working for a man named Captain what-is-his-name?"

"Wally-Wallace. Wally is the nickname, Lawless, L-a-w-l-e-s-s."

"Lawless?"

"Law, like 'law,' statute of the law, less, l-e-s-s. Lawless."

"Lawless. He was the man you were working for?"

"Yes, sir. He's dead now."

Answering Meshbesher's questions, Furman told about his training as a private investigator and explained that prior to that he had been a trucker. He told very little about being hired by Thomas Congdon as a bodyguard after the murders. As predicted by his attorney, he pleaded the Fifth Amendment to every pertinent question. It came out that Furman had charged Tom Congdon over $15,000, much of it in expenses for trips to Minnesota that were never made and surveillance that was never performed. He had defrauded Tom Congdon.

On cross-examination, Furman told DeSanto that Congdon hired him from June 27 to July 1, 1977. That was all he admitted to. By the end of Furman's testimony, he had pleaded the Fifth Amendment sixty times.

Next, DeSanto called Mannette Allen to the stand. She had never met Roger Caldwell. She told the jury about her relationship with Marjorie.

"Marjorie came from a wealthy family, and she had a considerable amount of money at her disposal. She spent it freely, but during those years she spent very little on herself." She recalled that prior to her divorce from Dick, Marjorie had never worn much jewelry outside of a string of pearls she said that her mother had given her. "No rings or bracelets. Marjorie was not a showy woman. The children had lots of lovely things. When each child reached driving age, they received a new car. They took skating lessons. She was very, very generous with her children."

She told him about how Marjorie had supported her when her daughter was in the hospital. When Mannette was asked how she would describe Marjorie's relationship with her mother, she said, "I would describe it as being very warm and very close. Her mother lived in Duluth, and Marjorie lived in Minneapolis, and she spent more time on the phone with her mother and going to see her than I did with mine, and mine lives right in town. They visited back and forth reasonably often and, as I said, mostly in the summer but in between, there were continual phone conversations. (Mannette did not explain how these phone conversations were possible since Elisabeth's stroke.) Probably a week didn't go by that Marjorie didn't talk about her mother, about this and that or another thing, and this is encompassing a period of maybe seven years.

"Marjorie was devastated after her divorce from Dick. She never wanted it. Eventually, we lost contact, as often happens when there is a divorce and you're not a 'couple' anymore. The next time I called her was after I heard about her mother's death on television. I believed that she really loved her mother. They were very close. Marjorie would say, 'Mother called me and told me such and such.' I remember she was very upset after her mother's stroke in 1965. She cried to me and told me how upset she was that Elisabeth wouldn't be able to be as active as she had always been.

"I was convinced at the time, but I also realize that Marjorie could lie and really believe the things that she lied about. She could embellish a real story as she told it and believe every word she was saying. She was charming, fascinating, bright, and illogical, all at the same time."

At the time of the murders, Mannette had known Marjorie for seventeen years.

In September or October of that year, as part of their investigation, the police had interviewed the Allens and wanted to know anything that Marjorie had told them about the murders.

Marjorie told Mannette that on that Monday, the day of the murders, she was looking at some property in Colorado. She said that Roger hadn't wanted to go so she dropped him off at the library and arranged to meet him later. She said that Roger later called the motel in Golden, where they were living, and told the girl at the desk to tell Marjorie that he was ready to be picked up.

Marjorie told Mannette that nobody seemed to know where Roger was that day, and she said, "Why would anybody remember him being in the library?" Mannette tried to get Marjorie to elaborate, but Marjorie said, "My attorney said I should not talk about this." Mannette said she was satisfied with that answer.

Mannette and Marjorie had also talked about the wicker basket that was found in the Bloomington hotel room. Marjorie told her, "It's ridiculous to say that it came into my hands in a strange way. You know how I am about my mother's house. If I see something I like, I take it." Mannette didn't think that Marjorie meant it the way it sounded, like "If I see something I like, I steal it." She said that when they were in Duluth for the funeral, she saw the wicker basket "lying around her mother's house" and she had always liked it, so she just picked it up and took it. She said, "It was my mother's. I figured I had as much right to it as anybody. I picked it up and took it." She told Mannette that she carried it around with her the whole afternoon.

Mannette had asked Marjorie about the jewelry that was found in the Caldwells' hotel room at the Holiday Inn. Marjorie said, "Someone must have planted it there because it certainly didn't come in there with us. Somebody wanted Roger and me to look bad."

"Did Marjorie tell you that she had nothing to do with her mother's death?" asked DeSanto.

"Yes she did. She made that very clear."

"Do you think Marjorie is intelligent or stupid?"

"Marjorie is very intelligent."

❧ Chapter Sixteen

Every day in the spring of 1979 Helen and Wally Hagen made the trip from their home in the Minneapolis suburb of Mound to Hastings, about an hour drive. Nancy was going through a divorce, and she and her son Michael lived with them. Each night she listened to her parents recount their day in court. She realized that since they had retired, this was the most exciting thing in their lives. Helen's friend was the most infamous woman in Minnesota. The Hagens exclaimed how Marjorie was so friendly to everyone as they entered the courtroom, greeting them as if they were guests in her home.

It was about this time that Helen began to get more and more forgetful. She was having difficulty expressing herself and oftentimes she would substitute words. Nancy and Wally would exchange looks as Helen tried to describe her day in court, and she would inadvertently say "kitchen" for courtroom or "teacher" for lawyer. She didn't seem to know that she was doing it, and this was frightening to Nancy who had always admired her mother for never mincing words, always being concise and easy to understand. A diagnosis confirmed their worst fears: Alzheimer's disease.

The trial was good therapy for Helen. It gave her a reason to get up in the morning. She was on twenty-some pills a day, uppers in the morning, downers at night. The trial stimulated her brain and kept her going. The trial was like a full-time job, complete with an hour-long commute each way.

Having her parents so involved with Marjorie took some pressure off Nancy and gave her some breathing room. She was working extra jobs to help pay for Helen's medical bills, while cooking and cleaning and taking care of her mom and dad.

But when the trial was over, Nancy knew the family would have to think about how they were going to take care of her mother. Nancy knew that Helen's condition would surely deteriorate, and there would be no way Wally could watch her twenty-four hours a day. And she had to work and care for her son. At least, thought Nancy, this trial is not going to be a quick one.

On June 8, 1979, Marjorie's oldest daughter, Suzanne LeRoy, testified for the prosecution. She was twenty-four years old. She was on the chunky side and had long, straight, dark brown hair and brown eyes. She was single and lived alone. A junior in the nursing program at the University of Minnesota, she was looking forward to becoming a registered nurse. On weekends, she exercised horses at the Helvetia Stables near Stillwater, Minnesota. DeSanto asked her how her schooling was paid for.

"Well, I get a fee statement from the university, and then I mail it to the Marquette National Bank, and they pay it. It's through the Marjorie LeRoy Family Trust."

She received between $500 and $600 a quarter, plus the cost of books. In addition to that she was allotted $300 a month from other trusts.

The trial was the first time Suzanne had seen her mother since Stephen's wedding in February 1978. She hadn't seen her grandmother Elisabeth since January 1976.

"Now, did you ever live at a residence on the St. Croix River in Stillwater?"

"Yes, in 1974. I was about twenty."

"Did you live with anyone?"

"I lived in a small house by myself. My brothers and sisters, Becky, Heather, and Rick, lived under the garage. There were three little bedrooms under there. My mother had a separate house there."

It seemed as though DeSanto was leading up to the fire at the house in Marine-on-St. Croix, but then he dropped the ball. He did not mention the fire. Everyone knew that Marjorie had been accused of setting it. There was proof. Wouldn't that have been an asset to him in defining her character? Instead, he wanted to know if Suzanne was familiar with her mother's jewelry. He showed her exhibits, a dragon pin that Marjorie had worn on the collar of her dresses, some heart-shaped earrings, some earrings shaped like flowers with a stone in the middle, some gold earrings encrusted with a sapphire that Marjorie frequently wore. He also showed her a pair of earrings shaped like a fox head. Marjorie had bought two pairs, one for herself and one for Suzanne. There were crystal earrings from a place in New York—Knoudes—that specialized in hand-painted crystals. Marjorie often shopped there.

DeSanto wanted to know if Suzanne had ever heard her mother and her grandmother discussing money.

"I can remember one time—in 1974, I think—when my grandmother was driven down by her chauffeur with Mrs. Pietila and we all met at the Helvetia Stables. My mother wanted to talk to her about getting money for the house in Marine-on-St. Croix. This was before we had moved there. My mother said in front of my grandmother, 'Well, we have Grandmother down here so we can get some help with the farm. We're going to show her what we're building."

"My grandmother could speak, but with difficulty. She said, 'We'll see, we'll see.' "

"Were there any other times that you witnessed your mother asking your grandmother for money?"

"The one I can remember best was when my parents got divorced—in about 1971—and my mother called my grandmother and she upset her very much. We still lived in the house on Fremont. My mother told my grandmother that she needed some money. She kept asking for it and asking for it. My mother was very demanding. Then she told me to get on the phone and ask my grandmother for money. I got on the phone and my grandmother was so upset, and she just kept saying, 'I can't, I can't.' I told my mother that I wouldn't ask her for any money."

"Could you relate any more instances of that nature?"

"Once, in 1972, my mother and I were coming out of a bank and we were talking about horses. At that time, we had fifteen or sixteen horses. I told her that we didn't need that many, and she said, 'Well, I just took out a hundred thousand dollar loan, and Grandmother won't be living much longer, so I can pay it back right away.'"

Meshbesher cross-examined Suzanne. He did his best to make her look like a thoughtless granddaughter because she rarely made the trip to Duluth. She tried to explain to him that her grandmother wasn't well. She told him that her brother Peter and his wife and two children went more often and that these were Elisabeth's first great-grandchildren. It was too taxing for her to have too much company, Suzanne explained. Meshbesher reminded her that the reason she saw her grandmother in 1976 was because she was in Duluth for a horse show anyway. That was his opening. He reminded her of her mother's generosity, buying her all those horses, spending thousands of dollars so that Suzanne could attend the horse shows, and buying her hundreds of riding outfits. Then he went back to the jewelry, and reminded her of all the gifts

that her mother had given her. Marjorie had purchased duplicates of many of the items that DeSanto
had shown so that she could give them to Suzanne.

Suzanne had not seen her father since his birthday,
one year ago, and she had not seen her brother Rick
since Stephen's wedding. She had been sixteen at the
time of her parents' divorce, and Meshbesher got her
to say that Marjorie had been very depressed for a
long time after the divorce. But, she didn't forget her
children. Besides the money that Suzanne received
from her trusts, she also got a $200 a month clothing
allowance, and when she got a car she was given an extra $100 a month to make the car payment. The other
children were also on generous allowances. Meshbesher elaborated on how Marjorie had the separate house
built for Suzanne, and how much money it must have
cost. The implication seemed to be that Suzanne was
an ungrateful daughter.

On DeSanto's redirect, he wanted to know if
Suzanne needed that many riding outfits.

"I told her that we only needed one or two or three
at the most, and she just kept saying, 'Oh, we can afford to get more,' and she kept buying more."

Suzanne had left home in April 1975. She said she
couldn't live with her mother anymore because Marjorie read her mail and listened in on her phone conversations. Soon after that, Marjorie moved to Colorado with Becky, Heather, and Rick. Suzanne had
been at the stables when her sister Heather called her
to tell her that their grandmother had been murdered.
The first time Suzanne met Roger Caldwell was at her
grandmother's funeral in Duluth. She remembered
that he had a cut on his upper lip.

Throughout the trial, whenever DeSanto seemed to
touch on an important issue, one that could help his
case, he'd dodge it as if he were sorry he'd brought it

up. And so it was when he called Marjorie's youngest son, Richard (Rick) Webster LeRoy, Jr., to the stand. He had graduated from Benilde, St. Margaret's, a private school in Minneapolis. He was eighteen years old and the only child still living with Marjorie. He explained that the first time he'd met Roger Caldwell was in the spring of '75 or '76, after they had moved to Colorado. Rick planned to go to college and law school, and he expressed an interest in veterinary medicine.

This disclosure may have raised some questions for DeSanto, but if so, he kept them to himself. According to Marjorie, Rick had been afflicted with severe asthma his whole life. The props were stationed in every house they lived in, the oxygen tank, the syringes, and the medication. She said they had moved to Colorado because the air was supposed to be better for Rick. However, under those circumstances, it would seem that veterinary medicine, outdoor sports, and horses might be something that Rick would strive to avoid. Asthma is usually caused from allergic reactions to things such as dust, pollen, or animals. Attacks of asthma often follow periods of heavy exertion such as horse riding, running, or weight lifting. The chest constricts, making breathing difficult, and sometimes asthma sufferers feel as though they are suffocating. They are afraid they will die. It's very frightening. Why would an asthmatic seek out activities that would bring on these attacks? Did Rick LeRoy really have asthma? DeSanto asked all the right questions, but failed to pursue this line of questioning. Why?

A smiling Meshbesher stood up and walked toward the podium. He knew that Rick was Marjorie's most loyal supporter.

"Rick, you are an asthmatic, are you not?"

"Yes."

"How long have you had asthma?"

"Ever since I was born."

"You had medication all your life for it?"

"Yes."

"Before you went to Colorado, how often were you hospitalized as a result of asthma attacks?"

"Probably two, three, four times a year."

"Did going to Colorado minimize your asthma attacks or cause you to become healthier?"

"Well, it was the treatment at the asthma center, not the locale, that helped."

"Have you grown substantially since you've been in Colorado?"

"Well, when I went out there approximately four years ago, I was about five feet tall with about a forty-inch waist; and when I came back to Minnesota, I was about five-nine with a thirty-four inch waist."

"How tall are you now?"

"About five-eleven, thirty-four inch waist, two hundred and ten pounds."

"Did you have to have oxygen on call when you were living in Minnesota?"

"Yes. I had two large tanks right in my room."

"Now you are getting along without oxygen?"

"Yes."

"What types of medication do you take?"

"Well, I take Slo-Phyllin, and I have an inhaler that I carry with me at all times."

"Do you ever give yourself adrenaline shots when the attacks start getting bad?"

"Yes."

"Do you have needles, syringes?"

"Yes."

"Has it only been in the last few years, since you have been in Colorado, that you have been able to engage in more strenuous activity?"

"Yes. Before I went to Colorado, I did a little bit of everything, but very little. Before I would start getting very asthmatic and had to stop, and now I can do pretty much what I want."

"Your track activities are limited to shot-put and discus, is that right?"

"Right. I can't do the running. My lungs are approximately like one-third the size of somebody that doesn't have asthma."

Finally, DeSanto spoke up. "Your Honor, I object to that, and ask that it be stricken. There's no foundation, there's no medical opinion here."

"Sustained."

Meshbesher continued his line of questioning with Rick, trying to establish that Roger was a mean drunk and that Marjorie was afraid of him when he drank. Other witnesses assured him that Marjorie loved her mother and was extremely concerned when Elisabeth Congdon had had her stroke. The judge disregarded most of DeSanto's objections, as Meshbesher's witnesses established Marjorie as a loving, devoted daughter.

Meshbesher called Stephen LeRoy to the stand. He was twenty-seven, had jet black hair, long arms and legs, and still looked like the skater he had been as a teen. An observer in the gallery described him as "drop-dead gorgeous." He had been married for a year and a half.

Stephen recalled for Meshbesher when he was notified of his grandmother's death. "I was at my office when my sister-in-law, Peter's wife, phoned me. It was about 10:00 Monday morning." Later, he heard about the murders on the newscast. The announcer said, "they were looking for a blond young man." Stephen told Meshbesher that he had cooperated fully with the Duluth Police Department at the time of the murders.

"I had just seen her the previous day. I'd spent the weekend with her at the Brule."

"When was the last time you'd seen her before that?"

"I believe it was November of the previous year." He told Meshbesher that he and his grandmother were very close, that their relationship was "excellent," but he didn't get to see her very often because his job kept him from making the drive up north on the weekends.

Meshbesher questioned him about Rick's asthma and Stephen assured him that he had seen Rick seriously ill many times. Stephen gave him shots of cortisone or adrenaline when it was necessary. Syringes were kept on hand, and Rick had an oxygen mask in case of emergency. Marjorie, he explained, was very concerned about Rick's health. Stephen described his mother as being "overprotective" of Rick. Stephen had left home in 1969, when he was seventeen, to go to college. During the summers, when he moved back home, he saw his mother making needlepoint gifts for his grandmother.

Meshbesher seemed to have a real interest in needlepoint.

"Was there a particular gift that she made that was more time-consuming and more complicated than others?"

Stephen told him about the needlepoint rug.

Stephen said that his mother had never said an unkind word about his grandmother. He told Meshbesher that Elisabeth loved it when their whole family visited her.

"It was disconcerting for her to have somebody missing."

Stephen did not remember his mother ever asking his grandmother for money.

DeSanto cross-examined.

"Mr. LeRoy, are you aware of the fact that there is a Marjorie Congdon LeRoy (MCL) Family Trust that is administered by the Marquette National Bank in Minneapolis?"

"Yes, sir."

"Is it correct that when you reach thirty, on May 18, 1982, that the principal in that trust goes into seven separate trusts for each of you seven children?" That meant that when Stephen reached the age of thirty, Marjorie would no longer be a beneficiary. The money would be disbursed among her seven children.

"Yes, sir."

Next Stephen told DeSanto that the weekend he was at Brule visiting his grandmother, he spent his time canoeing, eating, walking through the woods, and sleeping.

"Mr. LeRoy, you have been asked on prior occasions by authorities about your familiarity with some jewelry items of your grandmother's, is that correct?"

"Yes, sir."

"You have indicated a familiarity with a diamond and sapphire ring that she owned, right?"

Stephen said that he knew of the ring. He hedged about seeing it when he visited his grandmother at the Brule on the last weekend of her life. He said he could not remember. But, DeSanto reminded him of his answer to the same question at Roger's trial and produced the transcript. Stephen had to admit that, yes, he had seen the diamond and sapphire ring that weekend when he visited Swiftwater Farm.

After Stephen heard about the murders, he drove to Peter's house and called the Congdon offices in Duluth to try to find out how to reach his mother. He did not know where she was living. He had not spoken with her for two years. He got the number of the Holland House Motel from the attorneys at the Congdon office, but he still couldn't reach Marjorie. He left messages but Marjorie did not contact him that day. The first time that Stephen met Roger Caldwell was the day before Elisabeth's funeral at the Radisson Hotel in Duluth. He knew nothing about Roger until two or three months after his mother had married him. Yet, in spite of all this, he insisted that he was very close with her.

❦ *Chapter Seventeen*

It was in the last days of the Marjorie Caldwell trial that Ron Meshbesher suddenly found himself wondering whether he had just made a terrible mistake.

On the witness stand was Colorado fingerprint expert Steven Sedlacek, who had testified earlier that Roger Caldwell's thumbprint was found on the envelope mailed from Duluth on the day that Elisabeth Congdon and Velma Pietila were murdered.

Meshbesher knew how extraordinarily important the fingerprint was to both the prosecution and the defense. If there was anything resembling a "smoking gun" in this most circumstantial of murder trials, the fingerprint—the direct piece of evidence linking Roger Caldwell, and thus his wife, to the murders—was it.

Steven Sedlacek was forty-four years old and an agent for the Colorado Bureau of Investigation. He had worked there for over nine years, conducting examinations, comparing latent fingerprints, performing special I.D. photography, and conducting initial crime scene investigations. On June 20, 1979, under direct examination by John DeSanto, he detailed his years of specialized training in regards to the science of finger-printing. During his career, he had conducted over 60,000 fingerprint examinations and comparisons.

Sedlacek's fingerprint testimony was largely respon-sible for Roger Caldwell's conviction one year earlier. He had testified at Caldwell's trial that the thumbprint on the envelope containing the gold coin that had been mailed from Duluth to Golden on the day of the murders matched Roger's thumbprint.

Now, here he was again, at Marjorie's trial, going over the same information. He told DeSanto, as he had during Roger's trial, how he had worked from 8:30 p.m. until 1:30 a.m. on the envelope, trying to develop any identifiable prints.

"The nin-hydrin developed fingerprint—latent print partial is what it is known as—I found to be identical with the inked impression on the fingerprint card bearing the name Roger Caldwell. His right thumb-print."

Sedlacek said that he had not used the best methods for lifting fingerprints off of the gold coin because he was afraid that he would damage the valuable coin. The method that he decided on did not show any prints.

Meshbesher's cross-examination began. He elabo-rated on a preservative for nin-hydrin solution, or fixa-tive, which prevents deterioration of the fingerprints over a period of time. (Prints can deteriorate from hu-midity, temperature, and handling.) Sedlacek pooh-poohed the solution, claiming that his department did not use it and he didn't believe that it helped to pre-serve the prints. He handed the envelope in a plastic bag to Sedlacek and asked him to remove it from the bag. Then Meshbesher gave him a small magnifying glass and asked him to look closely at the envelope. Sedlacek ceded to the fact that the prints had deteriorated to a point where they were no longer identifiable. The prints would not be suitable for comparison purposes.

Meshbesher harped on the fact that Sedlacek had not brought a photograph of the original print to this trial. He asked, with DeSanto's permission, if Sedlacek could get the negative from that photograph. Meshbesher assumed that the negative had been destroyed. This is where his plans went awry. Sedlacek said that the negative *was* in his office in Colorado. Sedlacek admitted that he had not told DeSanto that the fingerprint on the Radisson Hotel envelope had deteriorated. This new information could spell disaster for DeSanto.

The court ordered that the negative of the thumbprint photograph be turned over to Meshbesher for further examination. Although he couldn't shake Sedlacek's identification of the print, he did hope to show that Sedlacek had not taken adequate precautions to preserve it.

"I thought this was very fishy," he recalled. "How come this critical print was no longer available for us to see?"

After grilling Sedlacek, Meshbesher planned to call his own fingerprint expert, Herbert MacDonell (who years later would testify in O.J. Simpson's defense) to describe the steps that should have been taken to preserve the print. He was afraid that MacDonell, who was from New York, might put off the jury, so he found a local expert, Walter Rhodes, who could corroborate his testimony if need be. Rhodes was sixty-three years old and had been a fingerprint identification officer with the Minnesota Bureau of Criminal Apprehension for ten years. Before that, he had been with the Minneapolis Police Department for twenty years and spent ten of those years as a fingerprint expert. He was impressive and he was exact.

But, Meshbesher now found himself in a very tough spot. If he got the negative and introduced it into evidence, the prosecution would undoubtedly ask MacDonell to confirm Sedlacek's identification of the fingerprint as Roger Caldwell's.

"I figured now I'm in trouble because if we want to use this guy (MacDonell), he'll look at the negative and corroborate their fingerprint, and you know, he shoots me out of the water."

On the other hand, Meshbesher knew that it would not look good to the jury if he didn't finish what he had started. He decided to get the negative.

"I figured I have to carry this through or my credibility is shot," Meshbesher said. "So I sent MacDonell the negative and my associate said, 'I think you made a big mistake,' and I said, 'Well, it's too late now, it's done.'"

On July 6, 1979, Meshbesher called Herbert MacDonell to the stand.

He told Meshbesher that he was director of the Laboratory of Forensic Sciences and a professor of criminalistics at two colleges. He had a Master of Science degree in chemistry along with numerous other credentials.

"What is forensic science, by the way?" asked Meshbesher.

MacDonell explained, "Forensic science is the application of any scientific discipline, such as pathology, psychiatry, or dentistry, to the court system. For example, a pathologist might determine the cause of death is asphyxia, and a forensic pathologist would go further and say not only is it asphyxia caused by what we call hypoxia or anoxia because of suffocation or strangulation or drowning. There are many ways a person can asphyxiate."

"You mentioned that you were a teacher of criminalistics. What is criminalistics?"

"Criminalistics is the application of science to the examination of evidence or general investigation of crime. Most specifically, it deals with physical evidence, whether it be fingerprinting, firearms, blood stains, hairs, fibers, anything that can be measured or examined or photographed."

"At my request, did you examine a fingerprint, a negative of a fingerprint that was taken off an envelope in this case?"

"Yes, I did."

At this point, Meshbesher held up the negative marked Exhibit 92 and asked MacDonell if he recognized it as the negative.

"Yes I do. This is the negative that you had sent to me and I prepared enlargements and contact prints from."

"Did I, at the same time, send you some fingerprint cards of Roger Caldwell so that you could compare the print in that negative with the prints on those cards?"

"Yes, you sent cards which had his name on them."

DeSanto sat at his desk, rubbing his chin with his forefinger as if remembering the law enforcement officer who had called Meshbesher the top graduate of the "Dial a Witness School." How did Meshbesher find this guy? Sedlacek had been so sure.

"Now, after you received the negative of those fingerprint cards, professor, what did you do?"

"I made photographic enlargements from the negative that I received, and I made my own negative of the fingerprint card, which is dated July 22, 1977, specifically of the right thumb area which had been identified to me by you, which was the print concerned with in this case."

"I had told you that Steve Sedlacek from the Colorado Bureau of Investigation had identified the fingerprint on an envelope, which is received in evidence here as State's Exhibit 227, is that correct?"

"Yes, you stated it was from an envelope."

"And I told you that there was testimony that the fingerprint that appeared under the letter *A* on the back side of the envelope was supposedly from the right thumb of Roger Caldwell?"

"That is correct."

"After you evaluated the fingerprint, what did you conclude?"

"I concluded that the fingerprint in the evidence photograph, the latent print developed with nin-hydrin, is not a print that could have been made by the thumb of Roger Caldwell. *It's an entirely different finger.* We have an area of the thumbprint, which does not show up on the latent, and an area of the latent print, which does not show up in the thumb. Gross discrepancies."

A small grin passed over Meshbesher's face.

MacDonell continued to Meshbesher's satisfaction.

"So all of those things together support each other that it could not be the thumbprint of Roger Caldwell."

"Yes."

DeSanto cross-examined Herbert MacDonell and spent much time trying to discredit the man. MacDonell was calm, clear, and consistent; his knowledge and experience were more than DeSanto could successfully dispute. The fingerprint evidence was in. Sedlacek was not only discredited, but was impeached as a reliable witness. This would be a key turning point in not only Marjorie Caldwell's trial, but also in Roger Caldwell's murder conviction.

MacDonell had shattered the only solid evidence the prosecution had had against him. Had this been Meshbesher's plan all along—to undo Roger's conviction? Could he be retried? If he was found innocent of murder, because the so-called expert had made such a gross error, obviously, Marjorie couldn't be convicted of conspiring with him. Would Meshbesher's strategy work?

Small victories had been adding up as the trial moved along. When the fingerprint revelation came just a week before the trial ended, Meshbesher felt his case was by then so strong that there was no need to put Marjorie on the stand.

"Marjorie wanted to go on the stand in the worst way," Meshbesher said. "We had to convince her that she shouldn't testify, and that was no easy task."

❧ *Chapter Eighteen*

On July 18, 1979, DeSanto began his closing arguments by thanking the members of the jury for the sacrifice of their time over the past several months, and reminding them of their responsibilities in the case: To regard the evidence that had been presented and not the closing arguments. DeSanto knew what he was up against with Ronald Meshbesher. DeSanto warned the jury that his summation would be lengthy, not realizing at the time that Meshbesher's would turn out to be twice as long.

"I'm sure that when we sit down after our final summation, Mr. Meshbesher and myself will forget things that we wish we had talked about. There is a saying among trial lawyers that each trial lawyer really has three final arguments—the one he prepares, the one he gives to the jury, and the one he wishes he had given when he sits down."

As if reminding the jury of the mistakes he was about to make, he continued, "We are here to persuade you, and because of that, we argue to the exclusion of perhaps some important points. But just because I don't touch upon something that Mr. Meshbesher touches upon, does not mean it is not important. Please ask yourselves, How would the prosecution look at this? Please discipline yourselves to look at the other side of the coin, because that is what our criminal justice system is all about, looking at both sides of the coin."

In this instance, "coin" may have been an unfortunate metaphor. DeSanto continued on with rambling sentences, so wordy that the jury may have forgotten what he'd intended to say by the time he was finished. He lectured them to pay close attention to all the exhibits, to read them and use them as proof of his case. He picked them up and waved them in front of the jury, the baggage tags, the envelope with Roger Caldwell's handwriting, the jewelry, and pictures of Elisabeth Congdon as she lay dead in her bed. He used a lot of legal talk, which may have confused the laypersons on the jury, and then said, "I hope I didn't confuse you. I'm sure the judge will make it a little more clear."

DeSanto, through his witnesses, had not been able to establish the exact time of the deaths of Elisabeth Congdon and Velma Pietila. "The exact time of the murders, or exactly how they happened, is not an essential element," he said.

"As to why Roger Caldwell mailed the coin to himself, we may never know. Was he attempting to get caught? Was it a signal? Was it just plain stupid? I suggest to you if you reach the conclusion it was just plain stupid, you cannot acquit this defendant because Roger Caldwell is stupid. I submit to you criminals make mistakes, and that is why they are caught."

DeSanto recited the meaning of "reasonable doubt" and expounded on what a tough task the jury had before them. He told them that reasonable doubt was a mental term, not an emotional one, and said they would have queasiness in their stomachs when they went back to deliberate this case. He cautioned them to be morally certain of their decision.

"Mr. Meshbesher wouldn't even get up here if there wasn't room for argument, and believe me, he'll argue to you, eloquently and articulately. But the fact that there are two views or two arguments or several arguments to the same evidence does not necessarily mean there is a reasonable doubt. If there weren't two opposing views, we wouldn't be here.

"I submit to you that Mr. Meshbesher is going to argue, 'Roger Caldwell did it, all right, but poor Marjorie, she didn't know what her alcoholic husband, who gets violent when he drinks, was going to do, she didn't know where he was.' I submit to you on the evidence here, it is not even reasonable that the defendant did not know where her husband was that weekend. Oh, sure, during jury selection Mr. Meshbesher made a point of asking you, 'Ma'am, or Sir, do you know everything your spouse does?' and you said, 'I'd like to, but I don't.' Based on that, he's going to say, 'Well, she didn't have to know what Roger Caldwell did.'"

Next, he jumped to Thomas Congdon's private investigator.

"I submit to you that there were certain times that William Furman was not frank, open, and honest in his testimony. Believe me, I am not vouching for William Furman. He may approach the scum of the earth, but what facts in evidence are you going to acquit Marjorie Caldwell on, saying that it was the Furman gang either fabricating evidence or committing these murders?"

DeSanto named the major inconsistencies in the trial: the different physical descriptions of Roger Caldwell from the clerks at the airport shop where he bought the suede garment bag; different opinions about the entry point at the Glensheen Mansion; and discrepancies in the police reports about their arrival time after the murders, and who found what on the staircase and when.

"These are human variances, which of course, you must use in judging credibility, but they do not, I submit, acquit Roger—I mean, Marjorie Caldwell. If the defendant has agreed with and actually procured Roger Caldwell to commit these murders, she does not have to know exactly how he was going to commit them in the sense of smothering Elisabeth Congdon and beating Velma Pietila to death. But she has to know beforehand that the objective will be carried out and she intentionally participates in that agreement.

"Further, the court will tell you that to be a member of a conspiracy, a person need not know all of the details of the conspiracy, nor the means by which the object was to be accomplished. Each member of the conspiracy may perform separate and distinct acts. As long as it is proven beyond a reasonable doubt that the defendant was aware of the common purpose and was a willing participant with the intent to advance that purpose, she is guilty of conspiracy.

"I submit to you, Ladies and Gentlemen, in regard to the accomplice charge and the aiding and abetting charge, that the State's evidence has overwhelmingly proven that Marjorie Caldwell was the woman behind the man who committed these murders. The evidence has shown that she persuaded Roger Caldwell to murder in return for an irrevocable assurance of . . . \$2.3 million.

"I believe that Mr. Meshbesher will tell you or argue to you, Ladies and Gentlemen, there have been two tragedies here: the deaths of Elisabeth Congdon and Velma Pietila, certainly terrible, terrible tragedies; and, he'll argue, the frame of Roger Caldwell and Marjorie Caldwell. Ask yourself, what evidence backs up that statement? I anticipate he may argue that it has not been easy for the defendant to sit here these fifteen weeks and control herself. Yet, I submit to you, based on the evidence, Ladies and Gentlemen, that how she spends, how she's able to obtain loans without one penny of down payment, and to engage in real estate transactions without just promissory notes, is unusual, to say the least. I submit to you that the defendant is a very, very good con artist. I ask you, Ladies and Gentlemen, not to be conned."

DeSanto didn't know when to stop. He reiterated every single witness's testimony, word by word, and then informed the jury, as if he were a seer, what Meshbesher would say about these witnesses. His closing arguments were like those of a prosecutor who did not have a case to begin with. Here was a mountain of evidence, admittedly circumstantial, but strong nevertheless. But his confidence from winning Roger's murder conviction seemed to disappear along with Steven Sedlacek's fingerprint expertise.

"Whatever fictitious villain the defense wants to rely on, I submit to you, is going to be based on innuendo and conjecture only. The evidence, I submit to you, Ladies and Gentlemen, convicts Roger Caldwell and Marjorie Caldwell.

"Marjorie Congdon LeRoy Caldwell is not a mere victim of circumstance. The circumstantial evidence convicts her. She has had her day in court, and she's been most ably represented by perhaps one of the best criminal defense lawyers in the state, if not the country.

"It is only common sense, Ladies and Gentlemen, that tells you that there is rarely going to be eyewitnesses to a premeditated murder. Certainly, because a man commits murder in the darkness of the night, where there are no eyewitnesses, does not mean he is home free. With your true and just verdicts in this case, Ladies and Gentlemen, you will tell Marjorie Caldwell it's not that easy.

"Thank you for your time and attention."

In his closing arguments, which make up 178 pages of transcript, DeSanto said, "I submit to you,"197 times. He said, "I anticipate Mr. Meshbesher will . . ." almost as often. DeSanto had given Ronald Meshbesher plenty of ammunition for a good rebuttal the next morning.

❧ *Chapter Nineteen*

Ronald Meshbesher's opening lines were like the preview for an exciting, up-and-coming movie. There was a rush in his voice, an excitement, as if DeSanto had paved the way for a performance that any actor would die for, and here it was handed to him on a silver platter. He smiled at the jury, like the proverbial cat, and glanced over at DeSanto as if to say, "Gottcha." "If it please the court, counsel, members of the jury, I'm going to deviate from the opening that I had originally planned because I think the argument of Mr. DeSanto yesterday calls for it.

"Let's analyze Mr. DeSanto's argument. I thought I was on trial. He spent three-quarters of his argument talking about defense tactics. I will tell you now if you think I did anything wrong, I want you to get me for it real hard. Of course, I don't want you to hold it against Mrs. Caldwell. She's stuck with me. I told you at the beginning sometimes I may cross-examine a witness and get a little bit tough, but you'll find out that paid off in this trial. I got tough with that fingerprint expert, and because I persevered I got that negative from Colorado, and but for that negative, Mr. DeSanto would be here today, or yesterday, telling you that this was Roger Caldwell's fingerprint, as he did in his opening statement, and you bet his face is red. Am I accusing him of being a co-conspirator? He was duped, and he was duped by an incompetent, opinionated fingerprint examiner, but he goes on and accuses everybody in the police force of being involved in this frame-up, and that is not the case. But let's talk about tactics a bit. Mr. DeSanto painted a real picture of himself and me, trying to give you the impression he was the underdog.

"Well, it's an unusual day when the State is an underdog in a criminal prosecution, I'll tell you that, and don't be sucked in by that because he certainly is not the underdog. He's an accomplished, well-trained, well-educated lawyer, and he knew exactly what he was doing in trying this lawsuit.

"But all I can tell you about tactics is that we did not throw away a broken window; we didn't have a witness whose arm got bigger four months before trial so it couldn't be measured." Then he wondered aloud why in the world the State had not taken a picture of the broken window from the inside. Their exhibit had only shown the window from the outside. "If you want to show that the finger could touch the latch, you want to take it from the other side, too," he explained as if to a group of children. Then he reminded the jury that one officer whose arm measured 33 inches could not reach the latch through the window. He gave the lengths and widths of his arms and Caldwell's arms—31⅝ inches—and proved that if the officer could not reach the latch, Caldwell certainly couldn't. The officer claimed to have been laid up with some accident since the murders, causing him to use his arms more and his arm got bigger. "That's kind of strange," said Meshbesher. Then he said that they saved everything in this case. "We could have a rummage sale with some of the stuff they saved here. They gathered little pieces of hair, stuff that was insignificant, yet the windowpane was destroyed. It's forever gone.

"We didn't offer a mistaken fingerprint into evidence.

"We did not say that blood qualified as Roger Caldwell's, but it was the same as thirty million other people. I don't know how many million qualified for the hair. Their expert told you that the blond hair at the scene wasn't dyed. Well, we know from Mr. Pietila that his wife's hair was dyed. Now, who had blond hair around there that wasn't dyed?

"And what about this gray hair? Well, Roger's hair is gray. They even listed it to the police as gray. The State's expert said that he found some black hair. There was black hair found in Mrs. Pietila's hand. Her husband came in and said she never had black hair. Now, whose black hair was that? Roger Caldwell did not have black hair. This same 'expert' even admitted that hair was a poor type of evidence.

"We didn't manufacture William Furman; we didn't authorize illegalities, as apparently Tom Congdon did; we didn't exaggerate the value of the inheritance; we didn't accept information from liars and scum of the earth, to use Mr. DeSanto's words, like the State did; we didn't give up on our investigation because we had more important things to do.

"Call those 'tactics?' Call those 'blunders?' Well, call those what you will, but the defense is not guilty of those, and I think I stuck to the facts. I am not talking about Mr. DeSanto as a human being, because I think he's a nice guy. Let's look at what happened in this courtroom.

"As I said earlier, if I have said or done anything throughout this trial that may have offended you, please don't hold it against Marj. She has nothing to do with the way I call the shots. She may try to help me, but I tell you, I am the one that calls the shots in this courtroom as far as the defense goes.

"Now, Mr. DeSanto told you in opening statement that he was going to prove certain things. Well, he did establish some of the facts in his opening statement, but he dwelled hard about the fingerprint he was going to show. Now, this was an unusual case because we proved beyond any reasonable doubt that these fingerprints were false, for whatever reason. He told you that he was going to show that Marjorie Caldwell was insolent, demanding, and rude to her mother, that she had a terrible relationship with her mother; and if you just stopped at opening statement, "My God, isn't that awful." Now, the best you hear from Dr. Bagley, who had seen Marjorie Caldwell with her mother twice in seven years, the best she could say is that she was demanding, at times. Now, that is how far the prosecution had to reach to get those words from one witness. And in his opening statement, he told you that Roger dominated Marjorie and that Marj ran the show, but I don't think you heard that from the evidence.

"Now, Mr. DeSanto talks about how ridiculous any claim of frame-up is. He says 'Don't buy it.' I'm not trying to sell anything. Let's talk for a minute about how the State believes that Roger Caldwell committed this terrible crime. Well, the first thing that Roger Caldwell does, and Marjorie Caldwell, apparently, is they write out an assignment that has been variously referred to as a will, and they go to a notary in a public courthouse, apparently, and get it signed a few days before they're going to commit this murder—a public disclosure to a notary!

"Well, then they figure out, 'What is the best way we can make sure everybody knows about our plan?' So they get up on Sunday morning and go down and have breakfast, and they make sure they tell the waitresses, 'We're in a hurry because we've got to go to the airport.' Marj wants to make sure that something looks fishy. And Roger, according to the State, is busy flying off to Minnesota, no evidence of when he flew or what plane he may have gotten on, but he's going to Minnesota without a murder weapon, apparently, walks into a house that he knows his wife is familiar with, that has a twenty-four-hour nurse present and numerous household help, gets into a house that he's been in for thirty minutes in his whole life and never asked to look around, and this is a man plotting the murder, by the way, and never wanted to take a tour of the house.

"Now, he didn't have a picture with him of what the house even looked like. So then he's going into this house, and he's going to break in a window and apparently not realizing there's some kind of a latch on the side that he has to reach, he breaks in the window and he goes up, with no weapon, and apparently, according to the State's theory, he's accosted either on top of the landing or by the landing by Mrs. Pietila, 'My God, where did she come from? I didn't know there was somebody around here.' He grabs a candlestick holder that just happens to be there, and starts beating her to death, in a terrible, horrendous fashion. Well, then he's not done, he goes up and he puts a pillow over Mrs. Congdon's face and drops some blood. Well, then apparently, and I don't know which came first, according to the State's theory, he ransacked the drawers and took some items. I think the State would have you believe he was so bloody from that beating on the stairwell that he had to clean up and change clothes. Now, that took a little bit of time. And where are these clothes? There is no other evidence of blood in the car but a fleck from a shoe. Then, he goes ahead and he decides he's going to take a wicker basket, even though this jewelry would fit easily in one's pockets. So he's taking a wicker basket with him, and now he thinks 'How the heck am I going to get out of here? There's a car there. That looks like a good spot. Maybe I can find the keys to that.'

"This is a planned, premeditated murder, and how he got to the house we don't know because every mode of transportation was checked. So he takes that vehicle, and, according to the State's theory, he's running away from two murders, 'by the way, I'll mail myself a coin to make sure that everybody knows that I am in Duluth when that letter with the postmark comes.' So I don't know if the theory is that he had this envelope prepared before; if he did, he had it in his pocket, and there is no evidence of crinkling or blood and he's been through heck that night; or if the State's theory is that he stopped at the Radisson Hotel on the way from the murders, had to go to the desk clerk to get these large envelopes, and then, for some reason, he writes his own name on there, puts a gold coin in it. Is he trying to tell himself he completed the job? He knows he's going back to Colorado, according to their theory, and he's going to beat the coin there.

"Mr. DeSanto told you, 'I can't explain that coin. I can't explain it. Maybe it's a signal.' A signal to who, or for what? 'Stupid,' he calls it. Well, indeed, it is stupid. There is no evidence here that either Roger or Marjorie were stupid. Someone said that Marjorie is very intelligent. So he decides to find the mailbox, and now he continues on his way to the airport.

"At the airport, instead of leaving the keys and the parking ticket in the Pietila car, if that is, indeed, the parking ticket, he decides to throw them in the wastebasket. Why did he do that? What does he care about the car? He just stole it, leaves it there, and hightails it into the airport. Where does he put the car? In the most conspicuous place in the airport, right by the handicapped parking, as close as you can get to the entrance on the lower level. You couldn't get any closer. Is he hiding it?

"So then he goes into the airport and decides he's got to buy some garment bag, the theory is, to put the wicker basket in, I take it, I don't think he was just doing shopping, and so he goes into the airport gift shop and he starts looking around and he's calm and collected, according to the clerks, nothing unusual about him, and he picks out one and one of them suggest, 'Maybe you want a different one,' so he gets this prettier one and he puts it on the counter, and he's trying to put this wicker basket in it and the clerk starts to assist him in putting the wicker basket in it with, apparently, the stolen jewelry inside. Now is he trying to call attention to himself? Is Roger committing suicide?

"Well, then apparently, he leaves in a hurry they say now, for the blue concourse, the theory being he went to catch a plane. Okay. Let's check the airline records. Roger, for a stupid guy, he covered up that track pretty good, didn't he?

"So then, Roger gets back and apparently his wife isn't too sure where he is because she's busy telling people different things about his whereabouts. This is a plan, you figure she'd have a nice, clean alibi as to where Roger is, but she told too many different things, sort of like a wife covering up for a drunk than someone trying to alibi for a murderer.

"So Roger gets back home and now, of course, he's got the garment bag with him, apparently the wicker basket, what-have-you, and the funeral is coming the next day. Now he gets home, we know it from the banker, corroborated by the other banker, that he was there at 9:30 in the morning, looked fine, no marks, no bruises, nothing, looked good that day. The next day he saw the marks and bruises. So Roger is going back to the funeral and he decides, 'Well, I'd better take the garment bag and the wicker basket, all that jewelry, back to Minnesota with me. What is the difference? You know, nobody is looking for that,' so he goes back to Minnesota, ends up in the Radisson Hotel room, and then decides in the Radisson Hotel that he's going to, for the first time, take this Host guest receipt out of the pouch of the garment bag and put it on the box in the bed. How come he decides there to take this Host receipt out of a pouch? It traveled the Horn, came around full circle now, and then he decides to leave some baggage claim checks in the wastebasket that other maids said was empty when they looked at it.

"He goes down to Minneapolis after the funeral, and he goes into the Holiday Inn. For some unexplained reason, he collapses on July 5th, 8:00 in the morning, is in the hospital, the room is empty for a long time, so when the police execute their search warrant, what is the first thing they see? It's a wicker basket, a garment bag, and they look in the nightstand and, not too well-hidden, they find this jewelry box with all this jewelry. You call that stupid, call it reasonable, whose theory does it fit in more with? And I don't have to sell you anything."

Meshbesher explained the law to the jury. He told them that an indictment was not evidence of anything, but merely a procedural device. He explained how indictments have to be filed by grand juries, but to bear in mind that grand juries do not have to hear all the evidence, but just what the prosecutor thinks is sufficient at the time. Then, he lectured them about the "presumption of innocence" being the "principle on which this country was founded." He reminded the jury how in the Perry Mason series, he never got a case to the jury because he always had someone in the back of the courtroom pop up right toward the end of the case and confess. "I have never seen that happen," smiled Meshbesher.

Then he explained what reasonable doubt meant, in lengthy detail, not taking any chances. He reminded them of the judge's special instructions: "In your deliberation, you should consider only the evidence, testimony, and witnesses adduced this trial. You are not to consider Roger Caldwell's trial, as that was a different trial, different evidence, testimony, and witnesses. You should base your verdict solely upon what you have heard and seen in this courtroom."

"If you think back, way back to April—it seems like years ago—I asked, I think, each one of you if you understood this concept about this robbery, and Mr. De-Santo used it, too, because it's a good one to explain what we are talking about, that if someone picks you up at your house, comes to your house and says, 'I need a ride to the bank,' and you say, 'Fine, I'll give you a ride to the bank, my car is here,' and you give this person, friend, or neighbor a ride to the bank, and he goes in the bank and robs it, and comes out and says, 'Now, give me a ride home, will you?' You give him a ride home and the next day, you found out this guy robbed the bank and you all agreed that you couldn't be guilty because you didn't know anything about it. Now, you aided and abetted, you bet you did, you drove the car—you had the getaway car. That doesn't make you guilty.

"Then, I change the example. What if this person said, 'Come on with me, I'm going to rob the bank.' Knowledge beforehand. 'I want you to act as a look-out.' Well, in a weak moment, you say, 'Yes,' and you go there, you act as a lookout, he comes out of the bank, 'Get out of here, I have the dough.' You are guilty as all get-out, you know that, because you had prior knowledge, you had intent, and you participated.

"Then, I change it a little bit. Let's say you take this person to the bank, he robs it, you don't know about it, he comes out, comes in the car and as soon as he gets in the car, he says, 'I robbed the bank,' and you look startled, and you realize that that wasn't good enough because it was after-acquired knowledge. You didn't plan with him, you didn't participate with him, you were an unwitting accomplice, and that is what that means and that is why it's important to understand. Sometimes analogies help us do it, and I hope that was helpful to you. Basically, if you agreed beforehand, you are a conspirator. If it comes afterwards, you are not."

Meshbesher continued, systematically and chrono-logically, to poke holes in every single witness's testimony in regards to Roger Caldwell's trial. It was as if he were killing two birds with one stone, defending not only Marjorie, but also making a good case against Roger Caldwell's guilt. One by one, he made DeSanto's witnesses look weak, accusing some of them of seeking publicity. He made the police officers that investigated the murders look like bumbling idiots. He disputed the prosecution's evidence, the airport ticket stub, and the Host International's receipt for the suede garment bag. It was Meshbesher's contention that Roger Caldwell had been set up, that all this evidence was planted.

Meshbesher continually referred to Sedlacek, the fingerprint expert who had wrongly identified Roger Caldwell's fingerprint. It was brilliant. Having proven the prosecution's key witness to be wrong, he planted doubts about every other witness the prosecution called. The jury had to wonder if Meshbesher was right and all of those witnesses were mistaken, lying, or both.

"Now, that is what gets me about some of these witnesses. They can be so dead sure about a fact, when we know from other evidence it is wrong, and they'll tell you so, too, and I don't think they are lying necessarily, but it's amazing what the mind can do for us. It plays tricks. You heard it time and time again. People say they are positive. Just like Sedlacek was positive.

"Now, let's talk about this fingerprint a little bit. Mr. DeSanto said I was going to talk about it until I was blue in the face. I think he did that to maybe hope I would forget about it. Well, I'm going to disappoint him because I am going to talk about the fingerprint, because the fingerprint really is the theme work for the credibility of all of the evidence in this case."

Meshbesher recapped the fingerprint fiasco.

"When I got the negative, we broke open the fingerprint, and I think we broke open this case because we called in Herb MacDonell. He comes, he looks at that print, and he comes into court, and here is a man, a noted criminologist, who testifies to you, and he's a bit arrogant, and I think maybe he's entitled to be, he knows his stuff, and he shows you graphically why that is not the same print.

"Well, I figure maybe you'd be a little suspect of this guy from New York, so I locate a local person, Walter Rhodes, who I know we all believe is a good honest witness. He's just too sincere and frank to be otherwise. He comes in and tells you that that is not the print, and I said, 'What do you see at that point?' 'I don't see nothing,' he said, 'nothing,' and then he says that the funny thing is that the guy had three points where there is only one.

"That is an awfully bad mistake. We gave them the courtesy of an interview, and it's perfectly proper, and they came in and they questioned MacDonell before he was brought into court, and Sedlacek was right there and he still disagreed after MacDonell went over that print point by point.

"It's either a mistake, or he's lying. Those are the only two explanations, and I prefer to think the former, but it is a frightening thing, Ladies and Gentlemen, when a fingerprint expert who you think has the qualifications and made a nice little impression in court, can come in and tell you that that is a fingerprint of the defendant or co-defendant, and it is not. Now, how many innocent people have been convicted on that type of testimony? We don't know because it very seldom comes out, because most lawyers, if they are like I am, they take those fingerprints for granted, but I'll never do it again."

Meshbesher then expounded on the envelope that contained the gold coin. He was on a roll.

"Now, Mr. DeSanto gives you a theory for the mailing of this gold coin, but I don't understand it. He said that maybe it was some type of signal. To whom? For what? If Roger did it and he was going back to the hotel, why would he have to signal himself? He gets there before the coin. The only reasonable explanation for the mailing of that coin is the frame. That is the only reasonable theory for it because the other explanations don't make sense, and I don't have to convince you my explanation makes sense. The evidence merely has to show a reasonable doubt, and if there are one of two theories, one points to innocence and one points to guilt, I remind you, you must adopt the theory that points to innocence, and even the State can't conjure up a reasonable theory for that coin other than stupidity.

"Good detectives look for clues, and then see where the clues take them. You don't look for a suspect and try to make the clues fit. That is too tailor-made. Marjorie thought she might be a suspect. They don't like her from last year. She's had running disputes with the trustees. So, for her to plot this terrible thing, knowing she'd be the first suspect, makes her stupid, too, but that is what the State would have you believe.

"Members of the Jury, the evidence itself suggests fabrication, suggests a frame-up. The baggage tags alone almost conclusively show a frame-up. The wicker basket and the closet photos corroborate it. You might ask yourself, What would be the motive for it? While the defense doesn't have to prove a motive, doesn't have to prove anything, I think you have to consider that this is an unusual case because of the unusual amount of wealth involved in the Congdon trusts, and that fact is stranger than fiction, and there are a lot of things that have happened in recent history that bear that out.

"Marjorie didn't trust these estate watchdogs. She was a gadfly, she was a troublemaker, she didn't take the word of these people, and she wanted to check the books. Now, the trustees got control of all of Elisabeth Congdon's assets in 1974. They created a living trust. Elisabeth Congdon was sickly. There is some indication that Marj was able to pull the wool over her eyes, but not the trustees and the fancy lawyers they had. What did Miss Congdon sign away? She gave away all of her assets to this living trust. This woman controlled a lot of money, and somebody wanted to control it for her, and they tied her into a document, and the only advisors were the trustees and the lawyer, who saw her once or twice. He prepared the documents and got the signatures, and that was his job. Now, who thought of these ideas, and why did they want to wrest complete control from Elisabeth Congdon? Well, I think that indicates something ought to be looked at a little more carefully than the prosecution is willing to admit. I think there was some evidence that even Elisabeth Congdon wanted an audit at one time, and Marjorie, of course, had been asking for it for years, but never got it."

If an Academy Award could be given for an attorney's closing arguments, Ronald Meshbesher would have walked off with the Oscar. Well-thought-out, orderly, plain-spoken, rehearsed to perfection, humorous, and professional, he had the jurors wrapped around his finger. They lapped up his every word. Like a seasoned actor, Meshbesher knew when he had a captive audience. He didn't let up. At this point, he apprised the jury of his "Colorado Connection" theory. He named Tom Congdon, Elisabeth's nephew; William Furman, the private investigator hired by Congdon; and others who supposedly spied on the Caldwells. Meshbesher wove a story, a page-turner, as the jury sat perched on the edge of their seats.

"We have heard too much about coverups in this country, to the highest places in the land. Would you have believed it if I had told you the Watergate story could ever happen? It did happen, in Twentieth Century America. The Congdon forty, fifty million bucks, was that enough for Furman? All the money in the world? Are you kidding? He'll do anything for a buck, and they had plenty of bucks at their disposal.

"What is Furman's reputation? He is dishonest; he is untruthful; he would fabricate evidence; he would plant evidence; he would do anything for a buck; he's used the badge improperly; he's used aliases, at times, even in registering at hotels, maybe used an alias on an airplane. Congdon didn't have enough money to get to Furman? Oh, no, I don't think the policemen were involved with Furman directly. They were duped and sucked in by Furman just as we would be unless we had uncovered him and started to dig at the facts here.

"Now, what do we do with Tom Congdon? He made a nice impression, smart guy, well-educated, controls a lot of money, trustee, active in the family business. Motives? Well, the trustees own much of the stock in the company he operates, controlled power money. That is what makes the world go around in high finance, and sometimes low finance, and you see money in the most gigantic amounts in this case, and power.

"He says he wanted Furman for a bodyguard. Now, there's no bodyguard in Duluth, and nobody is worried about that. If he's worried about the Caldwells, he knows they went to Duluth for the funeral. Marj told him on the twenty-seventh she's going for the funeral. What does he want a bodyguard in Colorado for? The Caldwells are in Duluth. That is just silly. Why didn't Congdon call a reputable detective agency like Wackenhut or Pinkerton? What kind of surveillance is going on of the Caldwells when they are in Duluth?

"Thomas Congdon supposedly was bilked for all the money, he's defrauded. That is the State's theory. Well, Congdon is no dummy. Now, what guy with that education gives out all that money without a statement? What guy with all that education says he hadn't even thought of suing Furman for the money back? My God, if someone stole fifteen thousand bucks from me, I'd be mad as a pistol, and I'd be out there any way I could to get it back. Very nonchalantly, hadn't even given it a thought. Strange? You bet it is strange.

"What were Congdon's motives, Ladies and Gentleman? I don't know. To control the estate? It's an awful lot of money. He *said* Marj didn't deserve the money. Now, *he's deciding* whether Marj deserves it or not.

"Here, picture Marjorie, she's really been painted very badly, I think, and you only get bits and pieces in a case as to what a person is. She was depressed after this divorce, and that was a divorce she didn't want. She had a family that she was involved with constantly, you heard it. She's raised some children. You have seen the children here. She was very lonely before the marriage to Roger. She told one of the witnesses here she wasn't really in love with Roger, that she wanted the companionship. Roger was good with Rick, and he could deal with the trustees for her money problems, which went back many years.

"They met at Parents-Without-Partners. She needed a man to relieve the loneliness she had suffered for those years. She was reluctant, too. She wanted him tested as to his drinking. One of the witnesses said, 'She wanted me to test him to see if he drank.' Well, Roger was probably on his good behavior. It didn't last long. On the wedding day, he took a drink and got abusively drunk. Nasty drunk.

He looked over at Marjorie, compassion in his eyes, and then faced the jury again, knowing they would sympathize with her plight.

"They deny, they deny, they deny, until the day when they have to admit it. Fortunately in that area, we are making progress. The stigma isn't there that much any more. People have come out of the closet; but for many years, and even today, people want to deny and cover it, and cover for the drinking spouse.

"Marj even said to someone, 'He doesn't drink, he always looks like this.' Well, she's covering for the man. She's embarrassed. She's ashamed, she's got a drunk on her hands.

"Now, Mr. DeSanto would have you believe that the

disheveled appearance is caused by the murder. Well, how come he looked so good at the funeral? Everybody said they didn't recognize him. He was all dressed up, cleaned up, looked good. Well, Roger is a drinker. One day he looks terrible; the next day, he looks pretty good.

"Now, Marj's financial history is important, because she always spent more than she had. She even had to balance the checkbook after the divorce. She couldn't handle it. Spending to Marjorie Caldwell is an emotional release, whether it's because of depression from divorce or family problems or a drunken husband. It's her way out of her depression, spend, spend, spend, and never really concerned about it. She's been doing it for twenty years or more.

"Now, I would like to believe that murder for money is done on the part of greedy people. Marjorie was generous to a fault. She liked money, but she liked to spend it. There was no greed in this lady. She lavished her children, maybe too much. At least some of them turned out pretty darn good. She spent $2,000 a month alone on Becky's skating, and $10,000 to $15,000 a year for Steve, and new cars, horses. Who were they for? The children. A lot of money was spent on Rick's asthma. There was the $200 a month clothing allowance for the kids, and $100 per month auto allowance. She bought them 250, 350 riding outfits. Preposterous. But was it on herself? The only thing on herself was real estate. Much of it was put in trust or was guardian for Rick, as you see here. Guilty people, greedy people, I should say, kill for money, not generous people."

He told the jury that Marjorie had bought a family burial plot for fifteen. "She spent twenty thousand bucks!" He exclaimed that she gave money to animal charities and even talked about donating the Brule property to the NAACP. She sent 75 to 100 poinsettias to hospitals for the elderly—every year!

Meshbesher rambled on about the trusts, reiterating how foolish it would have been to kill Miss Congdon for money when Marjorie had assigned the money from the Congdon Trust over to Roger. Chester Congdon provided in his will that one of his trusts would terminate immediately upon the death of his last surviving child. The trustees would have three years in which to distribute the money. Marjorie would have been left with little more than she had before the murders, he said. She would get $46,000 a year income. Chester ordered that the *principal* of that trust would terminate on June 27, 1998, twenty-one years after the death of his last child. Only then would Marjorie inherit a fortune. Meshbesher expounded on how Marjorie would have to be the biggest idiot in the world to hire a person to commit murder for money and then give all the money to the guy she's hired.

"Members of the Jury, the other trust stays in existence for twenty-one years after Elisabeth Congdon's death, and the beneficiaries only get the income from that trust. So if Marjorie gave away the major trust to Roger, she left herself in a financial position that was not much different than it was before the murders, because she had the benefit of Marquette Trust which was paying all of her expenses for many years. And I think the testimony was that she received over $30,000 or $35,000 a year from that trust. So what the State is trying to tell you is that for $11,000 a year more, Marjorie had Roger kill her mother. It just doesn't make sense. It just doesn't hold water.

"Marjorie did rely on her mother financially, there is no question about it, and she was probably brought up that way. She was given everything. Her mother was never married. She adopted Marjorie and gave her the world, if money is the world. I'm convinced it didn't help in this case.

"Marjorie appreciated the fact that she was adopted by her mother and spoke nothing but in the highest terms of her. She had made numerous gifts for her mother. She spent untold hours on needlepoint. Do you do needlepoint work for a woman who you don't care about or are not concerned about? If she were only there for the money, Ladies and Gentlemen, she wouldn't put hours and hours of her personality, herself as a person, into that kind of handmade work. It would have been just as easy to buy a gift and send it out, but that needlework takes time, it takes forethought, and you don't make them overnight. That shows a constant loving concern.

"I think we have proved the exact opposite of the prosecution's claim. Marjorie had a warm relationship with her mother. She was adopted as an infant, and that is the only mother she ever knew. And to think that the prosecution can twist and distort everything she does to try to make you think she could do this horrendous thing. It takes the most horrendous type of person to plot the murder of their own mother, and that is why I stress it, because you had to see a woman who was almost on the verge of insanity, lusting for greed, disregarding a woman that had given her everything in life, maybe too much, a woman who she had spent . . . many of her personal hours making private, personal gifts for, all in one fell swoop, all of that love had to go right down the drain in this dastardly plot; and if that is the picture of the woman, Marjorie Caldwell, I think we heard different evidence.

"Now, Mr. DeSanto tells you, with red face, he said that the fingerprint was false, as though that makes it go away. It is still there, Ladies and Gentlemen, a fingerprint that you would have been convinced of, had the defense not gone out and got a reliable expert to examine it, and you would have heard of that fingerprint until you were blue in the face, from the State, the same fingerprint that was used in the Roger Caldwell case.

"The phony fingerprint alone is a reasonable doubt. Furman is known as an evidence planter. The window hole is too small for Roger's arm. There is no motive for a killing for a woman . . . if she gives a lion's share away to a drunken husband. There is no transportation connection between Colorado and Minnesota for a killer who had to be on one of two flights, if that is the man.

"The alibi in Colorado is solid—not just a reasonable doubt, it's solid. The baggage tickets, the lack of the interline tickets, the wicker basket, the empty closet, they are all positive proof of a frame-up, and we don't have to give you positive proof. We just have to raise it to a reasonable doubt.

"Members of the Jury, you have been as patient with me as I could have hoped, and it's been a long, hard three and a half months. I don't know what to say to you, but you have got to be morally certain that Marjorie Caldwell plotted the murder of her mother before you can find her guilty. I don't want any sympathy. I want a clear analysis of the facts."

With tears in his eyes, he delivered his last plea, his final words to the exhausted jury. "Members of the Jury, I believe that you and I know there is only one verdict in this case, and I believe that you will do your duty, and your duty is to follow the law and follow the evidence and bring back a verdict of not guilty.

"Thank you very much."

Part III

"Now, we'll never know."

❦ *Chapter Twenty*

On July 21, 1979, after only a day and a half of deliberation, the jury came back and found Marjorie Caldwell *not guilty on all counts.* It was an emotional, climactic end to the sixteen week trial, the longest criminal trial in Minnesota history.

When the verdict was read, Helen and Wally Hagen clutched each other's hands. Tears streamed down Helen's cheeks. They jumped up and cheered along with the other spectators. A standing ovation. Marjorie gave Meshbesher, her savior, a huge, tight hug. It was more emotion than she had displayed throughout the whole trial. That night, the Hagens took Marjorie out to dinner to celebrate her freedom. Some of the jurors went with them.

Four days later, on July 25, Marjorie decided to revisit the Glensheen Mansion. She relived her childhood memories for a reporter. She remarked that to this day she prefers the company of animals to people. "My favorite spot at Glensheen was the stables, where I played with toy horses or spent hours lost in a book."

She said that she spent the day after her acquittal celebrating in solitude at the Como Park Zoo in St. Paul with a bag of White Castle hamburgers.

Of her spending, she said, "Of course I spent a lot. I never learned how to handle money. But I'll be damned if I'll be put up to a guilt trip for spending it on my kids." She added that she now realized that some of her children were "selfish pigs" who kept demanding more and more. "Obviously, I gave them too damn much."

Marjorie told the reporter that her natural parents

were very young and unmarried when she was born. They were a couple of farm kids of French and Irish descent, fourteen and fifteen years old. The illegitimacy was a thorn in the side of the Congdon family. Jennifer was legitimate, she said. Her parents were killed in a car accident. "When Jennifer came along, all she did was cut my share of the inheritance in half."

She said that she is "unsure what the future holds, but another trip to Duluth seems unlikely. I am two years tired," she said. Of her mother, "I can say this. She was the most incredible person. She was patient, kind, and an extremely active person. She was never bitter, never vengeful, and I never heard her say an unkind thing." She added, "There's nothing you can do. The hard part isn't that the wrong people were accused, but that the right people were not. I want to get away to where nobody knows me and just try to put my life together."

In acquitting Marjorie, the jurors in Hastings also, in effect, acquitted Roger based on the evidence they had heard. However, in Roger Caldwell's case, what the jury in Hastings thought didn't matter because he had already been convicted by another jury. He was already in prison.

Meshbesher believed that Caldwell would get another day in court. "I thought that if the jury in Brainerd had heard all of the evidence that the jury in Hastings heard with respect to Roger's involvement, they would have acquitted Roger too," he said.

On September 2, 1982, on the basis of the testimony from the fingerprint experts in Marjorie's trial, it was decided that he would be granted a new trial. Although he had been sentenced to two life terms in Stillwater State Prison, the Minnesota Supreme Court voted six-two to overturn the convictions. They cited the discrepancies in the evidence offered in both Roger's and Marjorie's murder trials. He was released without bond to await his second trial for murdering Miss Congdon and Velma Pietila. He was placed in the custody of his attorney, Doug Thomson.

DeSanto wanted a conviction. If the case went to trial again, the jury might have acquitted Caldwell. And DeSanto said that time had weakened his case. Thomson wanted his forty-nine-year-old client to remain free. Convictions for first-degree murder would mean another automatic sentence of two life terms.

Caldwell said, "I've been in prison for five years, and now I'm in a state of limbo. I'm just waiting to see what the State of Minnesota is going to do about me. I'm still accused of crimes I haven't committed. Being charged with two murders is hardly freedom. In a sense, I'm still in prison, no matter how pleasant the surroundings, until the criminal justice system recognizes my innocence."

"The deal was initiated," Thomson said, "when we met to discuss the mechanics of scheduling a new trial. One of us raised the question of whether the case could be disposed of without a trial. Caldwell's first trial lasted three months and cost at least $250,000." A plea bargain was struck.

Thomson and DeSanto agreed to two counts of second-degree murder. Caldwell had served sixty-two months in Stillwater State Prison, and by agreeing to this plea bargain, he would receive no further incarceration. His remaining sentence would be suspended. He would be free.

The conditions were that Roger Caldwell had to confess to the murders under oath, before a judge, John DeSanto, and Doug Thomson. DeSanto opened the proceedings. He recited the rules of the plea bargain, making sure that Caldwell understood the conditions.

Caldwell, DeSanto, Thomson, and the judge gathered in a small, windowless room in the Duluth County Courthouse to hear Caldwell's confession. It was a gloomy day outside and the weather seemed to pervade the walls as DeSanto began his questioning.

"Okay, Roger, let's go back to May 25, 1977, a month before the murders. Do you remember making the trip to Duluth to see Elisabeth Congdon?"

"Sure. The purpose of the trip was to try to get the trustees of the estate to loan my wife $750,000 to go into a horse breeding/racing ranch operation in the state of Colorado. I thought I should meet my new mother-in-law whom I had never laid eyes on. The trustees said that I could see her, but only for fifteen minutes."

"While you were there, visiting with Miss Congdon, did you have any thoughts of returning to the mansion to burglarize it?"

"No."

"To kill anyone?"

"No."

Then DeSanto asked Caldwell to explain how Marjorie happened to write him a note two days before the murders that would assign him her inheritance if anything should happen to her.

"Well, you know by now that Marjorie was no good with money. She just simply had no ability to control whatever it was that drove her to spend. Over the years, she had lost all credibility with her family, even her children. And I was always a fairly solid citizen with at least passable financial control of my own life. So, she got an attorney who thought it would be a good thing to show these trustees that Marjorie wouldn't be in control of this $750,000, but her husband would be the one who would handle the money. And that's where the Power of Attorney came from that you found in my safe deposit box in Colorado."

"Okay, that explains that. But what about the assignment of inheritance?"

"I don't know what prompted that. She got this wild hair idea, the way she did with other matters. If a little bit was good, then a whole lot was better. So, I guess she decided to write out this assignment to show how committed she was to her husband. I had nothing to do with it."

"After you received the assignment June 24, the Friday before the murders, did you then plan to commit murder so this could speed along the inheritance which would be yours if this was a valid document?"

"No. I don't know the law. I just did what she told me in order to avoid more confrontation with her."

Then, prompted by DeSanto, Caldwell told him of the day that he left Colorado to commit the burglary. He couldn't remember the airline, the flight number, or even the name he used to buy his ticket.

"I understand how it's hard to believe, but as you well know with the investigation you conducted, I am an old drunk. I have been on the sauce for a long, long time. There were many things I don't remember throughout my lifetime that were nearer and dearer to me than a false name I would give at an airline counter."

That may have been the most truthful statement that Roger Caldwell made that day. He relived his version of that night on June 26, 1977, for the judge and two attorneys. It was full of contradictions, but it was obvious that he believed what he was saying. This was his truth. It was a night that would be etched on his brain until the day he died, he said. It came to him at night when he couldn't sleep, he thought about it when he was driving or on escalators or eating. It didn't matter. He couldn't get it out of his head.

It had been warm. Even Duluth had summer, or so she'd told him. Ha, summer in Duluth? An oxymoron. He remembered thinking that while sitting in the bar that night. How did a forty-two-year-old man, a former high school football star, a law-abiding citizen who never forgot his parents' anniversary, end up in this predicament? If only he'd taken the time to answer. If only . . .

It had been a long day, first the flight, and then the bus ride from the Minneapolis-St. Paul International Airport. It was 180 miles to Duluth, but it felt like the other end of the world. He'd crunched up next to the window and pretended to be asleep, just in case the guy next to him got it in his head to tell his life story. It never failed. He remembered clutching his third vodka on the rocks. The booze gave him the courage he would need that night. He had another pint in his pocket for emergencies. It would be over soon, he'd thought.

It was almost dark when he hailed the cab. He cursed himself for not paying closer attention the last time he'd visited the Glensheen Mansion. He'd only been there one time before. In May. He hadn't even gotten past the first floor. He was so nervous that day that he hadn't noticed the stained glass windows, the floor-to-ceiling oak paneling, or the marble fireplace. He wouldn't have recognized Angora goat's wool wallcovering even if it had been labeled. How many times had she told him that the mansion—never the house, always "The Mansion"— had thirty-nine rooms?

The Superior Bar where he'd waited until dusk was on Eleventh Avenue at the end of London Road. Pretty seedy, he'd thought, considering how close he was to the wealthiest neighborhood in Duluth. He remembered her bragging to him that Sinclair Lewis had once owned a house down the street. That was after he'd won the Nobel Prize, she'd said. That was where Lewis wrote Cass Timberlane. He'd never heard of Sinclair Lewis, so once again, she had wasted her breath. She was good at that.

The cab slowly wound its way down London Road. Through blurry eyes, he saw a street sign, 26th Avenue East. Now he perked up. He remembered the address of Glensheen: 3300 London Road. Suddenly, the landscape changed from unkempt and tawdry to the aesthetic symmetry of elm-lined sidewalks that seemed to announce, You Have Arrived.

London Road runs along Lake Superior's edge, hugs it like a cloak. Some of the homes are tucked back so far from the road he had a hard time spotting them from the back seat of the cab. It was getting darker, and fog was rolling in off the lake. She'd told him how sometimes Duluth could be fogged in for days. He took a swig from his pint and wiped his mouth with the back of his hand. He craned his neck to the right as the cab driver slowly cruised by. He knew the house immediately.

The driver continued down London Road. About two blocks past 3300 London Road, he said, "This is good, drop me off." He noticed the look on the cabby's face from the rearview mirror. He could almost read his mind. "He must be lost." Then he caught a glimpse of his own face in the mirror. His five-o'clock shadow had turned into uneven stubble. He rubbed his chin and then smoothed back his hair. His eyes were bloodshot, but that was to be expected.

He paid the driver and got out of the cab. Then he back-tracked, sauntering, like a man out for a breath of fresh air, enjoying the warm June night. He heard a dog barking in the distance. A car passed him, the radio blasting through the open windows. Ronnie Milsap was singing "It Was Almost Like a Song." He loved Country. He was in front of the Glensheen Mansion. The house was dark, but the sky still had some light. It was too soon. This was no time to fuck up.

He walked past the long driveway to the Glensheen Mansion, not daring to glance down toward the house. Right next door he came to a wrought-iron fence. The gate was not locked and he strolled into a Swedish graveyard. If anyone ques-

tioned him, he could say he was there to pay his respects. *Roger* noticed a strong smell of clover. He sat down on the grass and leaned against one of the large headstones, dated 1899. He couldn't read the name. Just as well. Cemeteries gave him the creeps. He lighted a Camel and took another swig. He wondered if this is where they would bury Miss Elisabeth. He had a perfect view of the mansion next door. Soon, it would be pitch dark.

He didn't know how long he sat there. Had he dozed? He seemed to remember a dream about his wife. She was standing over him, bitching at him. "Let's see if just once in your life you can do something right. Just one thing. I highly doubt it!" Her voice rasped like a garbage disposal with a bottle cap caught in the blades. Then she was laughing like a clown in a funhouse. The laugh echoed. She was always laughing at him. Or sneering, which was even worse. He winced and looked all around him. Was she here? No way. That wasn't in the plan. It was only a nightmare.

It was dark now. He grasped the top of the gravestone and dragged himself up. Damn, his legs felt like Jell-O. Must be the booze. She would be pissed if she knew he was drinking. Shit, how did she think he could go into the old lady's house and rob her without a little help from his friend? He couldn't. Anyway, she'd never know. She'd sleep through the whole thing. He hoped. Why couldn't Marjorie wait for the goddamned jewelry? The old lady was eighty-three. Paralyzed. How long could she have to live? One year? Two? Couldn't Marjorie wait that long?

He wondered what he was doing standing in a goddamned cemetery in the middle of the night. He flicked his cigarette into the grass and wended his way to the mansion. The wrought-iron gates to the estate had been left open. Lush spruces and pines, forty feet tall, adorned the grounds. He had to watch carefully not to trip over the shrubs that seemed to jump out at him with every step. The house loomed over him like an imposing shadow. There were so many windows. Was *anyone watching?*

A long enclosed porch area ran the length of the back of the mansion. The exterior windows had been removed. He climbed onto the porch and cupped his hands against one of the interior windows. He could see a billiard table inside. He decided this would be a good place to enter the house, but when he tried to open the window it was locked. He'd have to break it. He jumped down off the porch and felt around on the ground until he came up with a large rock. Perfect. He picked it up, climbed back on the porch. He wrapped the tail of his shirt around his hand and punched the rock through the window. Glass shattered sixteen feet across the room. He waited a second. No alarm. It was dead silent. He stretched his arm through the broken glass, unlatched the window, and opened it. He climbed through. Mildew permeated the air. It was like being in a cave, a cave with Tiffany lamps hanging over a pool table and Oriental rugs strewn across the floor. He was startled by a crunching noise but then realized it was the sound of his own feet stepping on the broken glass. He was glad he'd worn sneakers instead of his cowboy boots. He edged around the pool table trying to get his bearings. Not exactly like the poolroom he'd hung out in as a kid back in Latrobe.

He rounded the first level of stairs, listening for any sounds. How could a house this big be so quiet? He cursed himself for not bringing a flashlight. He passed through the library, the one room he'd seen in this house the month before. He didn't know where the old lady slept, except that it was upstairs somewhere. But which room? She'd told him to watch out for the nurse. Her room was across the hall.

He climbed the second level of stairs. Small lanterns on the walls lit the hallway, sending eerie shadows across the floor. He heard a door open. Suddenly, without warning, a flashlight shone in his face. It blinded his vision. He tried to shield his eyes, and then there was a deafening scream. What in the hell was going on? He wanted to tear down the stairs and run out the door. She must be the nurse, and she saw his face. He *grabbed her by her shoulders and the flashlight flew from her hand. The small woman struggled with him, but he overpowered her and shoved her down the stairs onto the landing. He saw a look of horror in her eyes.*

Then it was as if someone else took over his body. There was no time to think. She wouldn't stop screaming. He had to shut her up. There was a sidetable next to him with a sculpture of a bird and two brass candlestick holders. He grabbed one of the candlestick holders and flew down to the landing where the woman was crouched, screaming, her hands flailing over her head. She clawed at his head. He pulled away from her and, swinging the weapon over his head, crashed the candlestick holder over her shoulder. Everything was blurred. He hit her again and again. "Shut-up," he hissed, "Just shut-up." Blood spattered the carved oak railing. It dripped down the Tudor rose design in the stained glass window like an eerie tentacle. A pool of blood saturated the oriental carpet. The woman lay in a small heap on the landing. Finally, she was quiet.

He wanted to run, but there was no turning back now. He panicked. He stepped over her body and ran up the stairs to the second level. He almost tripped on the broken flashlight and one of the nurse's shoes. Her bifocals lay on the floor at the top of the stairs. What was that noise? It sounded like a whining dog. Was someone else in the house?

He had to find the old woman. The hallway was long and formidable. There were doors everywhere. He got lucky. He opened the first door to the right of the stairs, and there she was. Was it possible that she had actually slept through all the screaming? She must be deaf. He saw a phone on her nightstand and ripped out the cord and stood over her bed. Her eyes were closed. The covers were pulled up neatly to her chin. As he peered down at her face, her eyes flashed, opened wide with terror. Her mouth opened as if to scream, but nothing came out. Her gray hair was perfect, not a strand out of place.

He grabbed a pillow out from under her head. Plunk. Her

head dropped like a cabbage. The lights from the hallway illuminated the pillow. Pink satin. The old lady had recognized him, no doubt about it. He could tell by the look in her eyes, even though they'd only met once. With both hands, he picked up the pillow and he laid it over her head so that she wouldn't hear, so that he could shut out the light and any noise. He pressed down as hard as he could and waited. Her left arm flailed in the air. He heard her muffled struggles for breath as her head jerked from side to side. He pressed harder. She fought for almost four minutes. Now, she was dead.

Caldwell's recollection did not sound like the viewpoint of an innocent man. His recriminations of Marjorie did not sound like a man in love with his wife. His memory of the murders did not seem to be that of a man who intended to commit burglary only. He had been almost trance-like as he described that terrible night at the Glensheen Mansion. There were long pauses, as if he was trying to decide what to admit and what to leave out. Or was he making it up as he went along? When he finished, he looked at Doug Thomson, as if for moral support. Finally, DeSanto broke the silence.

"With regard to Elisabeth Congdon . . . the physical evidence somewhat contradicts what you are telling us. Her nose was scraped. There were prints on the pillow indicating that it was firmly grasped. Was there somebody else in that house with you that actually killed her?"

Both DeSanto and Thomson were well aware of the many pieces of the puzzle that didn't fit. Besides the pillow, there were the dark hairs in Velma's hands; the longer, thinner arm needed to reach into the window, or the ability to walk through the front door and make a red herring of the basement window; and the probable guidance needed to know how to get from the amusement room in the basement to the upper stairway and Elisabeth's room in the dark.

"There was nobody else in that house with me. I had just completed beating a woman, and I was in a state of frenzy. I don't recall her struggling, but maybe I was more firm in placing the pillow than I recollect. My intention was never to kill the woman."

DeSanto and Thomson exchanged confused glances before DeSanto continued.

"Okay. After you put the pillow over Miss Congdon's face, what did you do in her room?"

"I ransacked the drawers to look for valuables, took what I could find, and left. I was obviously in a heck of a mess and wanted to get out of Duluth and out of Minnesota just as quickly as I could."

Caldwell went on to tell DeSanto that he did not recall taking the ring off Elisabeth Congdon's hand, or the watch off her wrist, or taking the wicker case. He said he did not remember taking the diamond and sapphire ring off her dresser. He had no recollection of the coin, nor did he remember the envelope with his handwriting on it. Drunk or not, how could he forget doing something so deliberate as stealing a Byzantine coin and mailing it to himself that same night? Could Marjorie have taken the coin from her mother's house? She had admitted to her friend that if she saw something that she wanted in the mansion, she took it. It would have been easy for her to get some Radisson Hotel stationery and forge Roger's handwriting. Caldwell told DeSanto that he couldn't imagine her doing such a thing.

DeSanto walked Roger through his drive to the Minneapolis-St. Paul International Airport where he said he didn't remember anything about where he had parked Velma's car or about throwing the keys in the trash can where they were later found. He didn't remember buying the airline ticket or which airline he took back to Denver. He didn't remember buying the suede garment bag. He didn't remember anything about the wicker case, much less stuffing it in the garment bag.

When he arrived back in Denver, Marjorie picked him up at the airport. He threw the garment bag in the trunk of the car. Then they went to feed the horses, and that is when the horse stepped on him, he said.

"I was hurt. That horse did a pretty good job on me. Oh, I have been stepped on and bitten and butted and kicked, and I never got along with those damned horses. Anyway, that's how I got the swollen hand."

"Roger, on June 28, when you went to open the safe deposit box, you knew that Elisabeth Congdon was dead, and that you had murdered her, right?"

"Right. I didn't know I had murdered her, no. I knew she was dead. I never thought it was murder."

DeSanto and Thomson looked confused. Where was this guy coming from?

"So now, you realized that this inheritance that had been assigned to you could be very important, didn't you?"

"No, I didn't. The only reason for putting those two documents in that safe deposit box was because we were living in a motel. You know what it's like, John. You were there. It's an odd—it's not a hotel, it's not a motel. It was a peculiar arrangement at best, but, along with it, we also had maid service, and we had people patiently waiting for us to vacate the rooms so they could come and make beds, change the towels, and what have you. We had stuff stacked and stored and piled and horse stuff, and it was a hell of a way to live. I am a rather private person, and it didn't seem to me that this was the kind of thing I wanted laying around to be viewed by the clean-up lady.

We didn't have a good relationship at the Holland House either. Marj had quarreled with virtually everybody in the place at one time or another, including the management, and when you live in a place like that, you don't know who has access to your rooms and who doesn't, and it just seemed to me that these documents were personal. I didn't want anyone getting their nose into them."

"Do you think you should be able to collect on that assignment of inheritance?"

"I never had any interest in Marj's money."

"Don't you think you're getting the short end of the stick right now?"

"I know I'm getting the short end of the stick, but not financially. I never had any claim to it. I didn't marry Marj for her money. When I married her, I didn't even know she had money. I had never heard of the Congdons."

DeSanto then asked Roger why he brought the jewelry, the suede garment bag, and the wicker basket back to Duluth when they attended the funeral. He said the garment bag was for his clothes and that he had no idea that the jewelry and wicker basket had been packed too. He didn't know how those items got placed in the nightstand in the Bloomington hotel. Marjorie knew from the police that those items were missing after her mother's death. She knew that Roger was a suspect. She knew that if those items were found in their hotel room, it would be enough evidence to arrest her husband for murdering her mother and Velma Pietila.

"Roger, what reaction did Marjorie have to you when she picked you up at the restaurant after your return to Denver?"

"Anxious, hurried. She had been real-estating again. She had seen properties and was telling me about them and wanting to hurry back up to the animals."

"And where did you tell her you had been?"

"She never had a great deal of interest. I told her that I'd been off tooting, and she didn't want to hear about it. She didn't like listening to stories of drunks."

"She knew her mother had been murdered, right?"

"Yes."

"Well, didn't you talk about it?"

"She was grief-stricken. You have to know Marj and how her processes work. She was upset and yet controlled enough to want to continue what had been our routine, and yet be left alone without being left alone. You have to know Marjorie."

"You understand that if she is involved, whether it be before the fact or after the fact, at this stage, she is not going to face any criminal consequences. She has the benefit of what we call the double jeopardy clause, do you understand that?"

"Yes, of course, I do, yes."

"Have you talked with Marjorie since you got out of prison?"

"No, I haven't."

"When was the last time you talked with Marjorie?"

"I haven't seen or spoken with Marjorie since approximately three weeks after her acquittal."

"Did Marjorie ever ask you if you did it?"

"No. She stood by me and supported me in every way she could. There was never any question that I was guilty. Never, from her. She knew I was innocent."

"But you, of course, knew otherwise."

"I did, yes."

"Did she ask you about where you were when it looked like what happened here was consistent with you committing the murders?"

"No. She never connected one with the other. As I say, it had long since stopped being a surprise when we would get into a real argument that I would go off and go out on a toot. She was used to me leaving her high and dry."

"Who do you think is getting left high and dry now?"

"Me."

❧ Chapter Twenty-One

Jim Klobuchar, a columnist for the *Minneapolis Star Tribune,* summed up the case on July 8, 1983:

From the beginning, the Caldwell case seemed freighted with characters and plots that borrowed equally from Agatha Christie and the old parlor game called Clue. There was a sea-side mansion and a wealthy old heiress and a prodigal son-in-law, there was greed and jewelry and a candleholder, and then came shrewd criminal lawyers and disputed evidence.

And now the man who did the killing has confessed.

And now the man is free.

The audience in a movie might walk away rubbing its eyes and looking annoyed, but this was for real, and the audience was entitled to ask, "Whatever happened to the jury system?" What happened in the Caldwell case is that the jury system suddenly scared everybody. Things like extra expense, the possibility that the jury might acquit Roger Caldwell because the evidence was old, the judge worrying that he might look unnecessarily hard-barked about the whole thing. So in the end the judge could not even prevail upon the agents representing the killer and the agents representing the county to settle for twelve more months of Roger Caldwell.

The agents—the prosecutor and the defense lawyer—said they were adamant. They had a deal that would make sure the prosecutor had it on record that Roger was the killer, and the defense counsel had his defendant safely walking the street. His ex-wife was exonerated because a piece of evidence didn't hold up. The effect of that was to throw out Caldwell's original conviction of murder after he served five years.

The principals came back before the court in Duluth, and the question was: Is the issue important enough to summon another jury to hear it through even though it might be essentially a reprise of two or three earlier trials? Or should reasonable and honorable people try to determine the public good and the interests of justice?

The judge is no doubt honorable, and the prosecutor might have been thinking about practical things like trial costs and such, but it is more likely that he was thinking about the horror of losing.

The defense lawyer was simply what everybody knew he was—a very smart and durable defense lawyer. It is not hard to understand where he was in the negotiation. Nobody has quite been able to explain where the prosecutor and the judge were.

There was a double murder, and it was big enough and brutal enough to warrant one more trial, even at the risk that the case might be lost. The worst scenario in that event was that Roger Caldwell might go free. So what happened is that after serving five years, he was allowed to plead guilty to second-degree murder. And he went free.

After Roger's release, he moved back to his hometown of Latrobe, Pennsylvania. Joe Kimball, a reporter for the *Minneapolis Star Tribune* who had followed the case closely, flew out there to interview the forty-nine-year-old Caldwell. His face betrayed the years of heavy smoking, drinking, and prison life. He wore a look of permanent sadness, loneliness, and disappointment. But he also had a calm about him, a resolve that nothing could be done to change the past. This article was published in the Minneapolis paper on July 7, 1983:

After spending five years in a Minnesota prison for two murders, Roger Caldwell has come home. He said Saturday that he wants to put the memory of those five years behind him. He said he wants to live quietly in the town he left thirty years ago, and where, he said, "I spent the happiest days of my life."

He said he is penniless. He said he spends a lot of his time in a couple of bars and walking the streets of Latrobe, a steelmill community of about 10,000 people in western Pennsylvania. He said he lives in a friend's house and eats meals with his parents.

"I've caused my family a lot of grief," he said. "I wouldn't do that for the world, but I was caught in circumstances I couldn't control."

Although the Duluth murders made Roger Caldwell a familiar name in Minnesota, they weren't publicized in Latrobe. The town's daily newspaper apparently had last mentioned his name in 1953 when he played on the Latrobe High School football team.

But the quiet life Caldwell sought in his hometown ended Friday, when the *Latrobe Bulletin* ran a front-page story under the headline, *Ex Latrobe Man Free in Bizarre Case.*

"The paper came to the door. My mother picked it up and came to me," he said. "She said, 'You made the headline.' She read it, then went into her room and collapsed. We called the doctor and he came to sedate her.

"That was the nastiest thing they could have done," he said. His seventy-seven year old mother was the first family member to see it. He was with her at the time. The newspaper detailed the murder case, including Caldwell's admitting that he committed the murders.

"There was just no reason to print that," he said. "No purpose to it."

"He won't talk about the case," a relative said. "He seems to be afraid that if he deviates at all from the statement he made in court they might charge him with perjury and try to put him back in prison. He doesn't want to go back to prison."

"I feel comfortable here," he said. "I'm home. I'm home."

Caldwell, who weighs about 180 pounds, has gained back about thirty of the pounds he lost in prison. He is about five-foot ten inches tall, and his hair is neatly cut with a distinguished silver tint. He is very soft spoken and appeared relaxed and content to talk about his life and about Latrobe.

But he seemed reluctant to talk to old friends and acquaintances. On one occasion yesterday, while strolling through Latrobe with the reporter, Caldwell recognized someone he said was a childhood friend who he hadn't seen in years. The friend apparently didn't recognize Caldwell, who said later, "I'm glad he didn't recognize me. I don't want to meet anyone I know right now."

Of the plea-bargain agreement that set him free in return for a confession, he said: "Nobody was happy about it. The idea was to wrap up the case. It's wrapped up."

He added, "There's no way I can make you believe anything, but I did not get one farthing, one promise or even the suggestion of a promise for saying that I committed the murders."

Of his hometown, Caldwell said: "This is a beautiful town. I'm very proud of it."

Caldwell yesterday pointed out houses; fences and stores that have been standing since before Minnesota became a state.

"My Uncle John used to live there," he said, pointing to an old house. "And there's where my grandfather's farm used to be."

At two cemeteries he pointed out tombstones with the names of his ancestors.

"We're not able to track it (his ancestry) all the way back," he said. "We get lost in the great-great-greats."

On Friday, the day when the *Latrobe Bulletin* published its big story about Caldwell, he visited two taverns with the Minneapolis reporter. In both places, patrons and bartenders warmly greeted him.

"I don't know who knows and who doesn't," Caldwell said of the Duluth murders. "If they do know, they aren't letting on. Irrespective of what the people in Minnesota will believe, there are people here who will never believe I did it. They say, 'I've known him since he was a kid. He's a nice fellow.'"

The people in Latrobe are like that. They are common-sense people with respect for others. His mother's high school class just held a fifty-nine-year reunion. Fifty-nine, because one of the few remaining class members had cancer and isn't expected to live long. "That's typical Latrobe fashion," Caldwell said.

Some of his relatives in Latrobe said last week that they never believed he was guilty. They said they believed that he was framed by people who didn't want him and Marjorie Caldwell to get their share of Congdon's inheritance. Those relatives said they were shocked when they learned from a Minneapolis reporter last week that Roger had confessed to the murders.

"I've always wanted to believe my brother was not guilty of such a heinous crime," said Howard Caldwell, Jr., one of Roger's three brothers. Howard Caldwell is a personnel manager for a steel mill in Latrobe. Another brother, Dave, is a city policeman. The third brother, John, is a librarian at Augustana College in Rock Island, Illinois. He regularly visited Roger in Stillwater Prison in Minnesota.

When they talked about the case last week, family members frequently used the word, if— "If Roger did it. If he's telling the truth."

"I just don't know what to believe," said Howard Caldwell's wife, Betty.

Her husband said, "Maybe Roger didn't want to take a chance on a new trial. Maybe he thought a bird in the hand is worth two in the bush. Maybe he wanted to agree to this and get on with his life."

Roger Caldwell said he spends a lot of his time walking around Latrobe, "reacquainting myself, ooing and aahing at the changes, trying to recall what has changed and what used to be there."

He said that, after being released from prison, he spent ten months not knowing when he would be called back to Minnesota for his second trial. "I couldn't permit myself to think of the future until Tuesday," he said.

He said that his drinking problems are over. "I still like my beer though," he said, adding that he spends a lot of time with friends at a couple of bars.

Some relatives say he has a strange, almost macabre, sense of humor.

For example, when Caldwell was released from prison, his lawyer asked about his future plans. Caldwell replied, "Maybe I'll become a tour guide at the Congdon mansion."

Also, one of his favorite Latrobe bars sells T-shirts that promote its name: Maggie's.

"I ordered one of those," Caldwell said. "I was hoping to get it in time to wear to court Tuesday." He explained with a grin that "Maggie" is one of his nicknames for Marjorie Caldwell.

"Marjorie is a unique person," Roger Caldwell said, "I can't be unfair to her, even though she was unfair to me."

That's all he would say about her last week. He expects a formal divorce proceeding soon. In the meantime, he said, he would continue to explore his hometown.

"I prefer to walk," he said. "I see better and I can stop to smell the flowers. In the spring I was in my glory. I smelled a lot of flowers. Pennsylvania is replete with flowers, from 'spring beauties' to 'dog tooth violets.'"

Caldwell said he plans to stay in Latrobe.

He explained: "Robert Frost said, 'Home is the place where they have to take you in.' I came home."

***

On May 17, 1988, fifty-three-year-old Roger Caldwell was found dead on the living room floor of his apartment in Latrobe where he lived with a girlfriend. She said that he had been depressed for six months. He told her that his criminal record kept him from getting a job. When she last saw him at 1:00 that afternoon, he was sitting on the living room floor and was visibly intoxicated. Holding a bottle of beer and a knife, he threatened to kill himself. She took the knife away and hid it before she left that day.

This was nine years after his murder conviction and Marjorie's acquittal. Roger Caldwell had bled to death from self-inflicted wounds on both wrists. He had used a straight-edged steak knife with a four-inch blade. Scattered around the room were three suicide notes, and in one of them Caldwell recanted his confession of murdering Elisabeth Congdon and Velma Pietila. "What you need to know is that I didn't kill those girls or to my knowledge ever harm a soul in my life." Perhaps he'd forgotten that just days before his suicide he had beaten up his girlfriend, sending her to the hospital. The other two notes were illegible.

Doug Thomson said, "I still don't know if he really did it . . . His statements were full of inconsistencies about his guilt."

DeSanto commented that he was shocked but not surprised by Caldwell's death. He imagined that Caldwell "had been living in his own personal hell since all this began eleven years ago. I had always hoped that someday he would tell the whole story. Now we'll never know."

❧ *Chapter Twenty-Two*

Helen Hagen's condition had deteriorated. Wally couldn't take care of her anymore. He and Nancy decided to place her in the Twin Birch Nursing Home near their home in Mound.

One day when Nancy visited her, Helen dropped a bombshell on her. She told her that she was sure that Wally and Marjorie were having an affair. Helen often rambled to Nancy, yammering about things that made no sense. It had become routine. Nancy looked at her mother and saw the fear, the frustration, in her eyes. There were tears streaming down her face.

Nancy held her hand and sat back and thought of all that she had read about Alzheimer's: the failing memory, the inability to communicate, using substitute words that the caretaker has to try to decipher. What else could she be trying to tell me? Surely, she doesn't mean "affair." The doctors had told her that when patients reach the severe stage of Alzheimer's they might become accusatory, reporting stolen food or possessions. But Helen wasn't that bad yet. And, Wally and Marjorie? That was too much to take in.

"Mom, that's ridiculous," Nancy said. But on this day, Helen was not rambling. She was as articulate as she'd ever been. She told Nancy that many times when Wally had taken her to the Country Kitchen with Marj, he and Marj had left for an hour or more, just left her sitting there.

If someone had told her that Marjorie was breaking up someone else's marriage, Nancy would not have bothered to blink. It wasn't that she trusted Marjorie. But she knew that her father would never let her down, never desert her mother. Surely, she'd have been able to sense something if there was any truth to it.

As hard as Nancy tried to convince her mother that Wally loved her more than anything in the world, and furthermore, Marjorie was her friend and would never do anything to hurt her, Helen could not be swayed. She grasped Nancy's hands and pleaded with her. "You have to believe me."

Helen had never shown a weakness in her life, had always been in control. This was a new side of her mother that Nancy had never seen. Obviously, the disease was eating away at her brain, gnawing away at everything that had always made her mother a secure and happy woman.

Nancy wished that her mother hadn't confided in her. There were some things that even grown children would rather not be privy to. Intellectually, she knew the disease was altering her mother's thoughts, that Helen had no control over what was going through her mind. But emotionally, she had sparked a ray of doubt in Nancy's mind. What if Marjorie had been trying to worm her way into her parents' relationship? Helen had always had wonderful intuition. She was a smart woman, not given to overreactions or emotional outbursts. It was just a small flicker of doubt, but Nancy couldn't shake it.

On Wednesday evening, March 26, 1980, Nancy went to the nursing home to see her mother. It was about 5:30, and she was going to feed her dinner because Helen had difficulty moving her arms. This was a good day because they could communicate. That night, Helen knew who her daughter was, and the old love that Nancy still yearned for shone through her mother's eyes. Nancy cut the baked chicken into small bites, and alternating with pasta and bland tomato sauce, slowly spooned the food into her mother's mouth. Nancy stayed for several hours, telling her stories about her son, Michael. When she got home, she told her dad what a wonderful evening it had been visiting with Helen and knowing she understood. Nancy didn't know that as she slept that night, Marjorie was paying her mother a visit.

She sat on Helen's bed in the nursing home, feeding babyfood to her old friend as if she were an infant. Marjorie could tell that Helen recognized her because she smiled when she saw her, grateful to have Marjorie's company. When Marjorie asked her how she was feeling, Helen's lips moved, but words did not come out. Marjorie smiled with relief.

She wondered what Helen was thinking as she slipped the spoon of mashed bananas into her mouth. Helen had always liked bananas. After her first bite, Helen's smile turned into a wince, and she got a frightened look in her eyes. The bitter Meprobamate could not be totally disguised in the bananas. What if she suspected something and called for a nurse? That would be a problem. That reminded Marjorie to gently move the call button away from Helen's hand and set it on the side table out of her reach. Helen turned her head toward the table and looked back at Marjorie as if she finally knew what was about to happen.

When Marjorie realized that Helen couldn't talk, she decided to have some fun. She reminded Helen that all those times Wally had gone out to do errands—or so she thought—he was really with Marjorie. "The drives he took by himself?

He was with me. Those weekends when you went on the skating tours with the kids and I said I couldn't go? I was home with your husband."

They had loved each other from the first time they met, she said. She told Helen that on those days when she and Wally left her alone at the Country Kitchen, they were back in Marjorie's bed making love. "Wally hated making love with you," she told her. "I knew what he liked."

She sat there smiling as she relived the past for Helen, telling her what a fool she'd been. She told her that the night she was acquitted for conspiring to kill her mother, Wally had promised her that now they could be together for the rest of their lives. They both knew that Helen was going downhill, and that he would have to commit her soon. "We planned it all," she whispered.

As Helen lingered in the nursing home, Marjorie became impatient. Wally was getting old. She wanted to get married. She wanted to travel and get the hell out of Minnesota. The winters were too long. Helen looked so pathetic, her thin hair all stuck to her head, tears streaming from her eyes, and her silent lips mouthing for help that didn't come.

As Marjorie visited, a nurse walked by the open door, but she didn't come in. No one did.

Marjorie knew from history how effective Meprobamate could be. Marmalade was a better mixer than bananas. It was tart, the perfect disguise for a bitter addition. When she had mixed the tranquilizer with the jam all those years ago, her mother, Elisabeth, hadn't seemed to notice. Of course, she was old and sick anyway.

Unfortunately, she hadn't known how much of it to give Elisabeth, or had she just panicked at the last minute when the nurses made such a big deal about Elisabeth's diabetes? It might have been enough to do the trick if only they hadn't called that damn Dr. Bagley. If her mother had closed her eyes and gone to sleep as Helen did, she might have died on the spot, and there would have been no need for Roger. She *wouldn't have had to put up with his drunken toots, as he liked to call them, or gone through that ridiculous trial. If only Elisabeth had died when she was supposed to, Marjorie would have had her inheritance and the life she deserved. When Helen closed her eyes, Marjorie slipped out of the room as quietly as she had come in.*

It was 10:30 the next morning when someone from the nursing home called Nancy at work. Her mother had gone into a coma. Nancy drove home, picked up Wally, and they went straight to the nursing home. On the way there, her dad discussed the possibility that Helen might die, and if she were going to die, they should allow her to do so and not attempt to use any life-support systems. Nancy knew he had been through a lot, gone through hell with her mom, and she knew that he was not one who dealt well with illness. But at the same time, she was shocked to hear her father talking about letting her mother go as if she were some employee who wasn't pulling her weight anymore. Nancy knew that Helen would not want to be connected to tubes in order to stay alive. But he sounded almost flippant. Where was his empathy? This was a side of her dad she had never seen before.

When they arrived at the nursing home, Nancy watched the doctor put a needle into her mother's foot. There was no response. The doctor was surprised. He said that her mother was in excellent physical condition, other than the deteriorating brain brought on by the Alzheimer's disease.

The next morning, March 27, Nancy was standing by her mother's bed looking at her medical chart when she saw a notation: In case of emergency, call Marjorie LeRoy, daughter of Helen Hagen. Nancy was shocked. She had no idea that Marjorie had ever visited her mother. Nancy informed the nurse that she was Helen's daughter, not Marjorie.

Then she discovered that when her mother went into the coma, the hospital had actually called Marj first. When they couldn't reach her, they tried Wally, but he didn't answer the phone, probably couldn't hear the ring, and finally, they found Nancy at work. Almost as an afterthought, the nurse told Nancy that just the night before Mrs. LeRoy had been in feeding her mother from babyfood jars.

🐝 *Chapter Twenty-Three*

Helen died on Sunday, March 30, 1980. She was sixty-four years old. She never came out of the coma. The doctor found her death a mystery since, physically, it had appeared that Helen should have lived for another twelve to fifteen years. Marj never came to the nursing home after Helen lapsed into the coma.

There was an autopsy. The results showed that Helen had died from dehydration and pneumonia. No one thought to ask for a toxicology report, to see if any drugs or chemical substances were in her body. Helen was buried in a cemetery plot, next to one reserved for her husband.

Seven days after her mother's death, Wally gave Nancy the shock of her life. She was sitting at the desk in the kitchen when her dad walked into the house. "Marj is out in the car," he said. His manner was abrupt, as if he'd had something on his mind for a long time and now he was going to rid himself of the burden. He could have been talking to a stranger on the street.

"I came to tell you that I hated your mother for the

whole forty-seven years I was married to her."

Nancy stopped what she was doing and looked up at him. "Then why did you stay with her?"

"Because of you kids."

"Dad, I'm thirty-two years old. I've been out of the house since I was eighteen. You'd better come up with a better reason than that."

Nancy's father just looked at her and then walked out of the house. Nancy almost fell over. As far as she'd known, her parents had had a wonderful marriage. She had lived with them during Marjorie's trial, and when she wasn't living there, she and her mother talked on the phone all the time. Even if her dad believed what he was saying, why would he tell her this? He knew how close she was with her mother and how devastated she was over her death. He seemed as detached as if he were talking about someone else. Not her mother, not his wife. This was only the beginning.

After her mother's death, Nancy was working forty hours a week at the University of Minnesota golf course, and doing inventory for Dayton's department store at nights. She had a young girl, Debbie, come out to their house and sit for Michael during the day in the summer. Other times, he went to daycare. She and her dad agreed that if she helped him—cook and take care of the bills—he would pick up Michael from daycare. One night, she got home about 11:00 p.m. from a conference in Wisconsin. She went upstairs to kiss Michael goodnight, and he wasn't in his room.

"I ran downstairs and asked my dad, 'Where's Michael?'"

"I didn't get him."

"What do you mean, you didn't get him?"

"Marj said I didn't have to."

"Are you crazy?"

She was frantic. She finally reached the woman who

ran the daycare center, who told her that nobody had picked Michael up at 6:00, the appointed time. They had tried to call the house, but there was no answer. Michael had wanted her to call Debbie, but the daycare center couldn't permit him to go to her because Nancy hadn't signed a release form. So, the daycare provider called social services. He had been made a ward of the state. Michael had spent the night in a foster home. He was only four years old. Nancy had to go down to the courthouse the next morning to get a court order to get her son back, and then listen to them accuse her of being a negligent mother for not having made arrangements for her child.

Wally started spending more and more time with Marj, alienating his children. Nancy's brother Tom and his family lived in Alabama. Her other brother, Dick, lived in Minneapolis but he was not as effected by his father's behavior. Tom and Nancy agreed that they wouldn't have begrudged Wally a relationship with anybody, at least after Helen's death, but he was shutting them out of their lives. It hurt.

Before her mother had gotten sick, Helen had handled all the finances with the house and their property. She had shown Nancy her will. They owned four lots. The big house would go to Nancy ("In case I married a bum"), so that she would have a roof over her head. Helen's sons would each get one of the other houses. Her dad, if he survived her mother, would have the right of survivorship. All these assets had been inherited from Helen's mother.

Helen's will was not probated. The will left Nancy as executor of the estate. After Helen's funeral, she invited everybody over to read the will, including Marj. She asked her dad what personal belongings he wanted. He said he didn't want any of it. Her mother had had several sets of diamonds that were to go to Nancy, but she did not want to cause dissension, so Nancy kept her grandmother's ring, which had been handed down through the family, but she gave the rest of the jewelry to her brothers. One week after that, she folded up the will and put it in the desk in the kitchen. When she came home, she noticed that things were missing. The house had been ransacked. There were fifty-four built in drawers upstairs and they had all been dumped. The will was gone. So were all of her papers, all the receipts—the proof that she'd spent over $50,000 on her parents' bills. It turned out that Wally had not been paying the bills with the money she gave him. He had been giving it to Marj. Nancy had mortgaged her own house, and she had no credit rating. Each of the Hagen children was supposed to get 30 percent of their mother's estate. Now there was no proof of that, either. Everything was gone.

"And then, there were the phone calls in the middle of the night. It seems that Dad's girlfriends were coming out of the woodwork. These calls started shortly after Mom died. One lady, in particular—she was an alcoholic—called all night long, and finally, one night she called me about 2:30 in the morning, and I said, 'He's not here, he's shacking up with his girlfriend, and here's her number.' I gave her Marj's phone number." Sometimes he came home, but sometimes he didn't.

Nancy had to leave her house at 3:00 a.m. in order to get to the golf course by 4:00. One morning, she got up to go to work and her dad wasn't home. What was she going to do with Michael? Torn between fury and worry, she called her brother Dick to see if he knew anything. She knew that her dad had night blindness and shouldn't be driving in the dark. She called the hospitals. She called her assistant to have her open the golf course for her, and told her she'd be there as soon

as she could. Wally showed up at about 9:00 that morning. When she accused him of going back on their
agreement, he just said, "Marj says I don't have to."

Nancy looked back at all the things that had happened since Marjorie had started seeing her father.
Several months before Helen had been sent to the
nursing home, she hadn't been able to wear her wedding rings because they didn't fit her finger anymore.
Nancy had had the rings resized and gave them back
to her. Two days later, she visited Helen and noticed
that she wasn't wearing them. When she asked her
mother about it, Helen looked down at her hand and
said she didn't remember where they were. Nancy
knew that since the Alzheimer's had started, Helen
had often taken her rings off in the middle of the night
in the bed. Nancy tore apart Helen's bed and searched
the house. No rings. Helen told her that she had visited Marj the day before and Marj had wanted to try on
the rings. That was the last thing she remembered.

Suddenly, Nancy wished she had requested a
toxicology report.

Just when she thought things could not get more
bizarre, she had another shock. Nancy was brushing
her teeth, and Michael, who was now five years old,
ran into the bathroom and said, "Mommy, Grandpa's
here, Grandpa's here."

Wally walked into the bathroom and said, "I wanted
to let you know, Marj is in the car, and we got married." Nancy still had the toothbrush in her mouth.
That was all he said, and then he patted Michael on
the head, the way he used to pat her on the head,
turned around, walked down the stairs, out to the car,
and drove away.

Wally was twenty-three years older than Marjorie.
He didn't have money. What would she want with
him? And, what would he want with Marj? Nancy

could not imagine her father being physically attracted to Marjorie. She couldn't imagine anyone being attracted to Marjorie. In her mind, she was dumpy, loud, and abrasive. The whole idea seemed impossible.

Marjorie and Wally were married in Valley City, North Dakota, on August 7, 1981. He was seventy-two years old, and she was forty-nine. When she applied for the marriage license, Marjorie was still legally married to Roger, and he was still serving time in Stillwater State Prison. She identified herself as Marjorie LeRoy and produced her divorce papers from Dick LeRoy in 1971. She listed him as her only previous husband.

After word got out that Marjorie had remarried, North Dakota officials charged her with bigamy. But in order to prosecute her, she would have to be extradited to North Dakota. It was too expensive. If she ever returned to North Dakota, though, she could be prosecuted as long as the complaint remained on file. Ron Meshbesher thought that was pretty funny. He said "You can never set foot in North Dakota? Yes, Marji, that would be a fate worse than death!"

She may have thought that since she was done with Roger, their marriage didn't count, like calories that don't count if you eat standing up. He was in jail so what difference did it make? Roger did not press charges. He probably thought the same thing. What difference did it make?

Part IV

"It was such a beautiful home."

❦ *Chapter Twenty-Four*

In March of 1982, Wally and Marjorie attended the Minneapolis Shrine Circus. In his wallet, Wally carried a ruby, which he had purchased in Venezuela for $500 twenty-five years ago. Somehow, in the midst of the circus, the stone must have fallen out of his wallet.

Just before the circus outing, he had taken the ruby to the Minnesota Independent Jewelry Appraisal Company in Minneapolis. The appraiser wrote a vague description of the stone and valued it at $16,000. Then, Wally insured the stone for that amount from North Star Mutual Insurance Company located in Cottonwood, a small town in southwestern Minnesota.

After Wally lost the ruby, the insurance adjuster for the First Adjustment and Survey Company received numerous calls from people who said they represented Wally Hagen wanting to know when the Hagens would receive their money. These calls raised a red flag to the adjuster. Then Marjorie called and said that she and her husband needed that money for a real estate investment. The adjuster held up the payment as long as he could, but in May 1982, he ended up settling with the Hagens for $10,000 for the lost ruby.

Marjorie and Wally decided to move to Mound, Minnesota, the same small town in which Helen and Wally had raised their family. The town is situated on Lake Minnetonka, one of the most affluent areas of Minnesota—Lake Minnetonka, that is, not Mound, which was a broken-down town in those days, a ghost town trying to come back to life. Main Street was cluttered with old brick storefronts dating back to the '50s and '60s. Mound was an off-the-lake, blue collar neighborhood.

As usual, Marjorie was broke. She found a house that she wanted to buy on Lynwood Boulevard, a red house, which she called the Cranberry House. The price was $59,000. The $8,000 down payment came from the insurance money from the "lost" ruby, and a bank loan provided $14,000. The original sellers helped them finance the house by giving them a $37,000 contract for the deed. The Hagens would have to pay them back on January 15, 1983, just a year away.

Marjorie nested, painted decals on the cabinets and curtain valances, and made needlepoint pillows for the sofas. If they really stretched their necks and stood on a chair in their living room, Marjorie and Wally could see a dot of beautiful, shimmering Lake Minnetonka two blocks away, literally on the other side of the railroad tracks where a Great Northern roared through every afternoon at 1:00. This was not the Glensheen Mansion perched above Lake Superior. Marjorie had apparently adjusted to living on the "edge" of affluence.

The due date for the contract for deed approached, and the Hagens still did not have the money. Marjorie had a solution. If they could sell the Cranberry House, she could get the $37,000 to pay off the debt. They sold the house to Randy and Janet Larson* for $89,000, a $30,000 profit in just one year. Marjorie explained that the reason she wanted to move from the Cranberry House was because Wally was ill—a heart aneurysm. They had already purchased another house on Phelps Road, about a mile away, that had a first-floor bedroom so Wally wouldn't have to maneuver stairs.

The Larsons agreed to purchase the property for $89,000 on the following terms: They would give the Hagens $15,000 cash; assume the bank mortgage of $14,000; assume the contract for deed that Hagens had with the original owners, now down to $36,000; and give the Hagens a new contract for deed for $24,000. The Larsons would be obligated to pay two contracts for deed totaling $60,000.

The closing date was scheduled for September 1, but they agreed that the Larsons would not move in until September 15 because the Hagens said they wanted to do a thorough cleaning of the house. Wally wanted to do some rewiring, even though the Larsons assured them that that was not necessary. They had other obligations, though, and did not mind delaying the moving date for a couple of weeks.

Since the Hagens had moved out, the Larsons periodically checked up on their new house. On September 4, they drove to the Cranberry House and noticed that the Hagens had left the dining room window opened. They worried that the Hagens had been careless about the security of the house. But that was not their only concern.

Now that the house was vacant, they saw huge water stains on the floors where the plants had been. Without telling the Larsons, the Hagens had refinished some of the wooden floors, varnishing right over water stains, rough spots, and even dirt. They'd used a high gloss varnish, instead of the matte finish that was on the rest of the floors. They had not bothered to sand the floors first, or between coats. It was "an atrocious job."

When the Larsons went back to the house on September 12, they noticed a pungent odor in the kitchen. They couldn't figure out what it was, but it smelled like chemicals. They thought it was coming from a wall-to-wall kitchen rug that Marjorie had told them she would shampoo. They hoped that no one would smoke in there before they got rid of it. When they went upstairs, they saw that the Hagens had now varnished the hall and the back bedroom with the same high gloss varnish, over stains and dirt, just as they had done on the first floor. They applied the varnish only six inches into another bedroom and stopped. It was thick, and all the brush strokes were visible. The Larsons were appalled. The back bedroom window was stuck open, and Janet couldn't budge it. The moving-in date approached, and they were worried. When they left the house that day, they made sure that all the doors were locked. When they got home, they called their realtor and told him to tell the Hagens not to do any more work on the house. And, they wanted the keys.

Wally gave the Larsons two house keys and a key to the padlock for the garage on September 14, the day before they were supposed to move in. He assured them that these were the only keys to the property. For some reason, the Larsons, who were upset about the shoddy work that had been done on their house, agreed to go out to dinner with Marjorie and Wally. Originally, Marjorie had set the dinner date for the 15th, but at the last minute, she changed it to the 14th, the night before the Larsons were to move in.

They all met at the Cranberry House. Randy and Janet noticed that the Hagens had a brand new black pickup truck. Wally said they had traded in their compact Chevy. He also mentioned that they'd bought an Airstream trailer. He did not say that the $15,000 check that they had received from the Larsons had paid for these toys.

When Randy and Janet walked into the house, it was obvious that someone had been there since the day they'd discovered the varnished floors. Some of the mess had been cleaned up. Paint cans that had not been there before were lined up against a wall. Also, the sticky windows had been closed. The house still smelled like chemicals. When the four of them left for dinner, Randy was the last one out of the house. He checked to make sure everything was secured, and he personally locked the front door.

The Larsons were dismayed about the condition of the house and thought they might approach the subject over dinner. They intended to ask the Hagens why they had varnished the floors and the windows. They wanted to ask Wally if he had actually rewired the house, and if so, why, when he was moving anyway? They went to a restaurant called the Ox Yoke, a little bar that served hamburgers. The couples did not ride together, but took their own cars. Marjorie had errands to do after dinner, she said.

Marjorie dominated the whole conversation, and seemed nervous. Janet and Randy were intimidated by her and decided it wouldn't be a good idea to broach the subject of the "work" they'd done. It might be better to leave it alone and just repair the damage after they moved in. They left the bar after one hour. They drove back to the Cranberry House, in their respective cars. The Larsons said goodnight in the driveway and the Hagens set out "to do errands." A short time later, the Larsons saw the Hagens heading back toward the Cranberry House.

The next day, at 6:30 a.m., a neighbor, Harold Pierson*, was driving down Lynwood Boulevard on his way to work when he noticed smoke billowing out of the trees.

"It was damp and rainy, I remember, and I thought, gee, that's kind of funny that somebody would be burning leaves this time in the morning."

He looked over and saw a house on fire. Pierson and his riding companion stopped the car and ran up to the house and pounded on the door, thinking that the residents must be asleep. The house was burning so quickly that he thought if anyone was in there, they would be overcome with smoke—or dead. The front door was locked and he was about to kick it in when he noticed a light on at the next door neighbor's house and ran over there and told them to call the fire department.

"Do you know if there is anyone in there?" Pierson asked.

"No," said the neighbor, "the house has been sold and it's empty."

"The house was an older home, narrow frame, red with white trim," he later told the investigators. "It was up on a little bit of a hill and it sat quite a way back from the road. There was a long driveway going up to the garage of the house, but I didn't see any cars. The flames were starting to come out of the top by the upstairs window and I could hear a little bit of glass falling out of the window as I was pounding on the door. I remember that the smoke was sort of a bluish gray."

The fire department arrived at the scene at about 6:42 a.m. Because the doors were locked, they forced their way in. By that time, flames were shooting through the roof. The fire was burning at an unusually rapid pace, considering that there was no furniture in the house. It would take the firefighters five hours to extinguish the fire.

Low burn and fire damage had occurred to the floor and floor joists. This burn followed up alongside the chimney, which was located in the center of the house. The burn pattern extended to the paneled walls on both sides of the chimney and to the bookshelves. On the second floor was a hallway, bathroom, a hall closet, and a master bedroom. This is where there was the most damage. The fire traveled vertically to the attic area and vented itself through the roof. A fire must have been started on the second floor at about the same time the fire on the first floor was ignited. On the second floor, there was deep charring and alligatoring, which is a burn pattern that indicates the presence of a flammable liquid poured on the floor. It turned out to be gasoline. There were no electrical defects that could have caused the fire.

Pat Shannon of the Minnesota Bureau of Criminal Apprehension was assigned to assist the assistant state fire marshal, James Hellerud, in the fire investigation. Shannon and Hellerud determined that there may have been two possible sources of the fire—one being close to the fireplace on the first floor, where they saw wires running up the wall adjacent to the fireplace. There were old wadded-up newspapers next to those wires, shoved up in the floor joist area at the base of the chimney. They said there was no logical explanation for newspapers to be placed there.

Janet Larson's sister, who lived near the Cranberry House, called her to tell her that the house was on fire. She said it was bad. Janet and Randy drove to the house as fast as they could. They got there at about 9:30 a.m. and saw that the four walls of the house, which was built around 1950, were still standing, but the majority of the house had burnt. It was gutted. They went to Janet's sister's house at 10:30 and stayed for a couple of hours.

They decided that they should go tell the Hagens what had happened. They were worried that a shock like this would be terrible for Wally with his heart condition. The Larsons drove to the Hagens' house on Phelps Road, but nobody was home. From there, they went home. They reached Wally by phone at 6:00 p.m. He told them he already knew about the fire and how sorry he was for them. Wally said that a friend had told him that the Cranberry House was on fire. He said that he had driven out to the scene that morning, apparently before the Larsons had arrived. He seemed distressed.

Another neighbor told the investigators, "On the day of the fire, at about 8:20 a.m., I was crossing the street to take my daughter to the bus stop. Before I crossed, a black pickup drove up with the window down. It was Marjorie. She asked me if I knew what was going on down there. She was very calm, but I noticed that her eyes kept shifting back and forth. I didn't know if she recognized me, so I said, 'The red house is burning.' When she didn't seem alarmed, I repeated, 'Well, your house is burning.'"

Marjorie said, "It isn't our house, we sold it. We moved out two weeks ago."

With her history of arson, Marjorie was an immediate suspect. On September 27, Shannon and Hellerud went to the Hagens' home on Phelps Road. Marjorie and Wally were in the driveway and invited them to come in. They all sat down and Shannon asked some questions about the wiring of the Cranberry House.

Marjorie said, "My husband is a master electrician, and he had just rewired the majority of the house."

"I heard about the fire on the morning of the 15th," said Wally. "An alderman friend of mine told me. I couldn't reach Marjorie till around noon and that's when I told her."

"I was shocked! I told him he was kidding. It was such a beautiful home," she exclaimed. "Wally and I put so much work into it, and it made us sick to see it all destroyed by a senseless fire."

Marjorie told Hellerud that on the day of the fire she was in Osseo, Minnesota, and knew *nothing* about it until she got home and her husband told her what had happened. She also said that on the evening before the fire, September 14, she and Wally had gone out to dinner with the Larsons. The Hagens told Hellerud that on that evening, they had given the house keys, *all of them,* to the Larsons.

Much to Marjorie's dismay, Ray DiPrima, an agent from the Minnesota Bureau of Criminal Apprehension (BCA) who had investigated the fire at Marine-on-St. Croix, was assigned to the case with Shannon. DiPrima, tall, lean, and balding, with sparkling brown eyes and a dark brown mustache, was married to a beautiful Chilean woman. He was a devoted father who spent as much time as possible with his two school-age boys. In his spare time, which was a rare commodity, he played tennis and golf, and enjoyed cooking and entertaining in his home. But his first love was his work. Ray was a problem solver. He was thorough. Interviewing suspects was his particular talent, which was why he was called to assist on this case. He knew what questions to ask and how to ask them, like Columbo, "Oh, just one more question, Ma'am." Ray DiPrima would be Marjorie's nemesis.

On October 5, DiPrima spoke with an agent from American Life Casualty Company and found out that Marjorie had called him several times after the fire to learn about insurance company protocol, the fire loss investigation, and claim and payment. She demanded to know whom the insurance company would pay for the fire loss, the Hagens or the Larsons? The Larsons had obtained insurance coverage on the house for $70,000. She also informed the agent that she and Wally had been planning a trip to Florida.

When the Larsons heard that Marjorie Hagen was a suspect, they thought of all the obvious clues that had never occurred to them prior to the fire. The chemical odor, the varnished floors, windows that were stuck open. Varnish is flammable, and fire needs air. Also, since the Hagens had already moved, what reason did they have to keep the Larsons from moving in on the closing date? None of that made sense. Had Wally actually rewired the house or was that another ploy to make the investigators think that the house had faulty wiring?

In the end, the $70,000 insurance money was not enough to pay everyone. The original owners and the Larsons would get their money before the Hagens. And because Marjorie and Wally's $24,000 contract for deed was the last to be paid, they took an $8,000 discount, but still received $16,000. Additionally, the Hagens had received $15,000 cash for a total of $31,000 on their original $8,000 down payment—insurance proceeds from the lost ruby.

❧ *Chapter Twenty-Five*

On October 6, 1982, Agents DiPrima and Shannon knocked on the Hagens' door armed with a police search warrant to seize "All business and financial records for Wallace and Marjorie Hagen, also known as Marjorie LeRoy, Marjorie Caldwell, and Marjorie Congdon; including but not limited to purchase agreements, work papers, financial statements, correspondence, insurance records, canceled checks, loan agreements, promissory notes or any other real estate documentation as they relate to 5850 Lynwood Blvd., Mound, Minnesota."

Trying to begin with good will, the investigators reintroduced themselves at the door. "It's good to see ya, Wally. Remember me? I'm Pat Shannon."

"And I'm the guy who's madder 'n hell," retorted Wally. He was wearing a three-fourths–length green plaid nightdress and a matching Rip Van Winkle hat with a long tassel. He had a long white beard and white hair. DiPrima would later describe him as Marjorie's LL Bean man, outfitted, tall, good-looking, distinguished. He called Marjorie the "Woolworth Lady." He described her thusly: "No class, tacky, five feet, two inches, weighing about 160 pounds, with short, dark hair, turning gray. She always wore baggy clothes, as if she could conceal her torpedo shape." He described her voice as shrill and screaming.

"When she was mad, it was scary."

DiPrima moved forward. "My name is Ray DiPrima."

"What are you boys doing here? You get me all upset when you start pickin' on my wife."

DiPrima explained to him that they wanted to close the case, and asked if they could talk inside.

Wally stepped aside, and they followed him into the living room. There was no place to sit down. The gold plaid couch was cluttered with needlepoint pillows, all sizes and all colors. There were two avocado green chairs on either side of the television. One had a needlepoint canvas on the seat with different colored yarns strewn over the arm, and the other one was stacked with newspapers. The television was blaring, and DiPrima took it upon himself to walk over and turn down the volume. The only sound, now, was the loud ticking of an old grandfather clock, which reached almost to the ceiling in the dining room. There was a rolltop desk on the opposite wall, which DiPrima noted would probably be a good place to start the search. Wally didn't make any attempt to offer the detectives a chair, so they stood there and began with their questions, the most obvious one first.

"Is Marjorie here, Wally?"

"No, she's not."

"Will she be back in a little while?"

"That, I couldn't say. She took off for her quilter's group. Look, I don't know what you're going to ask, but you probably know Marjorie's history."

"Well, to some extent, yeah, we know who she is."

"Yeah, and she's very sensitive."

"Well, we're lookin' at a fire here, sir. One thing I'd like to know is, how many keys were there for that place, do you know?"

"There were three."

"Three."

"Marjorie had one, I had one, and her son, Rick, had one."

"Okay, so the night before the fire, you went out with the Larsons, the people that bought the house from you, right?"

"Yep."

"And then did you all go back to the Cranberry House?"

"Yeah, I had a box to pick up there."

"Did you look at both the doors to make sure they were locked before you left?"

"I didn't check 'em, but I assume they were because the firemen had to break the windows on 'em in order to get in."

"Wally, you're sure that there were only three keys?"

"I'm sure of that, yeah. No, I beg your pardon, there were four keys. We gave one to the milkman."

Wally assured them that he had personally turned all the keys over to the Larsons. Because of that, Marjorie could not possibly have had a way to enter that house. They asked Wally what time he got up the morning of the fire. He said that he arose around 7:30 a.m. as always. Marjorie always made him breakfast before she took off for her various activities, he said. "She never leaves without fixin' breakfast for me."

"So, Wally, do you know of any reason your wife would be out and about the morning of the fire?"

"No, she was here. I'll tell ya what, I think she was here till almost 8:30. She doesn't have to be to her quilter's meeting until about 9:30. There's about six of 'em, you know. They charge people to do their quilting and then they turn that money over to a battered women's group or something like that. It's all charity," he bragged.

Just then, Marjorie walked in the front door.

"Hello, Marjorie," said DiPrima.

"I don't care to have you in my house. You get out. I mean it. You come back here with a court order that's signed. I want ya out."

"Well, we . . . "

"Leave!" She had a large bag of quilting paraphernalia.

"Marjorie, we want to close this investigation today, and if we could ask you one question, we could get this over with."

"One, you have no right to call me by my first name." She dropped her quilting gear on the floor, in front of the television, and then she whipped off her windbreaker and threw it on top of the bag.

"I'm sorry, Marjorie, but I have a search warrant here."

"Fine, then you talk to my husband about it. I don't want anything to do with you. Your behavior has been inexcusable."

He gave her his patient smile. "We just have to ask one final question, Marj, and we could wrap this thing up. You wanta settle the thing up with the insurance company?"

"I don't settle with the insurance company. I had a

contract. What do you want?"

"We just want to know where you were that morning."

And so, Marjorie expounded on how she was home in bed with her husband as Wally leaned on the door, listening. She told them about her quilting bee, corroborating his story, exactly. She said that she did not drive by the Cranberry House on the way to her quilting bee because she had to drop off a book at the library. Marjorie's old alibi. She had used that in her murder trial, too, when she was explaining her whereabouts on the weekend her mother was murdered. DiPrima noticed an old oak bookcase on the living room wall that was full of paperback books. He recognized some of the authors, Sheldon, Ludlum, Rule. There were stacks of *True Crime Magazine* on the bottom shelf.

DiPrima explained to the Hagens that he and his partner were about to search their house. Marjorie told DiPrima and Shannon that they would not be out of her sight.

"Just what are you looking for?" she demanded.

"We're looking for all financial documents for Marjorie Congdon, LeRoy, Caldwell, Hagen," said DiPrima, "as they relate to any type of transaction for the sale of that particular house."

"They are at the realtor's office. They aren't here."

"Okay. And you say you were asleep here all night before the fire, right?"

"I was here. You can ask my husband."

"Okay, so you went to the library. You didn't realize there was any fire or commotion or what have you?"

"No. You couldn't see any fire. I came down the back way and some gal said that the road was blocked off with water trucks. I wasn't anywhere near that. I just went on to my quilting bee."

"Marjorie," said DiPrima, "tell me, how many keys

were there to that residence?"

"I think I had one, you had one, and Rick had one," she said, looking at Wally.

"What's that?" asked Wally. He was a little deaf.

"Keys," she said.

"And the milkman," said Wally.

"The milkman? That's right, yeah, that's right."

Then, Wally explained to the detectives that he had turned all the keys over to the Larsons. He said that he had heard about the fire from a neighbor.

"We went over, drove by, and said, 'it doesn't look too bad.' This was before they boarded it up or anything. Then we walked up, there was a whole bunch of neighbors around, and we looked at it. Then we saw that it was worse than we had thought."

"Let me ask you, Marjorie," said DiPrima, "This can only help you two. Ah, financially are you in what I would call a precarious situation?"

"No."

"Are you pretty stable financially?"

"We have bills."

"So you're not financially strapped?"

"Well, we're not rolling in money, but we're comfortable. We can make it."

"Uh huh. Marjorie, did you go out on September 14 and buy some gas?"

"God, I could've. I don't know. I probably did."

"Mmm hmm. And did you buy gas and put it in a can or did you buy gas and put it in the car?"

"If I bought it, I would have put it in the truck. We don't even have a gas can."

"Yes, we have a gas can," said Wally.

"We do?"

"Yeah."

"Where? Oh, yeah, for your moped."

"Uh huh." DiPrima and Shannon exchanged looks,

trying not to smile. It was just too graphic, imagining seventy-four-year-old Wally wearing this Rip Van Winkle get-up speeding down the street on a moped.

"Anyway, I was with Wally that whole day before the fire."

"Marjorie, when you sign real estate documents and say that you're husband and wife, and you have it notarized, is that accurate to say that you're husband and wife?"

Wally answered, "Yeah, that's accurate."

"So, your other marriage to Caldwell was dissolved."

"That's right," Marjorie lied.

DiPrima asked Wally if Marjorie had seemed upset the morning of the fire. Did she smell of gasoline? Was there gasoline on her fingers? Does your wife ever talk about arson? Had she ever mentioned any other fires that she'd had? Wally answered no to everything. DiPrima asked him if he had been upset that morning to wake up and discover that his wife was gone. Wally dutifully repeated to DiPrima that his wife was there all the time. He was not about to be tricked. Marjorie accused DiPrima of twisting the truth.

DiPrima said, "I think that as we go through here, we're gonna find out that you people are flat busted. That you don't have any money. That you could never even live up to the standards that you lived before. Never in a thousand years."

"I made no pretense to live up to the standards that we lived up to before," she said. "We live comfortably."

"And it hurts, doesn't it?"

"No, it doesn't. I'm happier than I've ever been in my whole life."

"Are you?"

"I've never been so happy or so contented." She gave him a confident smile.

"Mmm hmm. Why is it then, Marjorie, that so many

of your houses end up burning to the ground or having considerable fire damage?"

"I don't know."

"Right."

Marjorie changed the subject. "Wally has lived in
this area for forty-seven years."

"Mmm hmm."

"You talk to people who know him. He's not gonna
tell you something that isn't so. And I'll tell you something. Anybody that represents the state government,
that deliberately forges a man's fingerprint in a trial,
deliberately lies and cheats . . ."

"That's neither here nor there," said DiPrima.

"Oh, yes, it is. Oh, yes, it is," she said. "I would not
put it past that same group to have deliberately set a
fire."

"I see. So you're thinking that ah, the State now,
this mighty . . ."

"No. I'm not saying the State. I'm just saying that I
wouldn't put it past anybody who decided they wanted
to frame me to do it. Just the way you are trying."

DiPrima asked her if she were taking any medication or if she was under psychiatric care. She didn't
lose her temper, as he expected, but calmly answered
'No' to both questions.

"Okay. Well, I guess we'll get on with the search
here."

Marjorie went into the kitchen and called Ron Meshbesher. DiPrima heard her ask for him but it didn't
sound as if her attorney was available. She stomped
back into the living room, though, with confidence, as
if she had just gotten a big boost.

"Remember, I know that you can only take what is
physically listed on the search warrant, and I want an
itemized list of everything you take," warned Marjorie.

She watched as DiPrima went through some keys.

"Say, Ray, you can check that key against, uh, the Ford key that's on my key ring, if you want to bring it back, and it should match one of those."

"I think we just went through all that," said DiPrima. "We will give you an itemized list of everything we take."

He walked over to the dining room and opened the rolltop desk. He started going through stacks of loose papers, receipts, old checks, needlepoint patterns, all mixed together. He came upon the Hagens' marriage certificate, and before he could get a good look at it, Marjorie grabbed it out of his hands.

He looked over at his partner. "I think we've got a problem here. Marjorie, uh, has taken her marriage certificate and put it down her pants."

"Hey, have you got eyes on the back of your head or what?" She glared at him defiantly. "I've spoken with my attorney."

DiPrima shook his head and said to Shannon, "She's refusing to give it to us. She has spoken with her attorney."

"My attorney says it is not listed on the search warrant. Unless it is specifically listed, he said that I do not have to give it to you. And he said to make no statements, no statements!" With that, she reached in and pulled the marriage certificate out of her pants.

"We'll take a look at that," said Shannon. "Make sure it's a marriage certificate and that there's no financial writings on it, whatsoever. Will you do that?"

"You want me to do that?" asked DiPrima, grinning.

Marjorie glared at them. "I will give it to you on one condition: That you give me your word of honor."

"He can't," said Shannon.

"That you will not reveal the state that licensed it," she said.

"Well, the only problem there is that if they subpoena

me I'd have to."

"All right, then I won't show it to you."

"Well, he can't promise," said Shannon. "Just hold your hand over the state while we look at it."

"Okay, I'll do that. That's no problem." She held it up with her hand covering the bottom half. Visible was Marjorie's age of forty-nine and Wally's age of seventy-two. The date of marriage was August 7, 1981.

DiPrima and Shannon glanced at each other, shook their heads, and then went back to the keys. Shannon took a key off the ring and asked Wally what it was for. Wally told him he didn't know, but it might be for a door. Shannon shook his head again.

Ray flipped through the keys as Marjorie watched with trepidation.

"Hey, Marj, what are all these keys for? Let's see here, what haven't we gone through here? Uh, those and those and . . . all these here."

Now Shannon was pulling some ledger-type books out of the desk drawer.

"Wait just a minute," Marjorie spitted, looking at Shannon, "What are you doing with those books?" She tried to grab them from his hand.

"Give me those!"

"I'll decide what we'll take, okay?" He told her to sit down and relax. Her eyes scanned the room and she said, "God, what a mess," as if she were used to a neat and orderly house.

"I'm finished with these books," Shannon said to DiPrima. He went back to the keys and started to flip through them.

"Give me those!"

"I can't believe how many keys you've got, Marjorie. She must have access to everything in the world out there," Shannon said to DiPrima.

Marjorie got up and stalked out of the room.

"Marjorie," yelled Shannon, "come back and sit in your seat. This will go a lot faster if you'll just cooperate." Then to DiPrima, "Now she's in the fuckin' kitchen. She's probably getting a knife. What do you wanna bet, she's going to come out here and stab us?"

"I wouldn't take that bet," said DiPrima.

She appeared in the kitchen doorway. "How do I know that you haven't taken stuff and hidden it? Huh? How do I know that?"

"Well, I'll do an inventory of what we've got right now," said DiPrima.

"Sure, of what you want us to see," she said. "I'm going to call my attorney."

"Again? Come on Marjorie, I'll show you what we've taken."

He followed her into the kitchen. The walls were painted a light yellow with stenciled flowers on either side of the wooden chair rails. A multicolored rag-rug was in front of the sink. The countertops were cluttered with canisters of coffee, flour, sugar, and a dusty pothos plant. Stuff everywhere.

"No. I have no way of knowing that what you say you're taking is all you're taking, so forget it."

"Sure, well that's your opinion," said DiPrima, "but I'd advise you to look at this list."

She grabbed it from his hand.

He explained to her that everything they were taking was already on the kitchen table. He assured her that he would dictate the items into his tape recorder, have the list typed out and a copy sent to her. He told her he'd even send a copy to Mr. Meshbesher.

Marjorie fumed. She said that she had just called Mr. Meshbesher and that he told her not to listen to them. He told her not to accept their "listings."

Shannon told her that she and Wally were welcome to watch them do their inventory. Wally had been leaning against the wall the whole time as if he were only a casual observer. DiPrima decided to start a conversation with Wally.

"How long have you been married? About a year and a half?"

"About."

"How many children do you have, Wally?"

"Three."

"Three, huh? How many does Marjorie have?"

"Seven."

"Seven, geez, really?"

"Does Marjorie see her children very often?"

"No. One boy is all."

"Oh, is he the one that lives in the basement down there? Rick, is that his name?"

"Yeah."

Shannon poked his head back in the living room. "Okay, I've got a list."

"Okay, let's wrap it up, now."

"Hey," said Wally, "I just want you to know that I've gotta be somewhere in thirty minutes."

"Right, we're almost done."

"Do you have any life insurance, Wally?"

"No."

"Not a dime, huh?"

"No."

"I can tell ya one thing. I'm not gonna leave anything for anybody," said Wally, defiantly. "I'll take it with me to the grave."

"That's too bad, Wally."

"Those kids took everything I had. Took me to the cleaners, all right. Left me with $18,000 after I worked for forty some years."

"Your kids don't contact you or anything?"

"No."

"I'm sorry."

DiPrima and Shannon finished the inventory and came up with shopping bags full of unpaid bills, and NSF checks. They also had a ring of keys, plus an extra one that they found in the cabinet above the stove. Just then, they saw Marjorie stuff a key down her pants.

"Oh, no. Give it up Marjorie."

She must have been worn out because she reluctantly pulled it out of her pants and slammed the key into Shannon's hand.

Marjorie glared at Pat Shannon. She stalked up to him, put her face close to his—spit actually flew out of her mouth and hit his glasses—"I hope that on the way home today, someone cuts your brake lines, that you go off a cliff, and burn a fiery death!"

As the two detectives walked back to their car, Ray said, "Hey, Pat, I think she's mad at you."

"No kidding."

"Is this your first arson case?"

"No, I had one a few years ago, but that was different. Some kid. Only way he could get it up was by setting fires and watching buildings burn to the ground. They put him in some juvenile detention center. I'm sure he's out now, doing it again. It got my curiosity up so I read a book about pyromaniacs. Did you know that women only account for 10 to 15 percent of firesetters?"

"So, how does Marjorie fit in?"

"Part man? Ha, ha. Money seems to be what motivates her. And control."

"Yeah, you're right. I'll bet she's started more fires than we'll ever know about."

"You're probably right."

When Ray DiPrima informed Nancy Hagen about the interview with Marjorie and Wally, she was incensed. What did he mean by telling them that his children had taken him to the cleaners? It was a low blow after all she'd done to help him. After her mother's funeral, she found out that her dad had told her brothers that she had run up thousands of dollars on charge accounts and stuck him with the bill. Why would he lie? Marjorie's modus operandi seemed to be Divide and Conquer.

Sure enough, the key DiPrima and Shannon confiscated belonged to the Cranberry House. Why did Marjorie keep the extra key? DiPrima wondered. Did she forget to throw it away? Perhaps she thought she was one step ahead of everyone else, smarter and craftier. Or maybe it was a game with her. But she had underestimated him. Ray DiPrima knew that they would not be able to prosecute her without evidence "in hand." She had to have possession of the insurance check. And so, they waited. In the meantime, the Larson's attorney told DiPrima that the Hagens had pressured Randy and Janet to get the insurance settlement because they were planning a trip to Florida.

Finally, on January 14, 1983, DiPrima was informed that American Family Insurance Company had paid. Marjorie and Wally received the check from the Meshbesher Law Firm's Trust Account that day. This was the evidence DiPrima was waiting for—the Hagens' profits for defrauding the insurance company and for burning their house down. An investigator had watched their every move. The Hagens' Airstream trailer was parked in a vacant lot on the corner of Afton Road and Brighton Boulevard, about one mile from their house on Phelps Road in Mound. That same afternoon, Marjorie and Wally were seen packing their 1982 black pickup with clothing which they'd removed from their home and transporting it to their trailer. They were going to run.

❧ *Chapter Twenty-Six*

Once DiPrima knew that the Hagens had received their money, he had to work fast. On January 15, 1983, at 11:00 p.m., he went to Judge Harold Kalina's house and had him sign four search warrants. The warrants included the Hagens' house on Phelps Road, a 1982 Chevrolet pickup, a 1978 Chevrolet van, and a twenty-foot Airstream trailer. The chief of the Mound Police Department was notified that these warrants would be executed the next morning, January 16. The warrants listed, among other things, the insurance check and gave permission to search "her person" for further evidence. One of the Hagens' neighbors in Mound had been helping the BCA on the case. The Hagens had told that neighbor they were planning to leave the state.

At 7:55 a.m., BCA agents, DiPrima, Shannon, Kohout, and Mound police officers knocked on the Hagens' door. They did not have a "no-knock" search warrant, which would allow the officers to blast down the door if need be. They depended on the element of surprise. Wally opened the door and was handed his copy of the search warrant for the house. Marjorie was getting out of bed. Agent Kohout informed Marjorie that she was under arrest for second-degree arson and for defrauding an insurance company. Agent Shannon read her her Miranda rights. Wally called Ron Meshbesher and told him that Marjorie was being arrested, and was enroute to the Hennepin County Jail.

Nothing listed on the search warrant was found in Marjorie's purse. DiPrima opened Wally's billfold and immediately found a check made out on the Meshbesher, Singer, Spence, Ltd. Trust Account, dated January 14, 1983, in the amount of $16,615.79. Bingo. DiPrima told Wally that they were taking that check because it "constituted fruits of the crime."

They found a plastic container of Carpet Magic cleaner and two cans of Rez varnish and sealer in the basement. Wally denied varnishing any of the floors. He said he had cleaned the kitchen rug. The container was three-fourths empty. Wally made them all a pot of coffee and started to chat with the agents. He told DiPrima that his deceased wife had been a good friend of Marjorie's and that after Elisabeth Congdon had died in Duluth, Marjorie had come to his wife asking for help. Wally said that Marjorie was so broke that she didn't have money to feed "her kid," and that he and his wife had helped her out.

He explained that the night before, after dinner with the Larsons, they did not go back into the Cranberry House. Wally said that he went to bed that night and slept until 2:00 a.m., when he got up to go to the bathroom. Marjorie was asleep, he said, and did not wake up until 7:00 a.m.

Wally told them that he never left his house to go look at the fire. He just stayed there all morning waiting for Marjorie to return from her quilting bee. Then, he said, they drove over to look at the burned house together.

DiPrima asked Wally if he or Marjorie had had previous fire losses. Wally said that he knew that Marjorie had had a fire in a garage on Fremont Avenue, but that her kids had set that fire. He said that Marjorie had told him that she had had a farm that burned down at Marine-on-St. Croix, but that she was in Colorado at the time of the fire. Marjorie blamed the Marquette Bank for failing to make the insurance premium payment on that insurance policy and claimed that she lost over $200,000 because of it.

At 10:37 a.m., Wally, two agents, and one police officer proceeded to the Airstream trailer. Wally was now served a copy of this search warrant. They found correspondence from American Family Insurance and Wally's union statement from the International Brotherhood of Electrical Workers. They thanked Wally and proceeded back to the house, where they arrested Marjorie and took her to the Hennepin County jail where she was booked for second-degree arson and for defrauding an insurance company.

The interviews and statements for Marjorie's trial began February 1983. Ray DiPrima interviewed some of Marjorie's children, both about the older arson charges and about the present. Heather LeRoy was twenty-four years old. Heather, Rebecca, and Rick had lived at the Homestead shortly before it burned down. Heather explained that her mother had decided to move to Colorado about two weeks before the fire. Her reason was to check Rick into an asthma clinic. Heather and Becky did not want to move because they were in school and didn't want to leave their friends, but Marjorie forced them to go. Heather said that her mother told everyone that Rick was dying, but it wasn't true. It was a hoax, she said.

Heather said she had never gotten along with her mother. She told of a fight that occurred between Rebecca and her mother when they were in Colorado. They were arguing over the car keys, and Marjorie ended up pinning Rebecca down on the floor with her hands around her neck. Marjorie was strangling her daughter. Heather had called the police, and they came, but nothing was done about it.

She said that her mother was telling everyone that she and Rebecca needed psychiatric help because they wanted their brother to die. At one point, Rebecca packed up one of their cars with their possessions and drove it back to Minneapolis. Then she returned to Denver intending to drive back to Minneapolis with Heather and her belongings. It was July 25, 1975. When the girls set out to leave, they discovered that Rick had let the air out of their tires. They abandoned the car and flew back to Minneapolis that night. They were terrified.

Heather then lived with her brother Stephen until she finished high school. After she graduated, she got her own apartment, worked as a secretary, and then joined the U.S. Army where she became fluent in German and was stationed in Germany for three years. At the time of Heather's interview, she had not seen her mother since Elisabeth's funeral in July 1977. Becky, twenty-five, was married and worked at Dayton's Department Store.

Peter, thirty years old, was interviewed that same day. He had worked for Warner Hardware as a warehouse man for ten years. He gave an update on his brothers and sisters.

Suzanne, twenty-eight, was a neonatal nurse at the University of Minnesota. Andy, twenty-seven, was married and studying mechanical engineering at the University of Minnesota. Rick was a student at Macalester College, studying to be an attorney. He said that his father, Dick LeRoy, was currently a limousine driver at the Metropolitan Airport.

Peter told DiPrima that before the fire at the Homestead his mother had come to his house asking for cash. She explained to him that she had several large traveler's checks that none of the banks would cash for her, and she needed $800. Against his better judgment, he had gone to the bank, got a certified check, and gave her the money in exchange for a personal check from her. The check was worthless. He had to submit it to the trust fund for collection. It took him three months to get his $800 back. He was irate.

Peter believed that at the time of that fire his mother was approximately $1 million in debt. He said that he had met Wally Hagen in 1982. He was vacationing at Swiftwater Farm with his family when Marjorie showed up with Wally. He saw Wally taking a dresser out of one of the guest cabins. He confronted him and told him to put it back. Then he called the Brule Sheriff's office. A deputy responded to the call and made the Hagens return all of the possessions that they had confiscated.

On February 11, Suzanne was interviewed. She claimed to know nothing about the Cranberry House fire. The last time that she had seen her mother was at her mother's trial, four years ago. She said that she had not talked to her since then and that she was "a little bit scared of her."

DiPrima asked her about the fire at the Homestead. Suzanne said that she had moved out of the guesthouse about a year before the fire. She visited the house a couple of days after the fire and noticed that the furniture from the main house had been moved to the guesthouse. There were "a lot of antiques, tables and chairs." Her silver trophies from horse competitions were there.

DiPrima asked her about any insurance claims that Marjorie may have made that were not true. Suzanne recalled that her mother had jewelry from her grandmother mixed in with her own. She thought that some of it might have been reported stolen. Suzanne did not want her address known and told DiPrima that if he needed to reach her, he could do so through her brother Peter.

Carroll B. Simmons, an antique dealer from Hastings, Minnesota, was questioned. Marjorie had been one of his customers since the days when she first got interested in eighteenth–century furniture. He said that she was an odd woman, and that she would buy something, not like it, and then sell it back. He told DiPrima that she had made several purchases from him just before the Homestead fire. Then she called him to come to the farm to appraise all of her household goods. This was just before she moved to Colorado. Marjorie's insurance agent called him and told him that the house had burned down. He went back to the Homestead and bought back some of the furniture that had not been destroyed. He had heard that the house was not insured.

On November 29, 1983, the day that jury selection began for Marjorie's arson trial, she took the witness stand to seek postponement of the trial until spring, saying she needed to be at home to care for her ailing, seventy-four-year-old husband. She said that Wally had been in the hospital for two weeks for heart tests and was on several medications, one of which caused dizziness and light-headedness. He had had heart surgery the previous spring.

She said they were living in a travel-trailer with no running water or sewer connection. Water to the trailer had been turned off because of the weather, and she had to haul water in five-gallon pails from a nearby building. She wouldn't get any of her inheritance until after the first of the year and had no money to hire someone to care for Wally or to send him to a warmer climate.

The judge said that he appreciated Marjorie's concern for her husband, but the court was not responsible for his care. She had been free without bond since her arrest one year ago.

On December 12, 1983, the arson trial began.

The prosecutor in this case was Dan Mabley. Mabley was in his thirties and had been a Dakota County prosecutor. He was handsome, debonair, and single. He was a sharp dresser who did not fit the stereotype of the rumpled prosecutor. Mabley had taught arson classes at the Bureau of Criminal Apprehension. He had a successful reputation for prosecuting arson cases. He was an artful orator—a legal actor who could hold a jury's attention.

Mabley had to prove that only someone with a key could get into the Cranberry House. The BCA had taken the door of the house to use as evidence in the trial. It would have been a dramatic moment and great visual prop to insert the key found in Marjorie's kitchen cabinet into the door's lock. However, one of the fire investigators had inadvertently thrown the door away and the prosecution was left with only testimonial evidence to prove their case. Mabley was up for the job.

Mabley associated with "match-heads," an insider's term for fire investigators and fire intellectuals. He was smart enough to want to learn from people who knew more than he did. He listened to expert witnesses, electrical engineers, Alcohol, Firearm Tobacco (ATF) agents, and cause and origin experts who attended his arson lectures. Ego did not get in Dan Mabley's way. It appeared that for once, Meshbesher was going to have some stiff competition. The trial was held in Minneapolis at the Hennepin County Courthouse.

Although Meshbesher objected, Mabley was allowed to introduce evidence from other cases to show a pattern of behavior. That evidence impressed the jury.

Wally was excused from appearing before the jury because he was ill. His deposition was video taped by Mabley in lieu of his live testimony. He stuck to his story that his wife was with him at the time of the fire. Marjorie sat next to Meshbesher during the trial, this time not so confident. It was obvious that Mabley had done his homework.

His arguments were carefully mapped out. The *opportunity* was there. Wally had admitted to getting up later than Marjorie had on the day of the fire. A witness saw Marjorie watching the fire from her truck—she had returned to the scene of the crime. It was only a seven-minute drive from her new house on Phelps Road to the Cranberry House. If the fire had occurred before the closing, the Larsons could have cancelled. The house was vacant during the two-week "holdover." The Larsons were to take possession the next day. They had insured the property. The Hagens had moved their belongings out of the house.

The *motive* was there. The Hagens were supposed to pay the "balloon" on January 15, 1983, and they didn't have the money. And, the Larsons would have to pay them immediately. No one but the Hagens had a motive.

The *means* were there. The house was locked securely on the 14th, and only a keyholder could enter. The house was still locked when the firefighters arrived, and only a keyholder could lock up when leaving. The only keyholders were the Larsons and Marjorie Hagen.

The *preparation* was there. Marjorie had changed dinner plans with the Larsons from the 15th to the 14th. She had sloppily varnished the floors at the last minute. The Hagens were still in the driveway of the Cranberry House when the Larsons pulled out the night of the 14th. They were later seen driving back toward the Cranberry House that same night.

Marjorie had made many false statements. She said that she had learned of the fire in the afternoon and that she was at her quilter's bee at the time. She said she was nowhere near the Cranberry House. She said she had turned all the keys over to the Larsons. She said she owned no gas cans. Her conduct was suspicious. She barely reacted when her neighbor told her that her house was on fire. She was supposed to have picked up another quilter friend that morning, but did not. She claimed to have returned a library book, but records showed that she did not have any books checked out. Wally did not contact her when he learned of the fire. Marjorie asked the insurance agent if the Larsons could rebuild, and when the insurance payment would come.

Mabley said the bank statements that had been removed from the Hagens' home showed Wally and Marjorie had a negative balance in their checking account in June, July, and August 1982, the period before the fire. Between June and September 1982, sixty-three checks for which there were insufficient funds were written.

To fight this onslaught of evidence, Meshbesher had to fall back on his "Marjorie Is Victim" technique. It had worked before. In his closing arguments, he explained that investigators had not suspected arson at the Cranberry House until they learned that Marjorie had owned the property. He stated that when the owner of the house was listed as Hagen, possible electrical problems were listed as the cause of the fire, but contended that when the investigators found out that Marjorie Hagen was Marjorie Caldwell Hagen, they shifted their investigation to arson.

"Most have heard her name," he said. "The finger of suspicion was pointed at her. Marjorie was picked on and the evidence was made to fit. This whole case stinks."

Even though expert witnesses for the defense and

the prosecution testified that gasoline was present in samples taken from the burned house, Meshbesher argued that their conclusions were not valid.

Marjorie spent her time at the trial sitting next to Meshbesher, her face buried in paperback murder mysteries. At one point, Marjorie disagreed with a witness's testimony, and Nancy Hagen, who was in the gallery, heard her mumble "Bullshit." Meshbesher was constantly putting his hand on Marjorie's arm as if that might control her. But after four weeks, it looked as though she was wearing even him out.

On January 13, 1984, after sixteen hours of deliberation, the jury of seven women and five men found Marjorie guilty of setting the Cranberry House on fire for the purpose of collecting insurance. While the verdict was being read, she sat with her arms folded, in an oversized gray sweater and blue galoshes, feet not quite touching the floor, staring at the court clerk. Meshbesher had failed her this time. He rubbed his eyes and looked down at the table.

The courtroom was packed. When the verdict was read, Nancy let out a sigh of relief. Marjorie turned and met her gaze, and Marjorie rasped under her breath, "I'll get you for this." Nancy had not been called to testify in the trial. She had not contributed to the verdict in any way. She was Wally's daughter. Nancy shrank back as if Marjorie might leap over the wooden railing and attack her, but right then, Meshbesher ushered his client out of the courtroom.

Outside the courtroom, hounded by press photographers, Marjorie's stoic composure melted away. Headed for the sanctuary of the probation office, walking as fast as she could, she tripped and fell. "He tripped me! You tripped me on purpose!" she bawled at a nearby photographer as she lay curled up on the floor. Her son Rick, with hair cropped just above his neckline, stretched out his forearm to block the photographer's view. "You fucking shit," he yelled. "Get the fuck out of here." Below, in the lobby, TV news camera crews and other assorted press jackals awaited their turn for the kill.

Marjorie's threat rang in Nancy's ears. What had she meant by "I'll get you for this?" Nancy was afraid that Meshbesher would get Marjorie out of sentencing. Stranger things had happened. Roger Caldwell's plea bargain came to mind. And if he didn't get her off altogether, what if Marjorie only got a light sentence? Or worse, some minor punishments like community service? Nancy hoped that Marjorie would go to jail for a long time, at least long enough to forget about those last words to her.

Ron Meshbesher promised the verdict would be appealed. Mabley was confident that the verdict would stand on appeal. Marjorie was allowed to remain free without bail while awaiting her sentencing. During this time, she and Wally lived in their Airstream trailer.

On February 9, 1984, Marjorie was sentenced to two and a half years in prison and fined $10,000 for her crime. She was now fifty-two years old. One of the issues in Meshbesher's appeal was whether the judge should have admitted the evidence of the two other fires since she was never charged. He stated that imprisonment was inappropriate and asserted that Marjorie presented no danger to the community and had no prior convictions.

In response, the judge described the crime as displaying sophistication and guile, and noted that it posed a risk to firefighters and cost an insurance company $70,000. Even so, Marj was allowed to go free on $50,000 bond until she was incarcerated. She left the courtroom this time looking like an aging Arabian queen, wearing large sunglasses and a white hood that covered her head and her forehead. Reporters surrounded her, and all she said was, "I am innocent."

On January 21, 1985, one year after her sentencing, the Minnesota Court of Appeals upheld Marjorie Caldwell Hagen's conviction and her two-and-a-half-year sentence for arson. The judge rejected all eight arguments made by Meshbesher saying, "It was not an overnight decision to torch a house and get insurance money. It was a long-term plan to conceal arrangements and benefit from complicated dealings." He went on to say that "Hagen was motivated by economic gain and caused significant damage to others." In spite of Meshbesher's objection, the appeals court agreed with the judge's decision to admit the evidence of the two other fires.

On January 25, 1985, Marjorie began serving her sentence in the Shakopee Women's Prison, in Shakopee, Minnesota. Although Meshbesher tried to get the judge to give her a ten-day extension so that she could make arrangements for Wally, the judge declined, saying, "This case has to come to an end sometime," and ordered that she be taken into custody immediately. Marjorie, wearing a parka and her now signature large-framed glasses, smiled for photographers as she was escorted into the prison.

The prison had just been renovated and was nicer than most college dormitories. State law required that each prisoner have a private room. The facility housed murderers, drug violators, thieves, and arsonists. Most of its residents had never lived in a home as fine as this institution. Not only did the prisoners have their own rooms, but they were furnished with trundle beds to accommodate their children on weekend visits. They were allowed TV sets and unlimited phone privileges. The prison was equipped with a gym where the inmates could exercise to Jane Fonda's workout, a three-lane bowling alley, and a heated pool. The library was equipped with all of the latest books, a craft room, and a computer room where the inmates could learn word processing. There was even a beauty parlor so that the women could get their hair done in red, burgundy, black—whatever they chose.

The inmates loved Marjorie. She started a quilting club, and taught the other women how to quilt and do needlework. She was housed in the newest, private wing of the prison. Marjorie was considered a model prisoner. Her sense of humor, her patience with the other prisoners, and her willingness to teach them made her very popular with the warden. That and the fact that she had flowers sent to the warden's office every week. Marjorie could afford to because she still collected money from her inheritance, even though she was in prison.

Wally lived in their Airstream trailer near the prison during Marjorie's term. The authorities believed that he—at the very least—knew that his wife had set the Cranberry House on fire. There were at least two reasons why the authorities decided not to prosecute him. He was old and did not have a previous record, and the investigators said that he had been brainwashed by Marjorie. They believed that he was a victim, and so there was no point in going after him. Prosecutors preferred to take on cases that they could win. He visited Marjorie regularly and waited for her release. He didn't have to wait long because Marjorie only served twenty months of her sentence. She was let out early for good behavior.

❧ *Chapter Twenty-Seven*

Ajo, Arizona, is an old, abandoned mining site, a collection of small stucco houses with cactus-filled yards sitting at the point where the desert flatness meets the mountain foothills. It is about 120 miles west of Tucson. It is surrounded by the Luke Air Force gunnery range to the north, the Papago Indian Reservation to the east, and Organ Pipe Cactus National Monument and the Mexican border to the south.

Overwhelming everything else, mountain and desert alike, is The Mine, as it's referred to in Ajo, a gaping, grayish white, open-pit copper mine one and a half miles wide. The town of Ajo grew along its rim the way many Minnesota towns developed along lakefront. It was The Mine that gave birth to Ajo and caused it to prosper in the early 1900s, thanks largely to Chester Congdon.

The town had 5,500 residents at its heyday, and sank to 2,500 after The Mine closed in 1985. Then, in a roundabout way, The Mine gave its town new life as the houses once rented to mine workers were offered for sale to the general public. "Retirement living at 1950s prices," advertised the sign outside of town. The houses, little boxes, some with copper roofs, sold for as little as $12,000. Senior citizens flocked to town, pushing the population back up to 3,500 in the summer and 4,500 in the winter.

This is also the town Marjorie and Wally chose to settle in after her release from prison. It was October 1986. Perhaps it was a subconscious desire to touch base with Elisabeth's father. Maybe not. In any case, Ajo was a screaming contrast from Duluth.

Marjorie and Wally traveled to Ajo in their Airstream trailer and bought one of the mining houses. The house stood out from the others because Marjorie applied her personal decorating touches. There were only four rooms inside—a kitchen with big Mexican paper flowers atop the refrigerator and a 1924 New Progressive Stove, which took up one whole wall. The living room had Mexican-style leather chairs, and the bedroom was crowded with a pale blue wooden bed and a "library" where Marjorie kept her collection of paperback mysteries and murder novels. The room was so small, Marjorie had joked to neighbors, that she could stand in the center and touch all four walls. She had painted a border of bright, folk-style flowers around the library ceiling.

Marjorie wanted to live in Ajo because it was close to the Mexican border where she could buy "alternative medicine" for Wally. According to her, his ailments included intestinal cancer, stomach cancer, two eye operations, and Parkinson's disease. Wally was eighty-two years old now. He was trim with rosy cheeks, a healthy tan, and a closely trimmed silver beard. It was hard to believe that he was in such bad health.

In June 1987, Wally's children decided to have a family reunion in Minnesota. They thought it might be a chance to reconcile with their father. Perhaps when Wally saw his grandchildren, he would want to rejoin with his family. He had missed so much. Nancy had particularly high hopes because Wally had been a father figure to Michael when they had lived with him.

Wally told Nancy that he would not come unless Marj came with him, and even though she did not want Marj in her house, she relented in order to see her dad. Wally and Marjorie flew to Minnesota for the reunion. While they were there, Marjorie never left Wally's side, and none of his children or grandchildren had a chance to be alone with him. He barely spoke the whole day. After three or four hours, he and Marjorie decided to leave. She waited in the car while Wally walked back in the house to say goodbye to his family. Although Wally was in Nancy's house for several hours, he never acknowledged her son, Michael. It was a terrible rejection.

The reunion had been Tom's daughter's idea. Heather was thirteen years old, and she wanted to know her grandpa. But every time she got near him, Marjorie would physically step between them. When Heather tried to talk to him, Marjorie would answer for him. When they left, Heather broke down in tears. The reunion had failed. Wally would never see his children or his grandchildren again.

The Hagens had lived in Ajo for less than two years when a series of forty-three fires plagued that small town in July 1990. Authorities believed that at least fifteen of the fires had been set by the same arsonist. No one could understand it. Crime was almost unheard of in Ajo. Everyone knew everyone else. People didn't even lock their doors. One of the fires destroyed a warehouse where the Hagens stored their Airstream. Marjorie became a suspect. The police had previously visited the Hagens to collect a second motor home and other property to satisfy judgments against the couple. They had been accused in a lawsuit of writing a bad check for $55,000 to pay for major repairs to one of the motor homes. The repair shop owner was given some of Marjorie's jewelry as partial payment of that judgment.

The neighbors were nervous because there were a lot of abandoned houses in Ajo, and there were many senior citizens who were sick and housebound. They were vulnerable. Ajo was afraid. The local newspaper ran announcements urging people to report their suspicions; residents took no chances and cleaned up firetraps near their houses. Most people suspected teenagers or derelicts.

On the evening of March 24, 1991, the Hagens' next-door neighbor, Mark Indivik, was home in his rented house packing his bags. He was going to Artesia, New Mexico, the next morning for two weeks of job training. Mark was a border patrol officer. He decided to go to bed early and had lain down in his bed for about five minutes when he heard a noise at the window. His lights were turned off. He got up and looked through the curtains and saw Marjorie leaving his backyard. She was with her dog, a combination German shepherd, malamute, and coyote named Wulf. Indivik didn't think much about it and went back to bed. A few minutes later, he heard a noise at the back window again. He saw Marjorie leaving his yard again and walking back to her own house.

Now he became suspicious and decided to crank open his window to see what she had been doing there. He saw an object, but it was dark and the screen prevented him from reaching out, so he went outside and walked around the house to the window. Stuck in the window was a rag that reeked of kerosene. Shocked and frightened, he realized that his neighbor, Marjorie Hagen, was going to burn his house down—with him in it.

Mark called the Pima County Sheriff's Department and Billy Ned, a police officer, came right over. They didn't know if Marjorie would come back or not, but they decided to set up a plan to catch her in the act if she did. If they could get a picture of her stuffing kerosene-soaked rags in the window, she'd be caught red-handed. They had two deputies in unmarked cars parked down the block where they still had a clear view of the bedroom window. They also got some night-vision goggles. It was 11:00 p.m.

Just before 2:00 a.m., Marjorie came out of her house with Wulf and walked down the alley and back into Mark's yard. Mark and Billy sat in the bedroom, and although they could barely see through the curtains, they heard the sound of a match being struck and then they saw a flame. The rag was lit.

Billy took four photographs and Mark quickly extinguished the rag, which had turned into flames that reached two feet high. One of the deputies stationed outside recognized Marjorie Hagen through his night-vision goggles. In a town the size of Ajo, everyone recognizes everyone, so there was no problem with making an identity. They watched her light the rag, and then they saw the flashes coming through the window as Mark snapped pictures from inside.

What had Marjorie thought when the flashes lit her face? She turned and ran back to the alley as fast as she could with the deputies in hot pursuit. They grabbed her, handcuffed her, and placed her under arrest right there in her alley. They neglected to do an in-depth search, but gave her the standard pat-down for weapons before placing her in one of the patrol cars. Later, the patrolman discovered a book of matches with one match missing in his backseat where she had been sitting.

The next day, the deputies served a search warrant on Marjorie's home. Wally was asked to leave while they searched the house. Billy Ned found rags underneath the sink that resembled the rag in the window. The officers also found kerosene lanterns. Marjorie became a suspect for the other fires that had occurred since she'd moved to Ajo. Even so, her trial was postponed for eighteen months because she pleaded to the judge that there was no one to take care of her ailing husband.

Wally was not able to raise the $50,000 bond to keep Marjorie out of jail. "All I have is my social security," he told the press. "They can't take it, thank goodness. All the rest is tied up in judgments. And Marj's kids won't help—they say she's gotten into trouble too many times before. I think that's terrible, don't you?"

Marjorie spent several months in the Pima County jail before she was able to come up with the $50,000 bond. It was believed that Rick came up with the money, which may have come from his share of the inheritance.

The rumors flew in Ajo. People said they remembered seeing one or both Hagens at the arson scenes. They remembered that Marjorie used to walk her dog around town at odd hours of the night. They gossiped over their fences, piecing together information.

One neighbor, Joan Graber, said, "Ajo is such an open, loving community. We took the newcomers in and welcomed them with open arms. They are retired people and they told us about their past lives, and we took them at face value. Marjorie worked at our taco dinners and donated two sweatshirts she'd painted for door prizes at our Valentine's Day party. We thought they were too good for door prizes, so we used them for silent auction items, and they brought $35, $40 each. Now, we wonder how gullible we were."

"I am shocked to the bone," claimed the justice of the peace, who had been roused at 5 a.m. to issue a search warrant for Hagens' house after her arrest. "I mean, I sat opposite that woman and did needlework with her at circle at Immaculate Conception Catholic Church." Apparently, Marjorie was a lapsed Methodist.

Wally continued to live in their house in Ajo. They

had no phone. He told the press that he had had four cancer operations in the past year, but he said he seemed to have licked it. "We lived in Mexico for a year to get special treatment we can't get in the United States," he said. The neighbors had seen Marjorie injecting her husband with "a concoction of vitamins and remedies" she said came from Mexico.

While Marjorie waited in jail for her release, Wally became noticeably healthier. Yet, he was no longer getting injections. He didn't understand it. Neither did their neighbors. He acted like a man in his early seventies. The neighbors said that he went from being a little guy in a wheelchair to a man about town, driving all around, flirting with waitresses. He had his old bounce back and was able to take walks around the neighborhood. Color returned to his cheeks, and he had newfound energy.

Wally remained loyal to Marjorie. "My wife is a doll. She loved fixing things up, not burning things down. Her mother was murdered, you know, but she proved her innocence. And she will again."

❧ *Chapter Twenty-Eight*

On October 22, 1992, Marjorie began yet another trial for arson, this time in Tucson. Courtrooms were Marjorie's milieu, but this one was different from the others in that it was curved like a horseshoe with a double row of seats upholstered in blue and green. The walls were dark wood paneling and there were no windows. The judge's bench was rounded to conform to the shape of the room. The industrial rug was orange. Witnesses would sit to the right of the judge's bench.

She had hired Edward Bolding to defend her this time. He was in his fifties, rather heavy, with a craggy complexion, glasses, and a salt and pepper beard. He had dark features, a receding hairline, and saggy chops. Nixonesque. Unlike Ron Meshbesher, he was arrogant and was disliked by his peers.

Prosecutor Bill Dickinson gave his opening statement. He described Mark Indivik's home and recapped the crime, emphasizing that Marjorie had set the house on fire with two men inside. In conclusion he said, "It's not required that the house burn to the ground in order to support the charge of arson. I ask you to bring back a verdict of guilty."

Bolding responded with a drawling, booming accent. "Something very, very strange, mighty strange, has gone on here for the last eighteen, nineteen months. And as I listen here, incredibly, to . . . the prosecutor, who is going to do an admirable job in the face and in the light of what I contend are insurmountable obstacles in front of him, you will see that he's a professional.

"Now, I have just been involved in this case for about ten months. Back in March of 1991, Mrs. Hagen was arrested, handcuffed behind her back, outside of her house, at 2:00 in the morning in nothing but a nightgown, with no underwear, no underclothes, a light jacket, and bedroom slippers. She's an animal lover and needed to take her dog out.

"She was made to stand there for forty-five minutes. She was thrown in a police car. And now they claim that some matches suddenly appeared with which she was supposed to set some kind of fire on that particular night. Now, think of that. This poor woman was thrown into jail and kept there until December of 1991.

"Marjorie and Wally Hagen. Marjorie is sixty years old. Wally is eighty-three years old. Peaceful, law-abiding. Community-loving, church-loving citizens of Ajo, Arizona, since December 18, 1990. They moved there for Wally's health. They have lived together, married many years, in a loving relationship."

Bolding talked about Wally's fight with cancer and his quest for the right drugs in Mexico. He bragged about their little house in Ajo—a $25,000 house that Marj had "fixed up so cute." He expounded on how she had no motive to set this fire. He laughed about the photographs that Mark Indivik had taken *which didn't turn out*. No evidence.

"So, was Marjorie Hagen out walking her dog on the night of March 25th? Yes, she was. Guilty. Did Marjorie Hagen's dog get out and head over to Mark Indivik's house? Yes. Marjorie had just finished watching *The Ten Commandments* with her husband, and the dog needed to go outside. Guilty.

"It's been a long time for Marj and Wally, and I am seething and outraged. I'm supposed to maintain my civility in the courtroom. I'll try to do that. I would ask that you listen to the evidence and see if those questions are answered. If they're not, she stays an innocent woman. Thank you very much."

Mark Indivik was called to the stand. He was a young man, twenty-eight years old, tall and thin with blond hair. He looked tired. He explained to the prosecutor, Bill Dickinson, that he had been a border patrol agent for four years. Dickinson showed him a picture and diagram of Mark's house so that he could point out the bedroom window to the jury.

At Dickinson's request, Mark pointed to the diagram showing what corner of the room his bed was in.

"What happened?"

"I'm just laying there and I started hearing some

scratching noises. My back was facing the window and was just lying and listening with my left ear and trying to figure it out. And then somebody starts yanking on my window. It sounded like they were trying to tear my window off the wall."

He explained that there were no lights on, and when he peeked through the curtain, he saw Marjorie walking away from the house.

"Why didn't you get up right when you heard the noise?"

"Well, I had an old metal frame bed and it made a lot of noise, and with these old houses, the walls are paper thin, and I didn't want whoever was there to hear me moving around inside the house."

He told Dickinson that he recognized Marjorie because he'd seen her many times, since they were neighbors. He said her walk was distinctive, and he also recognized her voice as she talked to her German shepherd. She was holding it by its collar, he said.

"My heart was pounding. I guess I was kind of scared because I thought somebody was trying to break in."

"You said that your lights were out. Did you make any noise that you're aware of?"

"My bed creaked when I crawled back in."

He told Dickinson how he and Billy Ned had waited for Marjorie armed with a fire extinguisher and a camera. "Me and Officer Ned were standing there, and he's poking through the side of the curtain and he says—he's whispering to me—he says, 'Be quiet, she's right here by the window.' And then we could hear what sounded like a match being struck, and you could see a faint glow through the curtain, and then the next thing I know there was a huge ball of flame coming up from that rag. The flames went up at least a couple of feet."

"What did you do then?"

"Officer Ned threw the curtain back. I gave him time to take a couple pictures and then I hit the rag with the fire extinguisher."

"Why did you put it out so quick?"

"It's a fire, it's not my house, I don't want to damage their house, I'm just renting. I don't want to wind up paying for something," Mark answered, as if it were the dumbest question in the world.

At this point, the attorneys asked to meet Judge Dawley in his chambers without the presence of the jury. This judge had a reputation for being a workaholic, and he was very unpopular with his peers. He was a temporary judge, hired on a daily basis, rather than a regular judge who was employed by the state full-time. He was a serious man, not one to chitchat or make small talk, and he had little patience with attorneys.

The argument in the chambers centered on whether or not Dickinson could introduce a picture of Marjorie, a mug shot, taken the night of her arrest. Bolding thought it would be prejudicial to the jury. Dickinson insisted that because Marjorie had been conspicuously absent from this trial—a constitutional right in Arizona—his case would be incomplete without the witness making a complete, positive identification in front of the jury.

Bolding promised that Marjorie would be there before the trial was over, and there was no reason for the jury to see her in a picture wearing prison garb, handcuffs, and a tag around her neck screaming "Pima County Sheriff's Department" in bold, black print. He said the picture would prejudice and inflame the jury.

Judge Dawley told Bolding that he couldn't quite understand what prejudice he was talking about since he'd "made a big deal" in his opening statement about her being cuffed and taken to jail. He decided that the picture could be admitted for the sake of the record, if needed, but would not be shown to the jury unless Marjorie Hagen didn't show up before the trial was over.

Returning to the courtroom, Bolding began to question Mark Indivik. He implied that Mark may have had too many beers that night before the arson attempt. He asked all the same questions as Dickinson, trying to change the slant, trying to make Mark look like a fool for not bouncing out of bed to catch Marjorie in the act. He even tried to make Mark look incompetent because he didn't immediately reach for his gun and start shooting through his bedroom window.

Mark answered, "Well, sir, like I said, I have a law enforcement background, and they teach us not to overreact."

Bolding's smirk turned into a frown, and he quickly changed his tack. "Frankly, to be honest with the jury here, that house you rent is not really in all that great of shape, is it?"

"It's an old house."

"Right. And it's got a lot of dings and a lot of dirt and a lot of this and that everywhere?"

"It's got a lot of dings in it, yes sir." Mark smiled shyly.

"And Mrs. Hagen's house, on the other hand, how would you describe that, sir?"

"She's done a lot of work to her house."

Bolding grinned as if he'd just received a compliment. "All right. Keeps up the outside beautifully, doesn't she?"

"Yes sir, if that's your opinion."

Bolding's smile vanished. "Is that your opinion?"

"I think it looks cluttered. She's got too many plants for my taste."

After more repetitive testimony, Mark Indivik was finally dismissed. The next witness to be called was

Wallace Hagen.

With great theatrics, Wally was rolled into the courtroom on a gurney, supposedly too ill to stand or walk. His loyal dog Wulf was by his side. Wally said he was eager to testify on his wife's behalf, never believing for a minute that she could have started that fire. He gave his testimony lying down.

Edward Bolding began his questioning. Wally told him that they had lived in Ajo for three years. He said that he was hard of hearing and because of that required a "hearing ear dog."

"And he's in the courtroom with you today?" Bolding asked, smiling down at the dog that posed on the floor next to the gurney.

"Yes, that's Wulf."

Wally told Bolding that he and Marjorie had been married for thirteen years, "or fourteen, somewhere in there." He said that he was almost eighty-four years old. He had known Marjorie for thirty years, had been introduced to her in 1960, he said.

When asked why he was on a gurney, he explained that he had a couple of bad discs and that he had an inoperable tumor "around them."

"All right. Other than that, sir, can you talk about your health and physical condition back in March of 1991?"

"I was in the hospital for quite some time. I had cancer operations, colon, intestine, and two-thirds of my stomach, and eye operations."

"Were you able to get up and around?"

"Very little, very little. Maybe I could walk to the end of the room here and back, but that would be it. . . . Excuse me just a minute." The dog sat up and growled at Bolding. "Wulf thinks I am raising my voice at you, evidently."

"He doesn't like that?" asked Bolding.

"No, he takes it personally." Wally tried to adjust his pillow so that his head would be raised more.

"All right," said Bolding with a slight smile on his lips. "Who was the person who cared for your medical needs at that time?"

"Marjorie. She is a registered nurse."

"Okay, okay." It was obvious that Bolding did not want to pursue that, probably realizing that all of his credibility could fly right out the door. Marjorie had never told him that she was a registered nurse.

He said that according to his prognosis he had had about six months to live.

"Well, you fooled them, didn't you?" Bolding smiled.

"I kind of did, yes."

"This bedridden situation that you're in now, this is of fairly recent origin, two weeks or so ago?"

"Yes. I had a physical here a couple weeks ago and they put me through the M.R.I.s and all this stuff, and they forgot to take out my hearing aid and that blew that all to pieces. Now I have to get new ones, so . . ."

Bolding interrupted, "All right, Wally, let's talk about you and Marjorie's life there in Ajo. What has that consisted of during the last two years, sir?"

"Well, we joined the Immaculate Conception Church, and I am more or less Catholic now, but I go to the Presbyterian Church because the pastor is a very good friend of mine. He also belongs to the Masons and so we go to lodge meetings and stuff, and Marj is very much active in the Catholic Church, with the altar guild and several other things in the church. We go to each other's Bible study classes."

"How do you get around, Wally?"

"I have a little three-wheel—I call it a wheelchair, but it's an electrically driven cart that I can ride all over town with. A mobility cart, it's called. Supposed to run about twenty miles between charges. I charge it up every night."

"Does Marjorie use the cart?"

"Occasionally, yes. Her arthritis is bothering her pretty much. She doesn't like to drive the car because of that, and with the cart, she can just push her hand back and forth."

"Tell me about her arthritis in her hands."

"Well, she has had to give up what little sewing and stuff she'd done. If she happens to pick up a dish just right and it slips, why, she cannot close her fingers enough to stop it and it falls on the floor and breaks. That's happened several times."

"Wally, is Marjorie capable of writing letters?"

"Well, she has some trouble with that because she can't hold the pencil very well. Looks like hen-scratching."

"Okay, Wally, let's go back to March of 1991 when Marj was arrested. Did she have problems using her hands doing fine tasks at that time?"

"Yes. I remember particularly because she had gotten a bottle of Gatorade for me because I can use the vitamins and stuff that are in it, and she picked up the glass and went to pour it, and it slipped right out of her hand. Gatorade all over everything!"

"Okay. Sir, in your opinion, was Marjorie capable at that time of holding and striking a match out of one of these paper book matches?" Bolding held a book of matches in front of Wally's face.

"I'm sorry, I didn't hear you," said Wally, cocking his head.

Bolding repeated the question.

"Well, the match would just slide over. It wouldn't keep on the igniting part of the match. She couldn't hold it between her fingers."

"You've seen that happen?"

"Oh, yes."

Besides wanting to show that Marjorie was incapable of starting a fire, Bolding wanted to establish that the fuel the Hagens had in their house was lamp oil, not kerosene. Oil lamps had been found in their garage, and Wally said that he had intended to wire them for electricity so that they could have some light on their patio.

Bolding went on about the structure of the houses on their block, the casement windows, how oftentimes the locks didn't work and the windows didn't always close. Wally said that he would have to go outside and push the window shut. To open it, he would have to go outside and use a screwdriver to pry it away from the casing before the handle inside would crank it open. Supposedly, Mark Indivik's windows were in the same shape.

"And would you agree if Mr. Indivik, on the witness stand, made the characterization 'There ain't no way anyone can open it up,' would you agree with that?"

"Yes."

Bolding showed him rags that had been taken from under his kitchen sink, and Wally agreed that, yes, they could be his rags. He didn't know who else they could belong to. Wally further explained that he had given some of the rags, which he had bought at Walmart, to Mark Indivik to use on his truck. (Mark had denied getting any rags from Wally during his own testimony.)

Bolding seemed to think Wulf was extremely important to his case because he allowed Wally to digress back to his dog's habits, repeatedly. Wally told him how the dog woke him and Marj up at night when he needed to go out. Sometimes, Marj took him out for his nightly run, he said.

"I wake up every time that Marj moves in that bed because my first wife, she had Parkinson's, Alzheimer's rather, and she would get up and get out of the house and I would have to run her down. . . . So I have trained myself. Any time that Marj would move, I would—even if she got up to go potty—I would be up and asking her, 'What's the matter?'"

"Okay, Wally, could you describe March 24th and 25th for me regarding Marj taking the dog out?"

"Well, Wulf came over—he always goes over to her side of the bed and nudges her. She's easier to wake up than I am, and when he does that, she will either wake me up or—I had a cold at that particular time and she said, 'Do you feel like going out?' and I said, 'Not particularly.' She said, 'Well, I will go, then.' And so . . .'"

"All right. Now I want you to refer to the last time that you saw Marj before she was arrested."

"Well, when she got up, I went into the kitchen and I said, 'I'll make hot water for tea and we'll have tea when you come back,' and so she started for the door, and I said, 'It's kind of chilly out there. Why don't you put my jacket on,' and I grabbed my jacket and threw it on her. It was hanging on the hook right alongside the kitchen door there. Then she snapped the leash on Wulf and took him out."

"And that's the last time you saw her before she was arrested?"

"Well, yes. As I stood in the door and asked them what was going on, a man said, 'We have taken care of her.' I said, 'What do you mean taken care of her?' He said, 'We have arrested her.' I said, 'What for?' He wouldn't say anything about what for, and then they threw this big light in my face. One of the young fellows gave me a push. He said, 'Put your hands behind your back,' and I said, 'I can't do that because I have got Parkinson's. I have to keep my hands out where they are free and I can keep my balance. Otherwise, I have to lay out there on the floor.'"

"All right, sir, then what happened?"

"Well, that was about the same time that one of the young deputies came running up, and he didn't judge the height of the patio from the place where he was at, and his foot caught on that, and he sprawled all over the patio. I think it was the tape recorder that he had in his hands, but anyhow, it wasn't much good after he got through because it was all smashed up."

Bolding couldn't resist a smile even though Wally was dead serious.

At this point, Dickinson began his cross-examination. He proceeded to go over the same questions regarding the oil lamps and the rags from Walmart. Dickinson sounded impatient and moved on to Wulf, who was the star of the show. He covered the length of the leash, the color of the leash, the type of collar, and the clip on the collar.

Wally told him that he and Marj were presently staying in a cabin located in an RV park. He admitted to Dickinson that Marj drove them from Ajo to Tucson. He said that it was over a two-hour drive.

"You didn't come by ambulance, did you?"

"No, we didn't."

Dickinson had no further questions. It was Bolding's turn.

"Where were you Wally, when Marj was making the drive?"

"I was in the back. I had built a platform for the dog and it has a rug on it, and it's large enough so I could lay curled up on it with pillows and stuff and that's where I rode over here. Me and the dog shared the back end."

"Okay. And where have you been since you came here to Tucson? In bed or where?"

"I've been in bed over in the cabin."

"On doctor's orders?"

"That's right."

"All right. Are you familiar with the movie *The Ten Commandments?*"

"The what?"

"The movie, *The Ten Commandments?*"

"Yes, I have heard of it, yes."

"All right."

"I don't recall anything about it, though."

"Okay. Was that movie on the night of March 24?"

"It could have been."

"You are not sure of that?"

"No."

After his testimony, Wally told the press that his wife was set up. "There's the culprit," he said, pointing to Wulf, who was pulverizing a beef bone from the butcher's shop. "I think someone put meat juice on the rag, and Wulf took it off the windowsill. She was just returning it." When someone asked him why anyone would frame his wife, he just shrugged his shoulders.

"The arson charges sound like a put-up job to me.

Her mother was murdered, you know, but Marj proved her innocence. And she will again. I'm standing by my wife," he said. "To my mind, she's innocent. I suppose you think it's strange I don't seem more upset. I suppose I should be, but things have always worked out in my life. I think this will, too."

❧ *Chapter Twenty-Nine*

Edward Bolding called Marjorie to the stand. She told him that she lived at 721 Palo Verde in Ajo. When he asked her if she was scared to be up on the stand, she exclaimed, "I am terrified." Bolding counseled her not to worry, that they would just have a little conversation.

"When and where did you go to school?" he asked.

"I went to grade school in Duluth, and I went with the nuns for junior high, and then I went away to boarding school in Massachusetts."

"All right. After that, did you have some college work?"

"Yes, I did. I went to St. Louis University . . . for undergraduate work, and then was going to finish my work after I was married and having children, and then about, oh—I didn't know you were going to ask me this and it dates about ten years ago. I finished my master's degree in theology."

Theology? Master's degree? Marjorie easily fell into the role of "witness." She bragged about her resumé, albeit a bogus resumé. She smiled at the jurors, knowing that they would be impressed. Theologists are not usually arsonists.

"And where was that?"

"That was with the University of the South. Swanee."

She told Bolding that she had been married to Wally for thirteen years and said that she and his first wife had been very close friends.

"And his wife died, is that correct?"

"Yes. She died of Alzheimer's." Marjorie explained that they had met in Minneapolis when they took their children to ice-skating lessons. "Back then you could afford it. It was . . ."

As if Bolding could sense Judge Dawley's annoyance, he cut her off.

He asked her about her children and grandchildren. She said that she had thirty-six grandchildren and would be having her fourth great-grandchild in about three months. She smiled again at the jury who might have expected her to bring the pictures out of her wallet. Grandmothers are not usually arsonists.

At his request, she explained that she and Wally had lived in Minneapolis and that he was a retired electrician. She explained that she had been a housewife, home raising her seven children.

"I did volunteer work at hospitals. I had some medical training, and from the time I had my first child I worked in the nursery and the Sunday school at the church and neighborhood groups. I was a real mother for each one of my children, and, you know, helped put on pageants and plays, and cooked for the P.T.A. and that kind of thing."

"Okay. Then there came a time in your life when you decided to move to Tucson or to the Ajo area, rather, is that correct?"

"Yes."

"What did you do between the time that you married and the time that you decided to move to Ajo, and what was the reason for that?"

"Well, Wally had always wanted to travel, and he had had tent campers and, you know, the little fold-up ones, and we bought an old trailer, and we started to travel. He found out on one of our trips that he had an aneurysm, but the doctor said that surgery would have been worse than letting it go. So while we traveled, we stopped at different hospitals and had them check it. And then when we were in West Virginia, the aneurysm started to leak, and he had to go in and have surgery, and they had to replace the entire aorta from the heart all the way down to the legs, and he was in the hospital there for a month. At that point, they told him that he should get out of the cold weather, and he should get someplace where he wasn't going to be under a lot of stress, so we went back and we sold our house, and he had the first of a series of strokes the following summer. That was in March."

"So this is why you ended up in the Southwest?"

"Yes. Wally and I like small towns. We wanted some place where we could walk or use a golf cart to get around and this type of thing.

"And so we looked around and we enjoyed driving down into Mexico, and we saw Ajo that way and just fell in love with it, and the houses were so reasonable, if you don't mind taking an old house and working on it. And so we found a house that's—you've seen it, Edward. It's the size of a two-car garage, and just thought this was exactly what we wanted. So we moved down there."

Bolding held up a picture of her house. "Is this your house?"

"Yes, it doesn't look like that now, though."

"Why not?"

"Well, because we put all this in. There was nothing there when we bought it, and we added the porches and transplanted all the bushes and the cacti, and we wanted them, and now they are up to the point where you can hardly see the house. See the back? Now we've got lattice work across the back, the back patio, so there is a private sitting area."

"But you and Wally together did all of the improvements on your house, I take it?"

"Yes, except we had one young man that helped us dig the big holes. And the patio too. Wally couldn't do that."

It was difficult to tell where Bolding was heading in his questioning. But it seemed that he was trying to gain the jury's sympathy. Obviously, his client had done everything humanly possible to help her husband get well.

"Marjorie, you said something about living near Mexico so that you could get medication for Wally. Tell me about that."

"Well, before we moved to Ajo he had four major

cancer surgeries in eight months and he had four or five strokes. He also has Parkinson's disease, and he had peripheral vascular disease, which means he couldn't take chemotherapy because it would blow his veins out. Our doctor is very good about trying things, and he talked with the cancer specialist and they said that they felt that there are some medicines that have not been approved in this country but are available in Mexico. This isn't Laetrile. That if we were willing to experiment and take a chance, he would put us in touch with both a clinic and a doctor and that it might work out."

"How far is it to Mexico from Ajo?"

"About forty miles."

"Okay. Now, Marjorie, I need you to tell the judge and the jury what your life has been, essentially, in Ajo, what you have done, how you have lived your life, what's gone on."

"Well, we get up early, or I do, because I never miss morning mass. If Wally is awake, I fix him breakfast before I go. If not, I do it when I get back after mass.

"Then I do a couple loads of wash and hang it on the line. I do my housework. We don't have carpet. We have cement floors because with his Parkinson's, he can't walk on carpet without tripping, so we have the old red cement floors, which I like." She smiled at the jury.

"I belong to two church groups. We have Bible study on Tuesday night. When my hands are good enough, I do needlepoint. I do quilting, sewing, and make a lot of my clothes. I do things for the grandchildren and the new babies. I paint, decorative painting, not a scene, but flowers and stuff. Wally cut me some borders for the kitchen and I painted designs on those and, oh, I wash windows and . . ."

"All right, Marj. Do you know a person named

Gordy Layman*?"

"Yes."

"Okay, who is he?"

"Gordy is the owner and broker of Ajo Realty. He is a bishop in the Mormon Church and a very close friend."

"Do you do some chores for Gordy?"

"Yes. Well, we keep an eye on empty houses that he has for sale, on the yards, make sure that they are kept up, watered, and weeded. He bought a house from somebody who left town and hired me to design how it should be remodeled inside and gave me the keys. I wanted the stove that they had and I didn't have the money for it, so we worked it out that way. I had been looking for a stove for three years."

The jurors smiled. Dickinson shook his head and looked at the table, and Judge Dawley tapped his pen on his index finger. Bolding slowly walked back to his table, as if to stall for time, wondering how he got into this line of questioning and wondering how he was going to get out of it. Marjorie was unpredictable. He decided to drop the subject all together and move on.

"All right, Marjorie. Let's talk about—as of March of 1991, some eighteen months ago, I need you to go back to that period of time and tell me about your medical and physical condition at that time."

"I had angina. The doctor terms it severe unstable angina. I had arthritis. I had cancer surgery. I was not at that time being treated for it, but I had had three major cancer surgeries."

"What were those surgeries, and how did they affect your body, your physical being?"

"They were lymphatic cancer and I had scarring on both arms up to the armpits. I have it on my hips down the leg and from the point of the hip around under the buttocks. They couldn't do it all in one surgery.

They did it three weeks in a row, and I ended up with fifteen hundred stitches for that."

Bolding did not look at the jury as if he were afraid to see what registered on their faces. He bravely continued with the line of questioning.

"All right, Marj, in March 1991 what were you able to do and not do?"

"I couldn't bend or do any heavy lifting. That's why we had to get the young man to do the digging."

"Right."

"Vacuuming was something that if I did it, it had to be done very slowly, and the doctor didn't want me to do it. When Wally had good days, he would help me. I could not reach above my head. Anything that I do up above shoulder level can precipitate severe attacks. Stress precipitates an attack. I am trying to avoid open-heart surgery. I no longer have any medical insurance and . . ."

"But I want to know how it affects you muscularly or physically."

"Oh. You can't lift. You can't do the things that you used to do. You get very tired. You are up a lot. I have a kidney problem that I have had for over fifteen years that is getting progressively worse. I have one kidney that doesn't function at all and one that has a tumor in it."

"Okay, back to March of 1991. How did your arthritis affect you physically?"

"Well, I have it in my ankles and in my hips and particularly in my hands. When I get up in the morning, they don't work until I soak them in hot water. They are swollen. They are pudgy and they just ache and I can't, for instance, I have a lever faucet and I can push it but I can't like grab hold of a faucet or anything and turn it. I can't pick up a hair brush to brush my hair."

"Can't pick up a hair brush? I'm sorry."

"You know, to brush my hair, until the hands got limbered up, and I can say to you, 'I am going to run across the room.' Well, my version of running is not like it was, say, twenty years ago. It causes me trouble even in church. I have had to many times—well, not many times, but a couple of times a month, I have to go to church without shoes on. I wear a pair of my husband's socks. My feet and ankles are so bad I can't get shoes on."

"All right. Now, Marj, are all of the windows in your neighborhood what they call steel casement windows?"

"Most of them."

"Okay, Marj, I forgot to ask you. How tall are you?"

"Oh, five one and a half if I stand very tall."

"Okay, Marj. Now, then, can you, in your house, standing outside the house when the windows are closed, when it's cranked shut, can you open that window?"

"No. I can't even reach the top of it."

"All right. But from the side, say, could a person pull on that window and open it?"

"No, because the windows are flat." She described the window frame, the lip around the frame, and how the window had to be cranked from the inside. She described the casing as if she had designed the window herself—or studied the construction of it for some time before giving her testimony.

Bolding questioned her about Mark Indivik's windows, which were just like hers. Since she had not heard Mark's testimony, Bolding told her that on the night of the fire, he had cranked the window shut and that it was flush against the frame. Marjorie told him that there was no way she was physically able to open Mark's window, in fact nobody could without a chisel and hammer. She smiled at Bolding and then at the jury.

"Okay, Marj you are, among other things, an animal person?"

"Very much." She prattled about her previous pets, and how Wulf was a replacement for the last dog that they'd put to sleep. Henry was his name. On and on.

Bolding looked like he wished that he had a muzzle for his client.

The no-nonsense judge said, "Please, just answer the question. The question was whether you got a replacement dog. The answer is yes."

"I am trying to explain."

"That's what I mean," said Judge Dawley. "You are not allowed to explain. Just answer the questions that Mr. Bolding asks you. If he wants you to explain, he will ask you a question that allows that. Proceed Mr. Bolding." Judge Dawley leaned back in his chair and sighed a little too loudly.

Bolding asked her about the replacement, which was Wulf, the new hearing-ear dog. "All right, and why do you have to have a dog for the deaf or a hearing dog?"

"Because Wally has hearing problems, and the hearing aids don't do much good for the type of deafness that he is progressively getting worse with."

"All right."

"I don't think that was said right."

"It came out all right."

Bolding had her describe her routine with Wulf during March 1991, and then he departed from his dog questions and asked Marjorie why she had rags in the house.

"Well, I used them to clean the stove . . . and Wally would tie like old golf balls and things into a rag and give it to Wulf. . . . There weren't any teeth, but he could get it back here and he would run and look silly with this thing hanging out of his mouth, and when we would get a bag of rags like that, I would used them to clean the stove—because it's a 1924 and you can't clean it like you do a new stove."

Marjorie finally got to talk about her stove. They'd stopped her earlier in her testimony, but it was as if she was bound and determined to tell the jury how old her stove was. She smiled proudly and Bolding looked exasperated.

He asked her about the oil lamps that she had in the house.

She explained that there were only four outlets in the entire house and none on the outside. Wally was adding outlets around the patio so that they could sit out there and read. She expounded on how the lanterns gave off a nice soft glow and that they still used them sometimes for atmosphere. She was intent on showing the jury that she had a very good reason to have lamp oil in her house and it had nothing to do with burning down the neighborhood. She denied having kerosene at all. "It smells."

She told Bolding that Wulf sometimes had a problem with taking things out of other people's yards. He'd even take Wally's stuff from his workbench and her sewing. "It wasn't his fault," she said looking at the jury, "he just didn't know any better."

Now, Bolding wanted Marjorie to re-create the night of March 24 for the jury. The jurors sat back in their seats, as if knowing that this could be a long haul. How could Bolding give her free reins like that, knowing how she rambled on and on? He was either overly confident or stupid. Ron Meshbesher would never have taken a chance like that. But, Marjorie had the floor now.

"Okay, Marjorie, I need you to tell this jury what you did on the evening of March 24," said Bolding.

"Well, I put things out for supper, and we usually watch *Sixty Minutes* and it's at 5:00. I think it's 5:00 if it's on Phoenix and 6:00 if it's on Tucson, or the other way around. We get both sets of stations in Ajo, and we were watching *Sixty Minutes*.

"Wally was in bed and a lot of times we will do that. We will have trays in bed and watch the TV. . . .The dog had to go out. So, I took the dog out for his walk and I noticed there was quite a bit of activity . . . and there was a lot of traffic, and particularly there was like a stationwagon, like an older one, pale yellow, not as yellow as your pad, but that kind of thing, that looked like a couple of cops in it. And as I came around the corner . . . it came flying up and looked at me and looked at Wulf, and turned around and went off again, and . . . I said something like, 'Well, they are out for somebody or something tonight,' and we just live down from Circle K and they have a lot of trouble with kids up there."

"All right, go on."

"Then I fixed supper, did the dishes, and *The Ten Commandments* was going to be on and it was right after *Sixty Minutes,* oh, unless there could have been news in there, I'm not sure.

"Anyway . . . in one commercial break, the dog wanted to go to the bathroom. Well, both Wally and I had been having colds and not feeling good generally, so there was no way, you know, that I wanted him to take the dog out.

"So, I took the dog out and it was kind of, you know—I went back where I usually do and I have to say, I didn't have him on a leash like I should have, and when we went out the back gate, he took off, and I heard him next door, so I walked into Mark's yard in the back and he was up by the back of Mark's house, and he loved to chase cats and I heard him like scrambling around at the back of the house, and Mark's truck was there and the house was dark. . . . So, I was trying to be quiet and not holler, 'Wulf.'"

"Did you believe that Mark was home?"

"Yes. His truck was there."

"Okay, go on."

"I went . . . around the back of the house, and he [the dog] was like scratching and scrambling and grabbing at stuff, and I thought, 'Oh, what have you got now.' Well, I thought, I couldn't go and bang on the door and wake Mark up. I will wait until tomorrow and tell him that if the dog has done any damage, please let us know."

"So, then did you leave?"

"Yeah. I got the dog, went back to our house."

"Was Wally aware that you had left?"

"Oh, yeah, because he said, 'Well, you missed some.' I was out longer than the commercials. So then, Wulf got into his bed and he has a bed right next to ours with a heating pad in it, and I must have gone to sleep before it was over because I didn't see the end of it.

"And then all of a sudden Wulf was over nudging me, and I thought, oh dear, you know, I felt like I had just barely gotten to sleep and Wally said, 'I will get up, I'm awake anyway,' and I said, 'No, you won't, you are not going outside with this cold,' and he said, 'I will get up with you and make some tea,' and so we got up and I had my nightie on and I go barefoot an awful lot. And he hollered at me and he said, 'You put on some shoes.' So, I put on my tennis shoes and walked out with Wally."

Bolding made her repeat what she was wearing. At first it seemed as though he was just tired of her diatribe, but she had forgotten to mention that Wally made her wear his jacket, so she rambled on about how Wally had made her "fasten it up."

"I took Wulf out. It was dark and I wasn't moving very fast, just kind of feeling my way, you know. There are no streetlights in the alley, and we are right in the middle of the block, and there are huge salt-cedars that block the light from the street.

"As soon as we got in the alley, Wulf took off—I just knew I should have put the leash on him—and I knew he had gone over to Mark's because that was his habit. So, I went over to Mark's back yard. He has a big double gate, like a vehicle gate, that was opened."

"So, what did you do next?"

"I went up to the house, because that's where Wulf had gone earlier. I didn't see him, and I put my hand out like this on the side of the house, to feel my way, and I don't know if it was right on the window or the edge of the window, but all of a sudden there were blue lights and sparks. It looked like if you have got a wire that's sparking off and going off. It scared me to death."

"What did you do then?"

"Well, I did what for me constitutes running. I moved out of there toward the fence. I was still in the yard, and all of a sudden, this cop grabbed me, and I mean, it was like a nightmare. He shoved me up against the fence, and the next thing I knew my hands were pulled around behind my back, and they had handcuffs on, just cutting into me. . . . I said something like, you know, 'What's going on? I am looking for my dog. Where is my husband?' or something like that. . . . And then he started searching me, putting his hands in my hair, putting his hands in the pockets of the jacket, and he ran them down my legs and he put his hands up under my nightgown. I said, 'You can't do that,' and he said, 'Yes, I can.'

"I never heard of a man being able to do that to a woman. He just went all over my body, down my arms.

He even went inside the jacket, unzipped it, and all the time my hands were way back like this as tight behind my back as they could get them with the cuffs on. I said, 'Those cuffs hurt.'

"Then he grabbed me by the arm and by the cuffs and pushed. I don't mean he threw me on the ground, but I mean he was pushing me over to the car, and somebody, I don't know who, but one of the policemen yelled, 'Don't hurt her.' Then they threw me into a police car. I can tell you I have never been so scared in my life. I mean, this is the kind of thing that you see on television."

At this point, Dickinson objected, and the judge reminded her to stop volunteering information.

Marjorie looked at the judge and said, "Your Honor, are you saying that I can't tell the truth?"

"No Ma'am. No one is precluding you from telling your version of what happened on the stand here today. Just answer the questions without volunteering anything extra. Do you understand?"

"I think so."

"Mr. Bolding, you may go on with your questioning."

"Thank you. Marj, do you or Wally smoke?"

"No—well, Wally smoked twenty years ago."

"Did you have some kitchen matches at your house?"

"Yes, the big, long wooden ones to light my stove and the lamps."

"You have a gas stove?"

She smiled at Bolding and then at the jury. "Yes. It's a 1924 New Progressive, and you have to light it because the thing that's supposed to make it light doesn't work. It's the only part that doesn't."

"Okay, Marj. When the detectives searched your house, they found a book match that said Circle K or something like that. Would you have ever used those particular book matches?"

"I couldn't."

"Why not?"

"My hands are too awkward on those little tiny matches. It's like at church. I have to use the long wooden stick. My fingers don't work well."

"All right, if somebody said that they looked through a curtain and saw you holding some book matches and striking them, would that have been possible?"

"No, I couldn't."

"Okay, did you see anything on the window sill of Mark Indivik's house on the morning of March 25th?"

"I didn't see anything. . . . I just felt something that wasn't like a window or a wall. It was soft."

"What ran through your mind at that time?"

"I thought it could have been a sweater. It was soft, you know. Sweat shirt. I thought Mark had something hanging there and I thought, you know, Oh Lord, if the dog has gotten this and then I have to find out what damage, I mean just—it wasn't a full thought—it was just . . ."

"Is that when the flashes happened?"

"Yes."

"Marj, shortly after you and Wally moved into Ajo, did you become aware that there was some type of reward offered for the arrest and conviction of somebody charged with arson?"

"Yes. Everybody in town knew and talked about it. It was in the paper and they asked for contributions. Wally and I gave to it or signed up for giving to it."

"Do you know the amount of that reward?"

"Something like $5,000 or $10,000."

Bolding then asked her if Wally could have set the fire. She looked at him as if he'd gone mad and said, "No, Wally had IV's in his arm hanging off a frame two and three times a week. Of course he couldn't do that."

It was Dickinson's turn to cross-examine.

"Is it true, Mrs. Hagen, that you had previously been convicted of a felony?"

"Well, everybody knows that. It's common knowledge."

"Yes or no."

"Yes."

"And that was in Minneapolis?"

"Yes."

"That was on February 9, 1984?"

"I don't know. It was about ten years ago. I'm sure you have the date."

Finally, after much prodding and arguing between the attorneys, Dickinson got Marjorie to admit to the date that she had been convicted in Minnesota. Then he went over all of the testimony again. She told him that she had been in Mark's yard many times prior to that night to clean up his beer cans and Dairy Queen wrappers. "His yard was a mess," she said. She reiterated her physical ailments and told him how she'd fallen "flat on my face in church, just the other day."

Dickinson didn't get anything new out of her, but it was obvious the jury was tired anyway. On redirect, Bolding got in one last shot:

"Marj, did you set fire to any rag anywhere anytime, or more particularly, in Mark Indivik's house?"

"No. No reason to."

Apparently the jury was unimpressed with Marjorie's testimony. They said she had overacted; she was too bold, too cocky. She had a history of arson. And if that wasn't enough, one of them had happened to look out the window on the day that Wally was to give his testimony. She saw him get out of the car, unaided, and watched as Marjorie helped him onto the gurney to be ushered into the courtroom for his testimony.

Marjorie was indicted by the Pima County grand jury in late November 1992 on four counts of arson of an occupied structure, four counts of criminal damage, insurance fraud, and engaging in a fraudulent scheme. She pleaded no contest to a criminal damage charge in the July 1990 fire at the Ajo commercial storage yard where she had kept her motor home. Marjorie admitted that the prosecutors would be able to prove that she cut through a security fence and started a blaze that damaged four vehicles in the lot, including her own Airstream. The grand jury also alleged that she ignited kerosene-soaked rags on the windowsills of two houses in her neighborhood. They belonged to members of her quilting club. Investigators testified during the hearing that she filed a $38,000 claim on a fire insurance policy that she had taken out on the motor home. Police said that she also might be responsible for a dozen other unsolved arsons in the town of 3,500. Prosecutors dropped the charges in exchange for her plea of no contest and agreed to recommend that she serve her sentence concurrently.

On June 11, 1993, Marjorie was sentenced to fifteen years in prison. Her first chance of parole would be in ten years. She was now sixty years old. Judge Dawley's sentence was considered harsh, but he took into account her previous fire conviction and the fact that she knew that Mark Indivik was home when she lit the kerosene rags at his window. He could have burned to death. Marjorie was given credit for the one and a half years she had spent in jail since her arrest.

Edward Bolding made a plea to the judge that Marjorie needed to make arrangements for her ailing husband, Wally. It was an old story, but with a new result. Dawley allowed her twenty-four hours of freedom. What harm could it do? It was only one day.

Marjorie was escorted home to Ajo from Tucson by two police officers. They could not have guessed that she had anything on her mind besides watering her plants and reuniting with her husband. She laughed and made small talk for the whole two-hour ride. She was lucky that Judge Dawley had understood just how important it was that she have time with Wally before being sent away to prison.

Part V

*Nothing would wake
him now.*

❧ *Chapter Thirty*

As long as she was with Wally, Marjorie knew she could control him and keep his daughter, Nancy, and his two sons away from him. But once she was back in prison, they might take Wally back to Minnesota. He'd be lonely. If she wasn't there to keep him drugged, they might be able to turn him against her. No one knew better than Marjorie did that Wally was like clay. She had spent all these years molding him. He was her own creation, set and cast, and no one was going to undo all that work.

A double-suicide would be reasonable. After all she'd been through, who wouldn't believe that she and her loving husband would rather die together than be apart while she was in prison. He was so old, he'd die before she got out in any case. Everyone believed he had battled cancer since the day they arrived in Ajo. She had made sure of that. It was common knowledge that she was his caretaker, and without her, he couldn't exist.

Wally would really be better off dead than without her anyway. All she had to do was write a suicide note and get him to sign it. He did everything she told him to do, so that wouldn't be a problem. First, she'd give him the usual dose of his tranquilizer, Xanax. No, she'd give him a few extras for good measure. Then, just before he went to sleep, she'd tell him, "Oh God, Wally, before you doze off on me now, you need to sign this paper. Those damn tax people are after us again. Just sign your name and I'll put this in the mail today. I don't want you to have to deal with those vultures while I'm gone. Here's a pen, dear. That's right, just put your name on top of that line. Good boy."

Or maybe she'd just tell him how much she loved him and that she'd rather die than spend the rest of her life without him. She could explain to him that if they died together, they could spend their afterlife together, and they'd never have to be apart again. He'd never be lonely. Maybe she would actually show him the note, and he would look at her with those big, sky-blue eyes and say, "You're right Marj. Let's do it. They'll never be able to bother us again."

But she also had another choice. Why tell the old goat anything at all? She had signed his name enough times over the years that she could do it blindfolded. She'd just write the note herself, put down his John Henry, and be done with it.

That night, she put her husband to bed, literally, tucked him in, as if he were a young child. He was, in a way, so vulnerable, so dependent. Then she put on her blue-and-white checkered cotton pajamas and crawled in next to him and turned out the light on her nightstand. She knew what she had to do, and how she was going to do it. Marjorie slept well.

When she awoke the next morning, it was hot and dry. Typical Ajo. If she had time, she'd water her flowers before she had to leave. She would miss the flowers. There wouldn't be anyone left to take care of them. She knew she'd better get moving before the police returned to take her back to Tucson. She went into the bedroom where Wally was watching The Wheel of Fortune. *She had just given him his lunch, chicken noodle soup.*

"It's time to take your medicine, Wally."

"I'll have plenty of time to sleep when you're gone, Marj."

"Well, dear, don't you worry. I'm going to take care of everything," she promised.

She went into the kitchen and opened the bottle of Xanax. She took out six capsules, broke each one in half and emptied the powder into a glass of gingerale. She stirred the mixture with a spoon until the powder had dissolved. Then she carried the glass back into the bedroom.

She handed Wally the glass of gingerale and two tranquilizers. "Here, dear, you just get these two little pills down, and you'll feel so much better. Now, drink up. That fizzy pop will settle your tummy. That's a good boy."

"Marj?"

"Yes dear?"

"I don't feel too good."

"Well, your medicine will kick in soon and then you'll be as good as new."

He put his head back on the pillow and closed his eyes. Vanna was turning four Es on the letter board. Marjorie took the glass back into the kitchen, rinsed it out, and placed it back in the cabinet. She put the childproof lid back on the bottle and stuffed it into her purse.

She couldn't take a chance on Wally pulling through this. He had to have a high tolerance for the medication that she'd been feeding him for so many years. Marjorie had a backup plan, one she had thought of during her trial. Plan B. The idea had just popped into her head, like a bubble in a cartoon, and she had it all figured out before the trial was over. The old gas stove that she had so painstakingly harped on during the trial was finally going to pay off.

Out in the back yard, hooked onto the side of the house, was a green, vinyl garden hose holder. She had nailed it up there herself. She had two green hoses screwed together that reached around her house so that she could easily water her desert marigolds, owl's clover, and brittlebrush. She had always enjoyed her garden. It looked like the neighbor, Mark, wasn't home. He'd probably never come back. Good. Her hands were feeling stiff and arthritic, but she managed to lift the heavy hose over the rack and unscrew the extension hose. Looking around to see if anyone was watching, she lugged one of the hoses through the back door and into the kitchen. Canned laughter from the bedroom TV startled her. She had forgotten to turn the set off. She peeked in to see Wally, who was out like a light. She stretched the hose from the kitchen to the bedroom and there were inches to spare. She went back into the kitchen and took a serrated knife from the kitchen drawer. She held up one end of the hose and sawed off the coupling.

313

The New Progressive stove stood on legs with clawed feet. It was black cast iron.

The left side was the oven, which was at eye level. It was imposing and out-of-place. Marjorie knew she had to have that stove the first time she had seen it in her realtor's house. It hadn't looked so big there. Gas burners sat on an extension table to the right of the oven. Each gas burner had its own white porcelain knob. The gas flowed through copper tubing that ran behind the burners.

First, Marjorie found the gas valve on the wall and turned the lever up, perpendicular to the gas line. The gas was turned off. She reached behind the burners and, with her right hand, tried to unscrew the flair nut that was attached to the copper tubing. It wouldn't budge. "Damn." She found her trusty pliers in the kitchen junk drawer, wrapped them around the flair nut and turned. Nothing. Try again. It moved. Again. Slowly, the flair nut turned with the pliers until it was detached, and she could slide it up the tubing. She let it go and it dropped, stopping at the end of the tubing. She picked up the hose and stretched the cut end over the tubing, sliding the flair nut up and out of the way. The hose was too loose and it dropped to the floor. She remembered that she had seen a roll of duct tape. But where? She hurried out to the garage, and there it was, on the ledge under the window. She rushed back into the kitchen. She cut off a long piece of tape, slid the hose over the tubing, and wrapped the tape around the hose, making sure that no gas could leak out. Quickly, she went back to the bedroom, and with her needlepoint scissors, she cut off several pieces of the tape and stuck them onto her arm.

Wally was snoring deeply and his chest barely moved. Nothing would wake him now. She took the end of the hose and stuck it under his nostrils. She removed the first piece of tape from her arm and secured it over the top of his nose and around the hose. It stuck. She proceeded to do the same with two more pieces of the tape. When the hose was secured, she went back into the kitchen and turned the gas valve parallel to the gas line. She heard the swishing sound of gas running through the copper tubing. She went back into the bedroom and sat down in her husband's rocking chair. Wally was going to die before her eyes.

Marjorie got up from Wally's rocking chair and walked over to the bed. He was still now. She put her fingers on his pulse just to make sure. Yes, it was over. She'd done it again. Actually, this was the easiest one of all. Wally was lucky to have lived as long as he did. He really should have thanked her for taking such good care of him, feeding him healthy foods, moving him to a nice, warm climate, giving him his medication. Especially that. At one time, she'd thought he was good looking. He had a nice smile. Now, as she stared at his dead body, she couldn't help notice how relaxed he looked, smooth and unwrinkled, almost healthier than he'd looked in life. Well, he wouldn't have to worry about her anymore, and she wouldn't have to worry about him.

He had been a good companion, though. It was too bad that it had to end this way. Unfortunately, Wally just knew too much. She had no choice. She had been collecting prescriptions of Xanax for months—it was the latest version of Meprobamate—telling the doctors that Wally needed something to help him sleep. The stress of the trial and of having Marjorie taken away from him was more than a man his age could stand. That was an interesting thought. Wally was the same age as her mother, Elisabeth, when she had died. Of course, she would have died sooner if Marjorie had been a bit smarter. She didn't make the same mistake this time. There were no nurses or doctors to interfere, and a simple coma wouldn't do. Yes, Marjorie was older and wiser. And Wally was dead.

She gently lifted the tape off of his nose, hoping that there would be no marks. The hose fell to the floor. She lugged it back into the kitchen, loosened the duct tape, and removed the other end of the hose off of the stove's copper tubing. She *reached behind the stove and turned off the gas valve. She wrapped the hose around her arm as if she had just watered the plants and took it back out to the side of the house and draped it over the vinyl holder. She set the hose over the hooks and put the extension hose on top of it. It looked tidy again. Then she went inside, put the serrated knife back in the drawer and her needlepoint scissors in her bag next to Wally's rocking chair. With the pliers, she screwed the flair nut back in place. Taking a quick scan of the house, she didn't see anything out of order.*

She only had one thing left to do. She took a pen and paper out of her desk drawer and sat down to write. She addressed the letter to Edward Bolding.

Dear Edward,

First, we both want to thank you for all you have done for us. No one could have done more and we leave our love and appreciation. Please don't blame yourself for our joint actions tonight. We both feel that with Wally's health and the type of political miscarriage of justice done to both of us, we have no choice. When a reward creates a situation where a sworn law officer and his friend can create a set-up to destroy the lives of two innocent people, and a prosecutor and judge deliberately withhold information and facts in order to prejudice a jury, we are left with no choice. I understand that some of the jury were so keen to exonerate a police official, we hope that for the rest of their lives they all remember what they conspired to do. I restate to you now at this moment, under the chance of eternal damnation for taking my life, that I am now and have been innocent of all charges put against me. We ask you to try your best to follow our last requests.

We wish to be buried together in a single coffin along with Wulf. As we have only the three of us in life, we wish to have three of us together in death.

Wally would like a Masonic service.

All material things that I have, including the Crucifix in the bedroom and the shrine of the Virgin in the living room are to go to my son, Richard LeRoy. Please let Rick know how much we love him and ask him to think lovingly of us sometimes.

We love the town of Ajo and would like to be buried here. Please ask Rick for a plain stone of two entwined hearts with only our names, Wally and Marj united in death as they were in life on it. [sic] No birth or death dates. Again, our thanks and love to you.

She signed the note, Wally Hagen and Marjorie Hagen.

Someone was knocking at the door. "Marjorie, are you in there?"

It was 1:00 p.m. and Sheriff's Lt. Tom Taylor had been riding his bike past the Hagen house. He thought he smelled gas. He was scheduled to take Marjorie into custody four hours later for her arson conviction. She answered him through the window.

"She told me that she'd left the gas burner on," he said. "I asked if everyone was okay. She said, 'Yes.' I said, 'I'll see you in a few hours.'"

❧ *Chapter Thirty-One*

Tom Taylor was in his office in Ajo at 4:30 p.m. when Tom Hagen called him from Minneapolis and told him that his father was dead.

"My name is Tom Hagen. My father is Wally Hagen and his wife is Marjorie Caldwell Hagen. Do you know who they are?"

Taylor assured him that he did.

"Well, Marjorie just called me and told me that my father passed away and I'd like you to go over there. I suspect that he did not die of natural causes, and I'm sure that Marjorie had something to do with his death."

Taylor asked Tom, "What else did Marjorie say?"

"I don't know, she seemed sad, I guess. I asked her how it happened and she said, 'He just slipped away and he was holding my hand, telling me he loved me.' I asked her when it happened. She just said, 'He died this morning.'" Hagen's voice shook as he repeated his conversation with Marjorie. "It's 4:00 in the afternoon now. She hadn't called anyone yet, and I asked her why." She said, 'Who should I call?'"

"I said, 'call the police.' There was a big silence there. And I said, 'If you can't call the police—knowing she has some little problems with the police—call a doctor.' She said, 'Okay, I'll call a doctor.' She hung up the phone and I called you."

Marjorie probably hoped that the drugs would kill him, but Wally had built up too much of an immunity over the years. Marjorie knew that it takes three or four hours for gas to dissipate from the body, a logical reason for her to delay calling Tom Hagen as long as she did.

After the police made the two-hour drive to Ajo from Tucson, they went through the house with a fine-tooth comb. They didn't find so much as a cash register receipt. They later discovered that Marjorie had cleaned out their checking account as well. When the detective first walked into the house, Marjorie said, "Here's the suicide note," and handed it to him as if it were a grocery list. She was weeping softly when she told them that she and her husband had been so distraught that they would have to be apart, that they had decided to die together. But, then, at the last minute, she lost her nerve. She just couldn't join her husband in death. Then she told him that she wanted to talk to her lawyer, Edward Bolding. The detective knew he had problems.

During their investigation, the police found the outdoor hose on the side of the house. It had been cut. Like piecing a puzzle together, they ran the hose from Marjorie's New Progressive gas stove to the bedroom where she and Wally had watched *The Ten Commandments* the night she had set Mark Indivik's house on fire. The hose was exactly the right length. A neighbor told them he had seen Marjorie lug the hose into the house. Later, the gas company would determine that there was no gas leak.

Marjorie was arrested and taken to a jail in Tucson. She did not resist. In fact, she was calm, as if she had done what she had to do, accomplished her mission. Perhaps she thought that she would get out of this too. So far in her life, the consequences that she had suffered, compared to the crimes she had committed, were minor. She had already accepted the fact that she would be in prison for at least fifteen years. If the prison in Tucson was anything like the Shakopee Women's prison in Minnesota, she could get used to that. She'd have no bills or creditors, she'd be well liked, and she'd have plenty of companions, all while her trust payments were accruing. She could read murder mysteries, watch TV, and needlepoint to her heart's content, biding her time until her 1998 inheritance.

Marjorie was charged with second-degree murder in her husband's death and held in lieu of $1 million bail. Not surprisingly, Edward Bolding, like her attorneys and husbands before him, defended her until the end. He said that the reason Marjorie took so long to call anyone was because she wanted to spend some time alone with her husband.

"She bathed him and wanted him to look presentable. Wally was highly distressed after his wife's conviction. You want to know what killed him? That's what killed him. Furthermore, I think it was an overreaction on the part of the law enforcement community and the county attorney," he said. "Just because she's got some kind of prior problems."

Bolding said, "I've been predicting all along that they didn't have anything. They simply don't have any kind of case to show there's been a crime by Marj." He said that the murder charges were simply a "payback" because prosecutors tried to convict Hagen of arson and the jury found her guilty only of "attempted" arson.

"If this had been anyone else who lived with her husband for years in a loving relationship and he was as ill as Wally was, life would have gone on as usual. There might have been a quiet investigation. Instead, they lock her up on $1 million bond," he said.

Nancy Hagen believed that Marjorie had been laying the groundwork with the neighbor's fire. "She was working her way to Dad." Nancy was sure that if she'd had more time, Marjorie would have set her own house on fire with Wally in it. Bill Dickinson, the prosecutor, agreed with her. Up to this point, Wally's children had always believed that one day they would be able to reconcile with their father, to reunite and start over. Now, he was gone and none of their questions would be answered. It wasn't so hard to understand how Marjorie could have swayed Wally. After all, their mother was ill and Marjorie was so full of life. She made Wally feel like a "young sprout" again. She dressed him in blue jeans and big belt buckles and cowboy boots. He had grown a beard. But, why couldn't he have done all those things without alienating his children?

Wally had drawn up a will on October 3, 1989. It stated, "I devise my estate to my beloved wife, Marjorie Congdon Hagen. In the event that she should die before me, the estate that she would have received shall go to The Arizona Boy's ranch." Wally willed nothing to his three children or his grandchildren.

The sheriff's investigators initially described Wally's death as either an assisted suicide or a murder. But charges of second-degree murder against Marjorie Hagen were dropped. November 19, 1992, was the deadline for prosecutors to obtain a grand jury indictment or to begin a preliminary hearing. But the coroners had not yet determined what killed Wally, and a homicide case could not proceed without a cause of death. She got away with murder, again.

Had the prosecutors missed that deadline without dropping the charge, a judge, under court procedure, would have dismissed it with prejudice, meaning that Marjorie could never again be charged with murdering her husband. But, because the charge was dropped, the case can be refiled at any time. Bolding predicted that this would not happen. To this date, he is right.

An autopsy was performed on Wally Hagen's body.

A toxicology report indicated that he died of a drug overdose. *No cancer was found in Wally's body.*

❧ *Chapter Thirty-Two*

On December 15, 1994, two years and two months after Wally's death, Marjorie Hagen once again appeared on the front pages of Twin Cities newspapers. The headlines read: "Marjorie Hagen Feuds Over Husband's Ashes." No one who knew her was surprised.

Marjorie wanted Wally to be buried in Arizona. His children filed a lawsuit to have their father's body sent to Minneapolis to be buried in his reserved spot next to their mother. They did not want Wally to be cremated—not in the beginning. From her jail cell, Marjorie fought as tenaciously as a pit bull.

Wally's children hired a lawyer to help them fight for their father's remains. Attorney Robert Hooker tried to prove that Marjorie and Wally were not legally married, so she had no right to his remains. Nancy was deposed and so was Marjorie. Depositions were almost a way of life for her; Marjorie was in her element.

Hooker began by asking her if she'd ever had her deposition taken before.

She said, "Yes."

He asked her if she knew the purpose of a deposition.

She answered, "For you to snoop."

He asked her if she understood that the court would rely on all the information that she gave.

She answered, "I understand that you will use it however you can turn it." The stage was set.

She listed for him all the places that she and Wally had lived, which just about covered the entire Midwest, parts of the East Coast, Mexico, and of course, Arizona. She didn't remember how long they had been at any one place, but they went wherever their Airstream took them.

"How many times have you been married, ma'am?"

"Three times."

She told him that Richard LeRoy was her first husband. When he asked when she married him, she replied, "I'm extremely bad on dates. I'm guessing '50, '51, something like that."

She explained that they were married for approximately twenty years but it ended in divorce. Her second husband was Roger Caldwell. She couldn't remember when she married him but, "It was sometime when I was in Colorado with a sick child."

He asked her if she had divorced Roger Caldwell, and she assured him that she had. "It was sometime after my acquittal in the conspiracy trial for my mother's death and previous to my marriage to Wallace Hagen." She said that she had gotten the divorce in Tijuana "at some type of official building." Her Spanish was poor and she didn't know one building from another. All of her legal papers had been stolen, she said under oath, so unfortunately, there were no records.

"I sent copies of the divorce file to Roger when he moved back to Latrobe, but I have no idea what he did with them. I had had no contact with him from the time of his release from prison, nor was I notified as to the time of his death."

Hooker asked her when she married Wallace Hagen, and she did remember that date, August 7, 1981. He asked her to verify the marriage certificate, which he put in front of her. Then he asked her who performed the marriage ceremony.

"Pastor Plaster."

"P-l-a-s-t-e-r?"

"I'm not sure if it's e-r." Somehow, she kept a straight face.

He asked if the subject of her divorce from Roger Caldwell ever came up during her arson trial in Minnesota. She told him no, except by a newspaper reporter.

"By what kind of newspaper reporter?"

"A nosey one."

"Oh. Aren't they all?"

"Yes, almost as bad as attorneys."

Her final answer to Robert Hooker when he asked her if there was any documentation available to prove that she had actually divorced Roger Caldwell was, "I believe that that is up to you to prove and to find out."

After they filed suit, Nancy and Tom decided to bare their souls to the *St. Paul Pioneer Press* and the *Minneapolis Star Tribune*. They said that their lives had turned nightmarish when their mother died in her bed in 1980 and Marjorie moved in with their dad. They remembered some of the bizarre occurrences after Marjorie's murder trial, listing the arson conviction in Minnesota, and the arsons in Arizona.

"The bottom line is, she took our father away from us," said Tom Hagen. "We think she killed our mother, she killed our father. And now we want him back." He said that he never believed it was coincidence that three people close to Marjorie died in their beds. Her mother, her friend, and her husband.

It had cost the Hagen children $40,000 in attorney's fees to reclaim their father's remains, money that was not easy for them to get. They hoped that someone would read the story and offer their help. That didn't happen. In the meantime, Marjorie's attorney and a judge suggested that the children and Marjorie divide up Wally's remains. They were horrified, but they had fought as hard as they could, used all of their resources, and it was time to get on with their lives. So they agreed. Because of the judge's decision, the Hagens had Wally cremated. It would be easier to divide ashes than to divide a body, they mused. What was the judge thinking?

Edward Bolding said, "It's a tragedy that Wally's wishes aren't being responded to by his children. Wally wanted to be buried next to Marjorie."

Robert Hooker said, "I think she enjoys making people miserable. There are always victims in her wake."

The Hagens planned to bury their portion of their father next to their mother, Helen. Edward Bolding said that Marjorie planned a Christian burial service for Wally in Arizona. Finally, after a three-year battle, Wally's ashes—half of them—were mailed to Nancy Hagen, UPS. She transferred his ashes into a marble urn, which she purchased at a funeral home and then she strapped him into the passenger seat of her car and drove him to the cemetery where her mother was buried. She put the urn on the ground next to her mother's grave and lectured her parents as if they were still alive. Tears streamed down her face and she realized that if anyone had seen her, they would have called the men with the straight-jackets. She didn't care. It was cathartic. She said that she felt good, standing there in the cold, knowing that her mother and father who had been married for forty-seven years were together again.

January 19, 1996: It was 20 degrees below zero, the sky was a sapphire blue and the sun shone bright on the trees. The bare limbs were weighted down with a thick skin of shimmering ice from an ice storm the night before. The trees resembled Steuben glass sculptures, their ice prisms capturing the sun's light. Cars lined up in the parking lot at the Westwood Lutheran Church in St. Louis Park, Minnesota. It was 3:00 p.m. The program read:

In Loving Memory of Wallace Howard Hagen
Born: February 17, 1909
Died: October 30, 1992

It listed the survivors: Dick Hagen and his wife, Tom Hagen and his wife, Nancy Hagen and her second husband, eight grandchildren, and three great-grandchildren.

The Hagens filled the front pews as the mourners filed in to their seats. Dick arrived late. He kept his head down, not as if in prayer, but as if he wished he were someplace else. The rest of the family looked straight ahead at the gray, marble urn and a framed picture of Wally that was taken when he was forty-five years old. He looked like he could have been Tom's brother. The male soloist sang "Amazing Grace" from the gallery.

Tom's beautiful twenty-one-year-old daughter, Heather, gave a moving eulogy for a grandfather she hardly knew. "When I first met him as a teen, I felt as though I was meeting a stranger. We had a family gathering, and, of course, he was the focus since he had been estranged from the family for nearly ten years. Rather than hugging all of the grandchildren and kissing them on the forehead as I had imagined, he reached out his hand to mine and asked, 'Which one are you?' Today my heart aches for the grandfather that I never got to know."

The reverend discussed "Separation."

"Was Wally really separated from his family in his

last years? Through the twists and turns of his life, we'll never know what was going on in his mind," he said. "But none of us are separated from God's love." He talked about Marj, about manipulation, about control. "Is there evil in this world? Knowing what I know about Marjorie Caldwell—he did not call her Marjorie Hagen—I have to answer my own question with 'Yes, there is evil in this world.' Wally shouldn't have died when he did. It was premature, untimely.

"This memorial service is one of remembrance, of resolution, of release. There is resolution: Wally's coming home to be buried next to his first wife of forty-seven years. It's the end of some of the twists, a resolution, a long struggle to win back Wally's ashes. And with this come release, closure, a time to put Wally Hagen to rest."

❧ *Update*

On January 5, 2004, seventy-one year old, Marjorie Congdon, LeRoy, Caldwell, Hagen, was released from Arizona State Prison in Perryville, after serving ten years of her fifteen-year sentence for arson. Her release had been scheduled for 2007, but was moved up because of new Arizona laws. No parole hearing was needed this time and she was released with "credit for good time served."

A careful reader will recognize that Roger Caldwell had to have an accomplice when he murdered Elisabeth Congdon and Velma Pietila. John DeSanto, who prosecuted Roger and Marjorie, Gary Waller, who led the police investigation, Doug Thomson, Caldwell's defense attorney, as well as members of Caldwell's jury, all believed that Roger Caldwell did not act alone. A forensic scientist determined that the hair found in Velma Pietila's hand was neither hers nor Roger's. Remember that Ron Meshbesher said in his closing arguments, "In Mrs. Pietila's hand, there was some black hair. Her husband came in and said she never had black hair...Now, who's black hair was that? Because Roger did not have black hair either."

Several years ago, John DeSanto told Ray DiPrima, an agent of the Bureau of Criminal Apprehension as well as Joe Kimball, a reporter for the Star Tribune, who wrote *Secrets of the Congdon Mansion*, that all evidence for that case had been lost or destroyed. In 2003, DeSanto acknowledged that he had boxed up the murder evidence, which included hair samples from the crime scene, saliva samples, and bloodstained clothing, and stored it in his basement.

With the knowledge that we have of the case and the availability of new DNA technology, we know that hair samples may be crucial in forensic homicide investigations. What if Caldwell was telling the truth when he wrote in his suicide note, "I didn't kill those girls?" One wonders why the case hasn't been reopened. Why isn't anyone looking for the accomplice?

❧ *Epilogue*

Star Tribune, Minneapolis
Friday, August 27, 1999

Congdon-Caldwell Tale Twists Again
by Joe Kimball

The array of bizarre behavior connected to the 1977 murder of Duluth heiress Elisabeth Congdon continued this month when the daughter of confessed murderer Roger Caldwell apparently killed her mother—Caldwell's ex-wife—then stored the body for days in 700 pounds of salt in a makeshift cardboard coffin.

Just as her father had suffocated his mother-in-law with a pillow 22 years ago, Chris O'Neil apparently used a pillow to asphyxiate her mother. Police found the body of Martha Burns, 65, Monday night in the basement of the home she had bought with Caldwell in 1967 in an unincorporated area next to Littleton, Colorado. The salt had drawn moisture from the body, leaving it almost mummified, police said. Stuffed animals and burning candles were found around the cardboard coffin. Burns was apparently killed two weeks ago. O'Neil, 44, one of three children of Caldwell and Burns, was found dead Tuesday, an apparent suicide. She had continued to live in the house until the day the body was discovered, according to police reports.

O'Neil's body was found inside her car early Tuesday in the garage of a partially completed townhouse about 12 miles from the home she shared with her mother. Police said she had strung a hose from the car's exhaust pipe into the car, then sealed the windows with duct tape. O'Neil reportedly was dejected over a recent divorce, a lost job and the mysterious death of her pet cat.

Arapahoe County Undersheriff Grayson Robinson said that O'Neil had a date on August 20, more than a week after the killing. He said that, as she was leaving the house, she called back over her shoulder in a light and happy manner: "See you later, Mom." Two weeks ago, O'Neil reportedly told a sister in California that she had dreamed that her mother had tried to smother her with a pillow, but that she'd killed her mother in the dream.

O'Neil's father, Caldwell, confessed to killing Congdon, who was 83 and partially paralyzed, by smothering her in her bed with a satin pillow. He also confessed to using a brass candlestick to bludgeon to death a night nurse who was trying to defend Congdon.

Caldwell had married Burns, his high school sweetheart from Latrobe, Pennsylvania in 1954. They moved to Colorado in the mid-1960's. They raised three children but divorced in 1974. At the time, he was an office worker; she was a computer programmer. Several times over the years, he said he regretted that he had no contact with his children in Colorado. It was one of many prices, he said, for the bad choices he'd made in life.

References

Arizona Daily Star

Brainerd Daily Dispatch

City Pages

Duluth Herald (Duluth News Tribune)

Ada Fourie, *Their Roots Run Deep*

Hastings Star Gazette

Roy Hoover, *A Lake Superior Lawyer*

Juli Kellner, *Album*

Joe Kimball, *Secrets of the Congdon Mansion*

Jim Klobuchar

Republic News Wires

Star Tribune (Minneapolis Star and Tribune)

The University of Minnesota, *Glensheen*

Virginia Soetebier, *Footnote to History*

St. Paul Pioneer Press

Acknowledgments

Writing this book has been a facinating journey—sometimes a roller coaster—but I wouldn't trade one day of it. I met some wonderful people along the way and certainly hope that we will stay in touch. There were many critiques, lots of advice, and tons of moral support, which every writer knows is essential. The "You Can Do Its" kept me going.

Thanks to Chris Aho, Duluth Public Library; Mannette Allen Rauth and all of the "Skating Moms" who shared their stories; Douglas Borghi, who encouraged me and inspired me from the beginning; Peter Brown, my writing pal, who always took the time to help; Kay Dodson, Babe Lind, Robyn Cook, Mardene Eichhorn, Bob and Sue Gilhoi for reading my drafts and offering invaluable advice and encouragement; Ron Meshbesher and Joe Kimball for taking the time to read and critique the manuscript; Damas Grebinowski, official court reporter for Marjorie's trial in Hastings, for hours of phone time and research; Marguarite Grams for sharing your American Red Cross memories; Judy Gilbert, Dakota County Jury Management in Hastings; Ann Hendrickson, Skyline Stables; Doug Thomson, Bill Dickinson, and Ann Paine Williams for sharing memories; Nancy Hersage, who knew what to do from Day One; Jill and David Kidwell, who always boosted my confidence; Steve Kohls, photographer, Brainerd Daily Dispatch, for your generosity; Linda LaCasse, graphic artist; Michelle Lyons, deputy court administrator, St. Louis County; and Paul Druckman and Doug Shidell who introduced me to MIPA.

Special thanks to Tom and Julie Hagen for sharing your memories, your family pictures, and for taking me into your home.

Special thanks to Nancy Hagen Kaufmann for your honesty and for sharing your pain.

Special thanks to Dick LeRoy, a survivor and a true gentleman.

Special thanks to Jennifer Congdon Johnson for sharing your family pictures and memories of your wonderful mother.

Special thanks to Nan Wisherd. Your knowledge, your curiosity and your generosity are exceeded only by your enthusiasm.

Special thanks to Ray DiPrima—a man who loves his work. This book would not have been possible without you.

I want to thank my editors—talented authors in their own right—who knew how to build my confidence even as I pored over hundreds of notations in the manuscript that screamed, "Rewrite!" I was fortunate. You took me under your professional wings and helped mold this manuscript into an actual book with a cover! You made me go the distance. Thank you, Mary Logue and Marybeth Lorbiecki. Thank you, Paula Schanilec, for all the fine-tuning.

About the Author

Sharon Darby Hendry has two grown daughters, and lives with her husband. They divide their time between Bloomington, Minnesota, and a cabin on a lake in northern Wisconsin. Ms. Hendry's first manuscript, *An Element of Truth,* a true story about another woman con-artist, was translated into a made-for-TV movie, starred Donna Mills, and aired on CBS on September 26, 1995.

Her newest book, *SoLiAh, The Sara Jane Olson Story* was published in May 2002.

Kathleen Soliah is serving twenty years-to-life for her role in planting powerful pipe bombs under two Los Angeles Police cars in 1976. For more than two decades she had lived in St. Paul, Minnestoa, as Sara Jane Olson, doctor's wife, mother of three, actress, and community activist.

SoLiAh revisits the emotional tensions that surrounded the Vietnam War, the Civil Rights movement, the Kennedy and King assassinations, and the radical culture of the '60s and '70s. It is a true story of idealism and misguided youth gone violently wrong.

www.glensheensdaughter.com

334

THE Sara Jane Olson STORY

SOLIAH

Sharon Darby Hendry

AUTHOR OF *GLENSHEEN'S DAUGHTER*

Unsolicited Responses for
SoLiAh, The Sara Jane Olson Story:

"I had been looking for some great summer reading and with *Glensheen's Daughter*, and *SoLiAh* in hand I headed to the beaches on the Outer Banks of North Carolina and found what I was looking for.

"Lying there on the sand feeling the hot sun, my eyes widened by the lies, deceit, and simply greediness and cruelty of these two women—and because they were loving moms and family members, I was further intrigued by their psychic makeup. You have found your "Scarlet O'Hara's"!

"You did a great job on these books. Congratulations on your triumph! They were an excellent read, and at times made me angry and scared—a sure sign of a winner. It's hard to say which one I liked better, as I think I like them both equally."

—Gloria Bozevich, Tookipaws Productions

"I very much enjoyed your book and much to my surprise. I thought I would be entering a lifeless rehash and instead got an information-filled, page-turning, authoritative history, fun and fascinating."

—Steve Kaplan, Editor of *Minnesota Law and Politics*

"On the matter of confusing criminality for politics, Hendry has it right when she quotes the *Minneapolis Star Tribune* saying the "demands of justice should be fulfilled just as readily for a doctor's wife from St. Paul as for a jobless wanderer from Detroit."

—*Los Angeles Times Book Review*